The World's Illusion

THE EUROPEAN LIBRARY
EDITED BY J. E. SPINGARN

Herr Was
Sax Ger

ico

entu
Virgi
Li
at

THE WORLD'S ILLUSION

BY

JACOB WASSERMANN

AUTHORIZED TRANSLATION BY
LUDWIG LEWISOHN

THE FIRST VOLUME:
EVA

NEW YORK
HARCOURT, BRACE AND HOWE
1920

CONTENTS OF THE FIRST VOLUME

THE WORLD'S ILLUSION

CRAMMON, THE STAINLESS KNIGHT

I

FROM the days of his earliest manhood, Crammon, a pilgrim
upon the paths of pleasantness and delight, had been a con-
stant· wayfarer from capital to capital and from country-seat
to country-seat. He came of an Austrian family whose landed
estates lay in Moravia, and his full name was Bernard
Gervasius Crammon von Weissenfels.

In Vienna he owned a small but beautifully furnished house.
Two old, unmarried ladies were its guardians—the Misses
Aglaia and Constantine. They were his distant kinswomen,
but he was devoted to them as to sisters of his blood, and they
returned his affection with an equal tenderness.

On an afternoon in May the two sat by an open window and
gazed, longingly down into the street. He had announced the
date of his arrival by letter, but four days had passed and they
were still waiting in vain. Whenever a carriage turned the
corner, both ladies started and looked in the same direction.

When twilight came they closed the window and sighed.
Constantine took Aglaia's arm, and together they went through
the charming rooms, made gleamingly ready for their master.
All the beautiful things in the house reminded them of him,
just as every one of them was endeared to him because it united
him to some experience or memory.

Here was the chiselled fifteenth century goblet which the
Marquis d'Autichamps had given him, yonder the agate bowl
bequeathed him by the Countess Ortenburg. There were the
coloured etchings, part of the legacy of a Duchess of Gains-

I

borough, the precious desk-set which he had received from the old Baron Regamey, the Tanagra figurines which Felix Imhof had brought him from Greece. There, above all, was his own portrait, which the English artist Lavery had painted on an order from Sir Charles MacNamara.

They knew these things and esteemed them at their true worth. They stopped before his picture, as they so often delighted to do. The well rounded face wore a stern, an almost sombre expression. But that expression seemed deceptive, for a tell-tale gleam of worldly delight, of irony and roguishness, played about the clean-shaven lips.

When night fell the two ladies received a telegram informing them that Crammon had been forced to put off his return home for a month. They lit no lights after that, and went sadly to bed.

II

Once it had happened that Crammon was dining with a few friends at Baden-Baden. He had just returned from Scotland where he had visited the famous trout streams of MacPherson, and had left the train at the end of a long journey. He felt very tired, and after the meal lay down on a sofa and fell asleep.

His friends chatted for a while, until his deep breathing drew their attention to him, and they decided to perpetrate a jest at his expense. One of them shook him by the shoulder, and when he opened his eyes asked: " Listen, Bernard, can't you tell us what is the matter with Lord Darlington? Where is he? Why is he never heard of any more? "

Crammon without a moment's hesitation answered in a clear voice and with an almost solemn seriousness: " Darlington is on his yacht in the Bay of Liguria between Leghorn and Nice. What time is it? Three o'clock? Then he is just about to take the sedative which his Italian physician, Magliano, prepares and gives him."

He turned on his other side and slept on.

One of the men, who knew Crammon only slightly, said: "That's a pure invention!" The others assured the doubter that Crammon's word was above suspicion, and they spoke softly so as not to disturb his sleep.

III

On another occasion Crammon was a guest on an estate in Hungary, and planned with a group of young men, who were visiting a neighbouring country-house, to attend a festivity in the next town. The dawn was breaking when the friends separated. Crammon, with senses slightly dulled, went on alone and longed for the bed from which half an hour's walk still separated him. By chance he came upon a cattle market crowded with peasants, who had brought in their cows and calves from the villages around.

The crowd brought him to a halt, and he stopped to listen while a bull was being offered for sale. The auctioneer cried: "I am offered fifty crowns!" There was no answer; the peasants were slowly turning the matter over in their minds.

Fifty crowns for a bull? To Crammon's mind, from which the wine fumes had not quite faded, it seemed remarkable, and without hesitation he offered five crowns more. The peasants drew aside respectfully. One of them offered fifty-six; Crammon bid fifty-eight. The auctioneer raised his three-fold cry; the hammer fell. Crammon owned the bull.

A magnificent beast, he said to himself, and felt quite satisfied with his bargain. But when the time came for him to pay, he discovered that the bidding had been so much per hundred weight, and since the bull weighed twelve hundred and fifty pounds, he was required to pay seven hundred and twenty-five crowns.

He refused angrily. A loud squabble followed; but his arguments were useless. The bull was his property. But he had

no such sum of money on his person, and had to hire a man
to accompany him with the animal to his friend's house.

He strode on wretchedly vexed. The man followed, dragging the unwilling bull by a rope.

His host helped Crammon out of his embarrassment, by
purchasing the bull, but' the incident furnished endless amusement to the whole countryside.

IV

Crammon loved the theatre and everything connected with
it. When the great Marian Wolter died, he locked himself in
his house for a week, and mourned as if for a personal
bereavement.

During a stay in Berlin he heard of the early fame of Edgar
Lorm. He saw him as Hamlet, and when he left the theatre
he embraced an utter stranger and cried out: " I am happy! "
A little crowd gathered.

He had meant to stay in Berlin three days but remained
three months. His connections made it easy for him to meet
Lorm. He overwhelmed the actor with gifts—costly bric-à-
brac, rare books, exquisite delicacies.

Every morning, when Edgar Lorm arose, Crammon was
there, and with a deep absorption watched the actor at his
morning tasks and his gymnastic exercises. He admired his
slender stature, his noble gestures, his eloquent mimicry, and
the perfection of his voice.

He took care of Lorm's correspondence for him, interviewed
agents, got rid of unwelcome admirers of either sex. He
called the dramatic reviewers to account, and in the theatre
looked his rage whenever he thought the applause too tepid.
" The beasts should roar," he said. During the scene in
Richard II in which the king addresses the lords from the
castle wall, his enthusiasm was so great that his friend, the
Princess Uchnina, who shared his box, covered her face with
her fan to escape the glances of the public.

To him Lorm was in very truth the royal Richard, the melancholy Hamlet, Romeo the lover, and Fiesko the rebel. His faith in the actor's art was boundless; his imagination was wholly convinced. He attributed to him the wit of Beaumarchais, the eloquence of Antony, the sarcasm of Mephistopheles, the dæmonic energy of Franz Moor. When it was necessary for him to part, he did not conceal his grief, and from afar wrote him at intervals a letter of adoration.

The actor accepted this worship as a tribute that differed fundamentally from the average praise and love with which he was beginning to be satiated.

V.

Lola Hesekiel, the celebrated beauty, owed her good fortune wholly to Crammon. Crammon had educated her and given her her place in the world and its appreciation.

When she was but an undistinguished young girl Crammon took a trip with her to Sylt. There they met Crammon's friend, Franz Lothar von Westernach. Lola fell in love with the handsome young aristocrat, and one evening, after a tender hour, she confessed her love for the other to Crammon. Then Crammon arose from his couch, dressed himself, went to Franz Lothar's room and brought the shy lad in. "My children," he said in the kindliest way, "I give you to each other. Be happy and enjoy your youth." With these words he left the two alone. And for long neither of them quite knew how to take so unwonted a situation.

VI

A curious occurrence was that connected with the Countess Ortenburg and the agate bowl.

The countess was an old lady of seventy, who lived in retirement at her château near Bregenz. Crammon, who had a great liking for ancient ladies of dignity and worldly wisdom, visited her almost annually to cheer her and to chat with her about the past.

The countess was grateful to him for his devotion, and determined to reward it. One day she showed him an agate bowl mounted on gold, an heirloom of her house, and told him that this bowl would be his after her death, as she had provided in her will.

Crammon flushed with pleasure, and tenderly kissed her hand. At every visit he took occasion to see the precious bowl, revelled in the sight of it, and enjoyed the foretaste of complete possession.

The countess died, and Crammon was soon notified concerning her legacy. The bowl was sent him carefully packed in a box. When it was freed of its wrappings he saw with amazement and disgust that he had been cheated. What he held was an imitation—skilfully and exactly made. But the material was base; only the setting had been copied in real gold.

Bitterly he considered what to do. Whom dared he accuse? How could he prove the very existence of the genuine bowl?

The heirs of the countess were three nephews of her name. The eldest, Count Leopold, was in ill repute as a miser who grudged himself and others their very bread. If he had played the trick, the bowl had been sold long ago.

It was easy to find a pretext for visiting Count Leopold at Salzburg. He sought distinction in piety and stood in favour at the bishop's court. Crammon thought that there was a gleam of embarrassment in the man's eyes. He himself peered about like a lynx. In vain.

He happened, however, to know all the prominent dealers in antiquities on the Continent, and so he set out on a quest. For two months and a half he travelled from city to city, from one dealer to another, and asked questions, investigated, and kept a sharp look-out. He carried the imitation bowl with him and showed it to all. The dealers were quite familiar with the sight of a connoisseur with his heart set on some object of art; they answered his questions willingly and sent him hither and thither.

He was on the point of despairing, when in Aix he was told of a dealer in Brussels who was said to have acquired the bowl. It was true. He found the object of his search in Brussels. Crammon inquired after the name of the seller and discovered it to be that of one who had business relations with Count Leopold. The Belgian dealer demanded twenty thousand francs for the bowl. Crammon at once deposited one thousand, with the assurance that he would pay the rest within a week and then take the bowl. He made no attempt at bargaining, much to the astonishment of the dealer. But in his rage he thought: I have snared the thief. Why should his rascality come cheaply?

Two days later he entered the count's room. He was accompanied by a hotel porter, who placed a box containing the imitation bowl on a table and disappeared. The count was breakfasting alone. He arose and frowned.

Crammon silently opened the little box, lifted the bowl out, polished it carefully with a handkerchief, kept it in his hand, and assumed a care-worn look.

" What is it? " asked the count, turning pale.

Crammon told him how, by the merest chance, he had discovered in a Brussels shop this bowl which, as he knew, had been for centuries in the possession of the Ortenburgs. It had, therefore, scarcely required the mournful memory of his dear and honoured old friend to persuade him to restore the precious object to the family treasury whence it came. He esteemed it a great good fortune that it was he who had discovered this impious trade in precious things. Had it been any one else the danger of loose tongues causing an actual scandal was obvious enough. He had, he continued, paid twenty thousand francs for the bowl, which he had brought in order to restore it to the house of Ortenburg. The receipt was at the count's disposal. All he requested of the count was a cheque for the amount involved.

He breathed no word concerning a will or a legacy, and betrayed no suspicion of how he had been tricked. The count understood. He looked at the imitation bowl on the table and recognized it for what it was. But he lacked courage to object. He swallowed his rage, sat down and made out the cheque. His chin quivered with fury. Crammon was radiant. He left the imitation bowl where it stood, and at once set out for Brussels to fetch the other.

VII

There were three things that Crammon hated from the bottom of his heart: newspapers, universal education, and taxes. It was especially impossible for him to realize that he, like others, was subject to taxation.

He had been summoned on a certain occasion to give an accounting of his income. He declared that during the greater part of the year he lived as a guest in the châteaux and on the estates of his friends.

The examining official replied that since he was known to live a rather luxurious life, it was clear that he must have a fixed income from some source.

"Undoubtedly," Crammon lied with the utmost cynicism. "This income consists wholly of meagre winnings at the various international gambling resorts. Earnings of that sort are not subject to taxation."

The official was astonished and shook his head. He left the room in order to consult his superiors in regard to the case. Crammon was left alone. Trembling with rage he gazed about him, took a stack of legal documents from a shelf, and shoved them far behind a bookcase against the wall. There, so far as one could tell, they would moulder in the course of the years, and in their illegal hiding place save the owners of the names they recorded from taxation.

For years he would chuckle whenever he thought of this deviltry.

VIII

The Princess Uchnina had made Crammon's acquaintance in one of the castles of the Esterhazys in Hungary. Even at that time the free manner of her life had set tongues wagging; later on her family disowned her.

He met her again in a hotel at Cairo. Since she was wealthy there was no danger of his being exploited. He had little liking for the professional vampire, nor had he ever lost the mastery over his senses. There was no passion that could prevent him from going to bed at ten and sleeping soundly through a long night. The princess was fond of laughing and Crammon helped her to laugh, since it pleased him to see her amused. He did not care to be loved beyond measure; he valued considerate treatment and a comradely freedom of contact. He had no desire for love with its usual spices of romance and disquietude, jealousy and enslavement. He wanted the delight of love in as tangible and sensible a form as possible; he cared less for the flame than for the dainty on the spit.

On the ship that took him and the princess to Brindisi there appeared a Danish lady with hair the hue of wheat and eyes like cornflowers. She was lonely, and he sought her out and succeeded in charming her. The three travelled together to Naples, where the Danish lady and Crammon seemed to have become friendlier than ever; but the princess only laughed.

They arrived in Florence. In front of the Baptistery Crammon met a melancholy young woman, whom he recognized as an acquaintance made at Ostende. She was the daughter of a manufacturer of Mainz. She had married recently, but her husband had lost her dowry at Monte Carlo and had fled to America. Crammon introduced her to the other ladies, but, for the sake of the Dane, who was suspicious and exacting,

passed her off as his cousin. It was not long, however, before
a quarrel broke out between the two, and Crammon was very
busy preaching the spirit of reconciliation and peace.

The princess laughed.

Crammon said: " I should like to see how many women one
can gather together like this without their thirsting for one
another's blood." He made a wager with the princess for a
hundred marks that he could increase the number to five,
herself of course excepted.

In the station at Milan a charming creature ran into him,
and gave signs of unalloyed delight. She was an actress who
had been intimate with a friend of his years before. She had
just been engaged by a theatre in Petrograd and was now on
her way there. Crammon found her so amusing that he
neglected the others for her sake; and although he was not
lacking in subtlety, the signs of a coming revolution in his
palace increased. The revolution broke out in Munich. There
were hard words and tears; trunks were packed; and the ladies
scattered to all the points of the compass,—North to Denmark,
West to Mainz, East to Petrograd.

Crammon was mournful; he had lost his bet. The little
princess laughed. She remained with him until another lure
grew stronger. Then they celebrated a cheerful farewell.

IX

When Crammon was but a youth of twenty-three he had once
been a member of a large hunting party at Count Sinsheim's.
Among the guests there was a gentleman named von Febronius
who attracted his attention, first by his silence, and next by
frequently seeking his society while carefully avoiding the
others.

One day Febronius, with unusual urgency, begged Crammon
to visit him.

Febronius possessed an extensive entailed estate on the
boundary between Silesia and Poland. He was the last of his

race and name, and, as every one knew, deeply unhappy on this account. Nine years earlier he had married the daughter of a middle-class family of Breslau, and in spite of the difference in age the two were genuinely devoted to each other. The wife was thirty, the husband near fifty. The marriage had proved childless, and there seemed now no further hope.

Crammon promised to come, and some weeks later, on an evening in May, he arrived at the estate. Febronius was delighted to see him, but the lady, who was pretty and cultivated, was noticeably chill in her demeanour. Whenever she was forced to look at Crammon a perceptible change of colour overspread her face.

Next morning Febronius showed him the whole estate— the park, the fields and forests, the stables and dairies. It was a little kingdom, and Crammon expressed his admiration; but his host sighed. He said that his blessings had all been embittered, every beast of the field seemed to regard him with reproachful eyes, and the land and its fertility meant nothing to him who had brought death to his race, and whom the fertility of nature but put in mind of the sterile curse which had come upon his blood.

Then he became silent, and silently accompanied Crammon, whose head whirled with very bold and equivocal thoughts.

After dinner they were sitting on the terrace with Frau von Febronius. Suddenly the lord of the manor was called away and returned shortly with a telegram in his hand. He said that an urgent matter of business required him to set out on a journey at once. Crammon arose with a gesture, to show his consciousness of the propriety of his leaving too. But his host, almost frightened, begged him to stay and keep his wife company. It was, he said, only a matter of two days, and she would be grateful.

He stammered these words and grew pale. His wife kept her face bent closely over her embroidery frame, and Crammon saw her fingers tremble. He knew enough. He shook hands with Febronius, and knew that they would not and dared not meet again in life.

He found the lady, when they were alone together, shier than he had anticipated. Her gestures expressed reluctance, her glances fear. When his speech grew bolder, shame and indignation flamed in her eyes. She fled from him, sought him again, and when in the evening they strolled through the park she implored him to leave next day, and went to the stables to order the carriage for the morning. When he consented, her behaviour altered, her torment and her harshness seemed to melt. After midnight she suddenly appeared in his room, struggling with herself and on the defensive, defiant and deeply humiliated, bitter in her yielding, and in her very tenderness estranged.

Early next morning the carriage was ready and drove him to the station.

That marvellous night faded from his memory as a thousand others, less marvellous, had done. The spectral experience blended with a host of others that were without its aroma of spiritual pain.

x

Sixteen years later chance brought him into the same part of the country.

He inquired after Febronius, and learned that that gentleman had been dead for ten years. He was told, furthermore, that during his last years the character of Febronius had changed radically. He had become a spendthrift; frightful mismanagement had ruined his estate and shaken his fortune; swindlers and false friends had ruled him exclusively, so that his widow, who was still living on the estate with her only daughter, could scarcely maintain herself there. She was beset by usurious creditors and a growing burden of debt; she did not know an easy hour, and complete ruin was but a matter of time.

Crammon drove over to the estate, and had himself announced under an assumed name. When Frau von Febronius entered he saw that she was still charming. Her hair was still brown, her features curiously young. But there was something frightened and suspicious about her.

She asked where she had had the pleasure of his acquaintance. Crammon simply regarded her for a while, and she too looked at him attentively. Suddenly she uttered a cry and hid her face in her hands. When she had mastered her emotion, she gave him her hand. Then she left the room, and returned in a few minutes leading a young girl of great sweetness.

"Here she is."

The girl smiled. Her lips curved as though she were about to pout, and her teeth showed the glittering moisture of shells to which the water of the sea still clings.

She spoke of the beautiful day and of her having lain in the sun. The broken alto voice surprised one in so young a creature. In her wide, brown eyes there was a radiance of unbounded desires. Crammon was flattered, and thought: If God had made me a woman, perhaps I should have been such an one. He asked after her name. It was Letitia.

Frau von Febronius clung to the girl with every glance.

Letitia brought in a basket full of golden pears. She looked at the fruit with greed and with an ironic consciousness of her greed. She cut a pear in half and found a worm in it. That disgusted her and she complained bitterly.

Crammon asked her what she cared for most, and she answered: "Jewels."

Her mother reproached her with being careless of what she had. "Only the other day," said Frau von Febronius, "she lost a costly ring."

"Just give me something to love," Letitia replied and stroked a white kitten that purred and jumped on her lap, "and I'll hold on to it fast."

When he said farewell Crammon promised to write, and Letitia promised to send him her picture.

A few weeks later Frau von Febronius informed him that she had taken Letitia to Weimar, and placed her in the care of her sister, the Countess Brainitz.

XI

On Crammon's fortieth birthday he received from seven of his friends, whose names were signed to it, a document written in the elaborate script and manner of an official diploma. And the content of the document was this:

" O Crammon, friend of friends, admirer of women and contemner of their sex, enemy of marriage, glass of fashion, defender of descent, shield of high rank, guest of all noble spirits, finder of the genuine, tester of the exquisite, friend of the people and hater of mankind, long sleeper and rebel, Bernard Gervasius, hail to thee! "

Gleaming with pride and satisfaction Crammon hung up the beautifully framed parchment on the wall beside his bed. Then with the two ladies of his household he took a turn in the park.

Miss Aglaia walked at his right, Miss Constantine at his left. Both were festively arrayed, though in a somewhat antique fashion, and their faces were the happiest to be seen.

CHRISTIAN'S REST

I

CRAMMON found the forties to be a critical period in a man's life. It is then that in his mind he sits in judgment upon himself; he seeks the sum of his existence, and finds blunder after blunder in the reckoning.

But these moral difficulties did not very much influence either his attitude or the character of his activities. He found his appetite for life growing, but he found loneliness a heavier burden than before. When he was alone he was overcome by a feeling which he called the melancholy of the half-way house.

In Paris he was overtaken by this distemper of the soul. Felix Imhof and Franz Lothar von Westernach had agreed to meet him, and both had left him in the lurch. Imhof had been kept in Frankfort by his business on the exchange and his real estate interests, and had telegraphed a later date of arrival. Franz Lothar had remained in Switzerland with his brother and Count Prosper Madruzzi.

In his vexation Crammon spent his days largely in bed. He either read foolish novels or murmured his annoyances over to himself. Out of sheer boredom he ordered fourteen pairs of boots of those three or four masters of the craft who work only for the elect and accept a new customer only when recommended by a distinguished client.

He was to have spent the month of September with the Wahnschaffe family on their estate in the Odenwald. He had made the acquaintance of young Wolfgang Wahnschaffe the summer before at a tennis tournament in Homburg, and had accepted his invitation. In his exasperation over his truant friends he now wrote and excused himself.

One evening in Montmartre he met the painter Weikhardt, whom he had known in Munich. They walked together for a while, and Weikhardt encouraged Crammon to visit a neighbouring music hall. A very young dancer had been appearing there for the past week, the painter told him, and many French colleagues had advised seeing her.

Crammon agreed.

Weikhardt led him through a maze of suspicious looking alleys to a no less suspicious looking house. This was the Théâtre Sapajou. A boy in fantastic costume opened the door that led to a moderately large, half-darkened hall with scarlet walls and a wooden gallery. About fifty people, mostly painters and writers with their wives, sat facing a tiny stage. The performance had begun.

Two fiddles and a clarionet furnished the music.

And Crammon saw Eva Sorel dance.

II

His anger against his friends was extinguished. He was glad that they were not here.

He was afraid of meeting any of his many Parisian acquaintances and passed through the streets with lowered eyes. The thought was repulsive to him that he would be forced to speak to them of Eva Sorel, and then to see their indifferent or curious faces, beneath which there could be no feeling akin to his own.

He avoided the painter Weikhardt, for the latter would rob him of the illusion that he, Crammon, had discovered Eva Sorel, and that for the present she lived only in his consciousness as the miracle that he felt her to be.

He went about like an unrecognized rich man, or else as troubled as a miser who knows that thieves lie in wait for his treasure. All who carried their chatter of delight from the Théâtre Sapajou out into the world he regarded as thieves. They threatened to attract to the little playhouse the crowd of the stupid and the banal who drag great things into the dust by making them fashionable.

He nursed the dream of kidnapping the dancer and of fleeing with her to a deserted island of the sea. He would have been satisfied to adore her there and would have asked nothing of her.

For Lorm he had demanded applause. But he hated the favour which the dancer gained. Not because she was a woman. It was not the jealousy of the male. He did not think of her under the aspect of sex. Her being was to him the fulfilment of dark presentiments and visions; she represented the spirit of lightness as opposed to the heaviness of life which weighed him and others down; she was flight that mocked the creeping of the earth-bound, the mystery that is beyond knowledge, form that is the denial of chaos.

He said: " This boasted twentieth century, young as it is, wearies my nerves. Humanity drags itself across the earth like an ugly clumsy worm. She desires freedom from this condition, and in her yearning to escape the chrysalis she finds the dance. It is a barbaric spirit of comedy at its highest point."

He knew well that the life he led was a challenge and a disturbance to his fellow men who earned their bread by the sweat of their toil. He was an enthusiastic admirer of those ages in which the ruling classes had really ruled, when a prince of the Church had had a capon stuffer amid the officials of his court, and an insignificant count of the Holy Roman Empire had paid an army that consisted of one general, six colonels, four drummers, and two privates. And he was grateful to the dancer because she lifted him out of his own age even more thoroughly than the actor had done.

He made an idol of her, for the years were coming in which he needed one—he who, satiated, still knew hunger with senses avid for the flight of birds.

III

Eva Sorel had a companion and guardian, Susan Rappard, a thorough scarecrow, clad in black, and absent-minded. She had emerged with Eva out of the unknown past, and she was still rubbing its darkness out of her eyes when Eva, at eighteen, saw the paths of light open to her. But she played the piano admirably, and thus accompanied Eva's practice.

Crammon had paid her some attentions, and the tone in which he spoke of her mistress gained her sympathy. She persuaded Eva to receive him. " Take her flowers," she whispered. " She's fond of them."

Eva and Susan Rappard lived in two rooms in a small hotel. Crammon brought such masses of roses that the close corridors held the fragrance for many hours.

As he entered he saw Eva in an armchair in front of a mirror. Susan was combing her hair, which was of the colour of honey.

On the carpet was kneeling a lad of seventeen who was very pale and whose face bore traces of tears. He had declared his love to Eva. Even when the stranger entered he had no impulse to get up; his luckless passion made him blind.

Crammon remained standing by the door.

" Susan, you're hurting me! " Eva cried. Susan was startled and dropped the comb.

Eva held out her hand to Crammon. He approached and bent over to kiss it.

" Poor chap," she said, smiling, and indicating the lad, " he torments himself cruelly. It's so foolish."

The boy pressed his forehead against the back of her chair. " I'll kill myself," he whimpered. Eva clapped her hands and brought her face with its arch mockery of sadness near to the boy's.

" What a gesture! " Crammon thought. " How perfect in its light completeness, how delicate, how new! And how she raised her lids and showed the strong light of her starry eyes, and dropped her chin a little in that inclination of the head, and wore a smile that was unexpected in its blending of desire and sweetness and cunning and childlikeness! "

"Where is my golden snood?" Eva asked and arose.

Susan said that she had left it on the table. She looked there in vain. She fluttered hither and thither like a huge black butterfly: she opened and closed drawers, shook her head, thoughtfully pressed her hand against her forehead, and finally found the snood under the piano lid next to a roll of bank notes.

"It's always that way with us," Eva sighed. "We always find things. But we have to hunt a long time." She fastened the snood about her hair.

"I can't place your French accent," Crammon remarked. His own pronunciation was Parisian.

"I don't know," she answered. "Perhaps it's Spanish. I was in Spain a long time. Perhaps it's German. I was born in Germany and lived there till I was twelve." Her eyes grew a little sombre.

IV

The lovelorn boy had left. Eva seemed to have forgotten him, and there was no shadow upon the brunette pallor of her face. She sat down again, and after a brief exchange of questions she told him of an experience that she had had.

The reason for her telling the story seemed to inhere in thoughts which she did not express. Her glance rested calmly in the illimitable. Her eyes knew no walls in their vision; no one could assert that she looked at him. She merely gazed.

Susan Rappard sat by the tile-oven, resting her chin upon her arm, while her fingers, gliding past the furrowed cheeks, clung amid her greyish hair.

At Arles in Provence a young monk named Brother Leotade

had often visited Eva. He was not over twenty-five, vigorous,
a typical Frenchman of the South, though rather taciturn.

He loved the land and knew the old castles. Once he spoke
to her of a tower that stood on a cliff, a mile from the city;
he described the view from the top of the tower in words that
made Eva long to enjoy it. He offered to be her guide, and
they agreed on the hour and the day.

The tower had an iron gate which was kept locked, and the
key was in the keeping of a certain vintner. It was late afternoon when they set out, but on the unshaded road it was still
hot. They meant to be back before night fall, and so they
walked quickly; but when they reached the tower the sun had
already disappeared behind the hills.

Brother Leotade opened the iron gate and they saw a
narrow spiral staircase of stone. They climbed a few stairs.
Then the monk turned suddenly, locked the door from within,
and slipped the key into the pocket of his cowl. Eva asked his
reason. He replied that it was safer so.

It was dim in the vaulted tower, and Eva saw a menacing
gleam in the monk's eyes. She let him precede her, but on a
landing he turned and grasped her. She was silent, although
she felt the pressure of his fingers. Still silent, she glided from
his grasp, and ran up as swiftly as she could. She heard no
steps behind her in the darkness, and the stairs seemed endless. Still she climbed until her breath gave out, and she
panted for the light. Suddenly the greenish bell of the sky
gleamed into the shaft; and as she mounted, the circle of her
vision widened to the scarlet of the West, and when she stood
on the last step and on the platform, having emerged from
the mustiness of the old walls into the balsamic coolness and
the multiform and tinted beauty of earth and air, the danger
seemed wholly past.

She waited and watched the dark hole from which she had
come. The monk did not appear. His treacherous conceal-
ment strained her nerves to the uttermost. The brief twilight

faded; evening turned into night; there was no sound, no tread. Not until late did it occur to her that she could call for help. She cried out into the land, but she saw that it was a desolate region in which no one dwelled. And when her feeble cry had died away, the shape of Brother Leotade appeared at the head of the stairs.

The expression on his face filled her now with an even greater horror. He murmured something and stretched out his arms after her. She bounded backward, groping behind her with her hands. He followed her, and she leaped upon the parapet, crouched near the pinnacle, hard by the outer rim of the wall, her head and shoulders over the abyss. The wind caught the veil that had been wound about her head and it streamed forth like a flag. The monk stood still, bound to the spot by her eyes. His own were fixed relentlessly upon her, but he dared not move, for he saw the determination in her face: if he moved toward her, she would leap to her death.

And yet a rage of desire kept flaring in his eyes.

The hours passed. The monk stood there as though cast of bronze, while she crouched on the parapet, motionless but for her fluttering veil, and held him with her eye as one holds a wolf. Stars gathered in the sky; from time to time she glanced for a second at the firmament. Never had she been so near to the eternal flame. She seemed to hear the melody of a million worlds singing in their orbits; her unmoving limbs seemed to vibrate; the hands with which she clung to the harsh wall seemed to upbear the adamantine roof of the cosmos, while below her was the created thing, blind and wracked by passion and sworn to a God whom it belied.

Gradually the rim of heaven grew bright and the birds began to flutter upward. Then Brother Leotade threw himself upon his face and began to pray aloud. And as the East grew brighter he lifted up more resonantly the voice of his prayer. He crept toward the stairs. Then he arose and disappeared.

She saw him issue from the gate below and disappear in the
dawn among the vineyards. 'Eva lay long in the grass below,
worn and dull, before she could walk back to the city.

"It may be," she said at the end of her story, "that some
one looked on from Sirius, some one who will come soon and
perhaps be my friend." She smiled. ,

"From Sirius?" The voice of Susan was heard. "Where
will he get pearls and diadems? What crowns will he offer
you, and what provinces? Let us have no dealings with
beggars, even though they come from the sky."

"Keep quiet, you Sancho Panza!" Eva said. "All that
I ask is that he can laugh, laugh marvellously—laugh like that
young muleteer at Cordova! Do you remember him? I want
him to laugh so that I can forget my ambitions."

Hers is a virtue that hardly begs for pennies, thought Crammon, and determined to be on his guard and seek security while
there was time. For in his breast he felt a new, unknown,
and melancholy burning, and he knew well that he could not
laugh like that young Cordovan muleteer and make an ambitious woman forget her striving. ,

V

Felix Imhof arrived, and with him Wolfgang Wahnschaffe,
a very tall young man of twenty-two. There was an elegance
about the latter that suggested unlimited means. His father
was one of the German steel kings.

Crammon's refusal of his invitation had annoyed Wahnschaffe, and he was anxious to secure the older man's friendship. It was characteristic of the Wahnschaffes to desire most
strongly whatever seemed to withhold itself from their
grasp.

They went to the Théâtre Sapajou, and Felix Imhof agreed
that the dancer was incomparable. Plans at once flew from
his mind like sparks from beaten iron in a smithy. He talked

of founding an Academy of the Dance, of hiring an impresario for a tour through Europe, of inventing a pantomime. All this was to be done, so to speak, over night.

They sat together and drank a good deal—first wine, then champagne, then ale, then whiskey, then coffee, then wine once more. The excess had no effect on Imhof at all; in his soberest moments he was like others in the ecstasy of drunkenness.

He celebrated the praises of Gauguin, of Schiller, and of Balzac, and developed the plan for a great experiment in human eugenics. Faultless men and women were to be chosen and united and to beget an Arcadian race.

In the midst of it all he quoted passages of Keats and Rabelais, mixed drinks of ten kinds, and related a dozen succulent anecdotes from his wide experience with women. His mouth with its sensual lips poured forth superlatives, his protruding negroid eyes sparkled with whim and wit, and his spare, sinewy body seemed to suffer if it was forced to but a minute's immobility.

The other two nearly fell asleep through sheer weariness. He grew steadily more awake and noisy, waved his hands, beat on the table, inhaled the smoky air luxuriously, and laughed with his gigantic bass voice.

Five successive nights were spent in this way. That was enough for Crammon and he determined to leave. Wolfgang Wahnschaffe had invited him to a hunting party at Waldleiningen.

It was at eleven in the forenoon when Felix Imhof burst in on Crammon. In the middle of the room stood a huge open trunk. Linen, clothes, books, shoes, cravattes were scattered about like things hastily saved in a fire. Outside of the window swayed in flaming yellow the tree-tops of the Park Monceau.

Crammon sat in an armchair. He was naked but for a pair of long hose. He had breakfasted thus, and his expres-

sion was sombre. His square Gothic head and his broad,
muscular torso seemed made of bronze.

The day before Felix Imhof had made the acquaintance
of Cardillac, ruler of the Paris Bourse, and was on his way
to him now. He was going to embark on some enterprise of
Cardillac to the extent of two millions, and asked Crammon
in passing whether the latter did not wish to risk something too.
A trifle, say fifty thousand francs, would suffice. Cardillac was
a magician who trebled one's money in three days. Then you
had had the pleasure of the game and the suspense.

"This Cardillac," he said, " is a wonder. He began life
as an errand boy in an hotel. Now he is chief shareholder in
thirty-seven corporations, founder of the Franco-Hispanic
Bank, owner of the zinc mines of Le Nère, ruler of a horde
of newspapers, and master of a fortune running into the hundreds of millions."

Crammon arose, and from the heaps on the floor drew forth
a violet dressing gown which he put over his shivering body.
He looked in it like a cardinal.

"Do you happen to know," he asked, thoughtfully and
sleepily, " or did you by chance ever observe how the young
muleteers in Cordova laugh? "

Imhof's helpless astonishment made him look stupid. He
was silent.

Crammon took a large peach from a· plate and began to
eat it. You could see drops of the amber juice.

"There's no way out," he said, and sighed sadly, " I shall
have to go to Cordova myself."

VI

On their journey Wahnschaffe told Crammon about his
family: his sister Judith, his older brother Christian, his
mother, who had the most beautiful pearls in Europe. " When
she wears them," he said, " she looks like an Indian god-

dess." His father he described as an amiable man with unseen backgrounds of the soul.

Crammon was anxious to get as much light as possible on the life and history of one of those great and rich bourgeois families which had won in the race against the old aristocracy. Here, it seemed to him, was a new world, an undiscovered country which was still in the blossoming stage and which was to be feared.

His cleverly put questions got him no farther. What he did learn was a story of silent, bitter rivalry between this brother and Christian, who seemed to Wolfgang to be preferred to himself to an incomprehensible degree. He heard a story of doubt and complaint and scorn, and of words that the mother of the two had uttered to a stranger: " You don't know my son Christian? He is the most precious thing God ever made."

It was cheap enough, Wolfgang asserted, to praise a horse in the stable, one that had never been sent to the Derby because it was thought to be too noble and precious. Crammon was amused by the sporting simile. Why was that cheap, he asked, and what was its exact meaning?

Wolfgang said that it applied to Christian, who had as yet proved himself in no way, nor accomplished anything despite his twenty-three years. He had passed his final examinations at college with difficulty; he was no luminary in any respect. No one could deny that he had an admirable figure, an elegant air, a complexion like milk and blood. He had also, it was not to be denied, a charm so exquisite that no man or woman could withstand him. But he was cold as a hound's nose and smooth as an eel, and as immeasurably spoiled and arrogant as though the whole world had been made for his sole benefit.

" You will succumb to him as every one does," Wolfgang said finally, and there was something almost like hatred in his voice.

They arrived in Waldleiningen on a rainy evening of October. The house was full of guests.

VII

Wolfgang's prediction came true sooner than he himself would perhaps have thought. As .early as the third day Crammon and Christian Wahnschaffe were inseparable and utterly united. They conversed with an air of intimacy as though they had known each other for years. The difference of almost two decades in their, ages seemed simply non-existent.

With a laugh Crammon reminded Wolfgang of his prophecy, and added, " I hope that nothing worse will ever be predicted to me, and that delightful things will always become realities so promptly." And he knocked wood, for he was as super-stitious as an old wife.

Wolfgang's expression seemed to say: I was quite prepared for it. What else is one to expect?

Crammon had expected to find Christian spoiled and effem-inate. Instead he saw a thoroughly healthy blond young athlete, a head and more taller than himself, conscious of his vigour and beauty, without a trace of vanity, and radiant in every mood. It was true, as he had heard, that all were at his beck and call, from his mother to the youngest of the grooms, and that he accepted everything as he did fair weather —simply, lightly, and graciously, but without binding himself to any reciprocal obligation.

Crammon loved young men who were as elastic as panthers and whose serenity transformed the moods of others as a precious aroma does the air of a sick room. Such youths seemed to him to be gifted with an especial grace. One should, he held, clear their path of anything that might hinder their beneficent mission. He did not strive to impress them but rather to learn of them.

It was in England and among the English that he had found this respect for youth and ripening manhood, which had long

become a principle, with him and a rule of life. The climate
of a perfectly nurtured understanding he thought the fittest
atmosphere for such a being; and made his plans in secret.
He thought of the grand tour in the sense of the eighteenth
century, with himself in the rôle of mentor and guide.

In the meantime he and Christian talked about hunting,
trout-fishing, the various ways of preparing venison, the advantages of each season over the others, the numerous charms of
the female sex, the amusing characteristics of common
acquaintances. And of all these light things he spoke in a
thoughtful manner and with exhausting thoroughness.

He could not see Christian without reflecting: What eyes
and teeth and head and limbs! Nature has here used her
choicest substance, meant for permanence as well as delight,
and a master has fitted the parts into harmony. If one were
a mean-spirited fellow one could burst with envy.

One incident charmed him so much that he felt impelled to
communicate his delight to the others who had also witnessed it. It took place in the yard where early in the morning the hunting parties assembled. The dogs were to be
leashed. Christian stood alone among twenty-three mastiffs
who leaped around and at him with deafening barks and yells.
He swung a short-handled whip which whirred above their
heads. The beasts grew wilder; he had to ward off the fiercer
ones with his elbow. The forester wanted to come to his help
and called to the raging pack. Christian beckoned him to
stay back. The man's assumed anger and all his gestures
irritated the dogs. One of them, whose mouth was flecked
with foam, snapped at Christian, and the sharp teeth clung to
his shoulder. Then all cried out, especially Judith. But
Christian gave a short sharp whistle from between his teeth,
his arms dropped, his glance held the dogs nearest to him, and
suddenly the noise stopped, and only those in front gave a
humble whine.

Frau Wahnschaffe had grown pale. She approached her

son and asked him whether he was hurt. He was not, although his jacket showed a long rent.

"He leads a charmed life," she said that night after dinner to Crammon, with whom she had withdrawn to a quiet corner. "And that is my one consolation. His utter recklessness often frightens me. I have noticed with pleasure that you take an interest in him. Do try to guide him a little along reasonable ways."

Her voice was hollow and her face immobile. Her eyes stared past one. She knew no cares and had never known any, nor had she, apparently, ever reflected concerning those of others. Yet no one had ever seen this woman smile. The utter absence of friction in her life seemed to have reduced the motions of her soul to a point of deadness. Only the thought of Christian gave her whole being a shade of warmth; only when she could speak of him did she grow eloquent.

Crammon answered: " My dear lady, it is better to leave a fellow like Christian to his own fate. That is his best protection."

She nodded, although she disliked the colloquial carelessness of his speech. She told him how in his boyhood Christian had once gone to visit the lumbermen in the forest. The trunk of a mighty pine had been almost cut through, and the men ran to the end of the rope attached to the tree's top. The great tree wavered when they first noticed the boy. They cried out in horror, and tried to let the tree crash down in another direction. It was too late. And while some tugged desperately at the rope and were beside themselves with fright, a few headed by the foreman ran with lifted and warning arms into the very sphere of danger. The boy stood there quietly, and gazed unsuspectingly upward. The tree fell and crushed the foreman to death. But the branches slipped gently over Christian as if to caress him; and when the pine lay upon the earth, he stood in the midst of its topmost twigs as though he had been placed there, untouched and unastonished. And those who were there said he had been saved literally but by the breadth of a hair.

Crammon could not get rid of the vision which he himself had seen: the proud young wielder of the whip amid the unleashed pack. He reflected deeply. "It is clear," he said to himself, "that I need no longer go to Cordova to find out how the young muleteers laugh."

VIII

At the castle of Waldleiningen there was a wine room in which one could drink comfortably. In it Crammon and Christian drank one evening to their deeper friendship. And when the bottle was emptied of its precious vintage Crammon proposed that, since it was a beautiful night, they should take a turn in the park. Christian agreed.

In the moonlight they walked over the pebbles of the paths. Trees and bushes swam in a silvery haze.

"Gossamers and the mist of autumn," said Crammon. "Quite as the poets describe it."

"What poet?" Christian asked innocently.

"Almost any," Crammon answered.

"Do you read poetry?" Christian was curious.

"Now and then," Crammon answered, "when prose gets stale. Thus I pay my debts to the world-spirit."

They sat down on a bench under a great plantain. Christian watched the scene silently for a while. Then he asked suddenly, "Tell me, Bernard, what is this seriousness of life that most people make such a fuss about?"

Crammon laughed softly to himself. "Patience, my dear boy, patience! You'll find out for yourself."

He laughed again and folded his hands comfortably over his abdomen. But over the lovely landscape and the lovely night there fell a veil of melancholy.

IX

Christian wanted Crammon to accompany him and Alfred Meerholz, the general's son, to St. Moritz for the winter sports; but Crammon had to attend Konrad von Westernach's wedding in Vienna. So they agreed to meet in Wiesbaden, where Frau Wahnschaffe and Judith would join them in the spring.

Frau Wahnschaffe usually spent January and February in the family's ancestral home at Würzburg. She had many guests there and so did not feel the boredom of the provincial city. Wolfgang had been studying political science at the university there; but at the end of the semester he was to go to Berlin, pass his examination for the doctorate, and enter the ministry of foreign affairs. Judith said to him sarcastically: "You are a born diplomatist of the new school. The moment you enter a room no one dares to jest any more. It's high time that you enlarge your sphere of activity." He answered: "You are right. I know that I shall yield my place to a worthier one who knows better how to amuse you." "You are bitter," Judith replied, "but what you say is true."

When Christian arrived in Wiesbaden in April his mother introduced him to the Countess Brainitz and to her niece, Letitia von Febronius. The countess was ostensibly here to drink the waters; but her purpose was commonly thought to be the finding of a suitable match for her niece among the young men of the country. She had succeeded, at all events, in gaining the confidence of Frau Wahnschaffe, who was distrustful and inaccessible. Judith was charmed by Letitia's loveliness.

Christian accompanied the young ladies on their walks and rides, and the countess said to Letitia: "If I were you I'd fall in love with that young man." Letitia answered with her most soulful expression: "If I were you, aunt, I'd be afraid of doing so myself."

Crammon arrived in an evil mood. Whenever one of his

friends so far forgot himself as to marry, there came over him an insidious hatred of mankind which darkened his soul for weeks.

He was surprised when Christian told him of these new friends, and wondered at the trick by which fate brought him into the circle of Letitia's life. He had a feeling that was uncanny.

He was anything but delighted over the Countess Brainitz. He was familiar with the genealogy and history of the dead and living members of all the noble families of Europe, and so was thoroughly informed concerning her. "In her youth," he reported, "she was an actress, one of those favourite ingénues who attune souls of a certain sort poetically by a strident blondness and by pulling at their aprons with touching bashfulness. With these tricks she seduced in his time Count Brainitz, a gentleman who had weak brains and a vigorous case of gout. She thought he was rich. Later it turned out that he was hopelessly in debt and lived on a pension allowed him by the head of the house. On his death this pension passed to her."

She was blond no longer. Her hair was white and had a metallic shimmer like spun glass. Its hue was premature, no doubt, for she was scarcely over fifty. She was corpulent; her body had a curious sort of carved rotundity; her face was like an apple in its smooth roundness; it gleamed with a healthy reddish tinge; and each feature—nose, mouth, chin, forehead—was characterized by a certain harmless daintiness.

From the first moment she and Crammon found themselves hopelessly at odds. She clasped her hands in despair over everything he said, and all his doings enraged her. With her feminine instinct she scented in him the adversary of all her cunning plans; he saw in her another of those arch enemies that, from time to time, spun for one of his friends the net of marriage.

She asked him to dine merely because of Letitia's insistence.

The girl explained: "Even if you don't like him in other ways, aunt, you'll approve of him as a guest. He's very like you in one way." But Crammon's dislike of the countess robbed him of his usual appetite, so that the reconciliation even on that plane did not occur. She herself ate three eggs with mayonnaise, half of a duck, a large portion of roast beef, four pieces of pastry, a plate full of cherries, and additional trifles to pass the time. Crammon was overwhelmed.

After each course she washed her hands with meticulous care, and when the meal was over drew her snow-white gloves over her little, round fingers.

"All people are pigs," she declared. "Nothing they come in contact with remains clean. I guard myself as well as I can."

Letitia sat through it all smiling in her own arch and tender way, and her mere presence lent to the common things about her a breath of romance.

X

Her estate having finally been sold at auction, and she herself being quite without means, Frau von Febronius had gone to live with her younger sister at Stargard in Pomerania. In order to spare her daughter the spectacle of that final débâcle she had sent the girl to the countess in Weimar.

The three sisters were all widowed. The one in Stargard had been married to a circuit judge named Stojenthin. She lived on her government pension and the income of a small fortune that had been her dowry. She had two sons who strolled through the world like gipsies, wrapped their sloth in a loud philosophy, and turned to their aunt the countess whenever they were quite at the end of all their resources.

The countess yielded every time. Both young men knew the style of letter-writing that really appealed to her. "They will get over sowing their wild oats," said the countess. She had been awaiting that happy consummation for years, and in the meantime sent them food and money.

It was not so simple to help Letitia. When the girl arrived she possessed just three frocks which she had outgrown and a little linen. The countess ordered robes from Vienna, and fitted out her niece like an heiress.

Letitia permitted herself calmly to be adorned. The eyes of men told her that she was charming. The countess said: "You are destined for great things, my darling." She took the girl's head between her two gloved hands and kissed her audibly on the porcelain clearness of her forehead.

Nor was she satisfied with what she had done. She desired to create a solid foundation and help her niece in a permanent way. That desire brought to her mind the forest of Heiligenkreuz.

On the northern slope of the Röhn mountains there was a piece of forest land having an area of from ten to twelve square kilometres. For more than two decades it had been the subject of litigation between her late husband and the head of his house. The litigation was still going on. It had swallowed huge sums and the countess' prospects of winning were slight. Nevertheless she felt herself to be the future owner of the forest, and was so certain of her title that she determined to present the forest to Letitia as a dowry and to record this gift in proper legal form.

One evening she entered Letitia's bedroom with a written document in her hand. Over her filmy night dress she wore a heavy coat of Russian sable and on her head she had a rubber cap which was to protect her from the bacilli which, in her opinion, whirred about in the darkness like bats.

"Take this and read it, my child," she said with emotion, and handed Letitia the document according to which, at the end of the pending lawsuit, the forest of Heiligenkreuz was to become the sole property of Letitia von Febronius.

Letitia knew the circumstances and the probable value of the piece of paper. But she also knew that the countess had no desire to deceive any one, but was honestly convinced of the importance of the gift. So she exerted her mind and her tact to exhibit a genuine delight. She leaned her cheek against the mighty bosom of the countess and whispered entrancingly: " You are inexpressibly kind, auntie. You really force a confession from me."

" What is it, darling? "

" I find life so wonderful and so lovely."

" Ah, my dear, that's what I want you to do," said the countess. " When one is young each day should be like a bunch of freshly picked violets. It was so in my case."

" I believe," Letitia answered, " that my life will always be like that."

XI

In the vicinity of Königstein in the Taunus mountains the Wahnschaffes owned a little château which Frau Wahnschaffe called Christian's Rest and which was really the property of her son. At first—he was still a boy—Christian had protested against the name. " I don't need any rest," he had said. And the mother had answered: " Some day the need of it will come to you."

Frau Wahnschaffe invited the countess to pass the month of May at Christian's Rest. It was a charming bit of country, and the delight of the countess was uttered noisily.

Crammon, of course, came too. He observed the countess with Argus eyes, and it annoyed him to watch the frequent conversations between Christian and Letitia.

He sat by the fishpond holding his short, English pipe between his lips. " We must get to Paris. That was our agreement. You know that I promised you Eva Sorel. If you don't hurry more than fame is doing, you'll be left out in the cold."

" Time enough," Christian answered laughing and pulling a reed from the water.

" Only sluggards say that," Crammon grunted, " and it's the

act of a sluggard to turn the head of a little goose of eighteen and finally to be taken in by her. These young girls of good family are fit for nothing in the world except for some poor devil whose debts they can pay after the obligatory walk to church. Their manipulations aren't nearly as harmless as they seem, especially when the girls have chaperones who are so damnably like procuresses that the difference is less than between my waistcoat buttons and my breeches buttons."

"Don't worry," Christian soothed his angry friend. "There's nothing to fear."

He threw himself in the grass and thought of Adda Castillo, the beautiful lion-tamer whom he had met in Frankfort. She had told him she would be in Paris in June, and he meant to stay here until then. He liked her. She was so wild and so cold.

But he liked Letitia too. She was so dewy and so tender. Dewy is what he called the liquidness of her eyes, the evasiveness of her being. Daily in the morning he heard her in her tower-room trilling like a lark.

He said: "To-morrow, Bernard, we'll take the car and drive over to see Adda Castillo and her lions."

"Splendid!" Crammon answered. "Lions, that's something for me!" And he gave Christian a comradely thwack on the shoulder.

XII

Judith took Letitia with her to Homburg, and they visited the fashionable shops. The rich girl bought whatever stirred her fancy, and from time to time she turned to her friend and said: "Would you like that? Do try it on! It suits you charmingly." Suddenly Letitia saw herself overwhelmed with presents; and if she made even a gesture of hesitation, Judith was hurt.

They crossed the market-place. Letitia loved cherries. But when they came to the booth of the huckstress, Judith pushed forward and began to chaffer with the woman because she thought the cherries too dear. The woman insisted on her price, and Judith drew Letitia commandingly away.

She asked her: " What do you think of my brother Christian? Is he very nice to you? " She encouraged Letitia, who was frank, gave her advice and told her stories of the adventures that Christian had had with women. His friends had often entertained her with these romances.

But when Letitia, rocked into security by such sincere sympathy, blushed, and first in silence and with lowered eyes, later in sweet, low words, confessed something of her feeling for Christian, Judith's mouth showed an edge of scorn; she threw back her head and showed the arrogance of a family that deemed itself a race of kings.

Letitia felt that she had permitted herself to slip into a net. She guarded herself more closely, and Crammon's warnings would have been needed no longer.

He offered her many. He sought to inspire in her a wholesome fear of the bravery of youth, to attune her mood to the older vintages among men who alone could offer a woman protection and reliance. He was neither so clever nor so subtle as he thought.

With all his jesuitical cultivation, in the end he felt that something about this girl knocked at his heart. No posing to himself helped. His thought spun an annoying web. Was he to prove the truth of the foolish old legend concerning the voice of the blood? Then he must escape from this haunted place!

Letitia laughed at him. She said: " I'm only laughing because I feel that way, Crammon, and because the sky to-day is so blue. Do you understand? "·

" O nymph," sighed Crammon. " I am a poor sinner." And he slunk away.

XIII

Frau Wahnschaffe had decided to arrange a spring festival. It was to illustrate all the splendour which was, on such occasions, traditional in the house of Wahnschaffe. Councils were held in which the major-domo, the housekeeper, the mistress' companion and the countess took part. Frau Wahnschaffe presided at the sessions with the severity of a judge. The countess was interested principally in the question of food and drink.

" My own darling," she said to Letitia, " seventy-five lobsters have been ordered, and two hundred bottles of champagne brought up from the cellar. I am completely overwhelmed. I haven't been so overwhelmed since my wedding."

Letitia stood there in her slenderness and smiled. The words of the countess were music to her. She wanted to lend wings to the days that still separated her from the festival. She trembled whenever a cloud floated across the sky.

Often she scarcely knew how to muffle the jubilation in her own heart. How wonderful, she thought, that one feels what one feels and that things really are as they are. No poet's verse, no painter's vision could vie with the power of her imagination, which made all happenings pure gold and was impenetrable to the shadow of disappointment. Her life was rich—a pure gift of fate.

She merged into one the boundaries of dream and reality. She made up her mind to dream as other people determine to take a walk, and the dim and lawless character of her dream world seemed utterly natural.

One day she spoke of a book that she had read. " It is beautiful beyond belief." She described the people, the scene, and the moving fortunes of the book with such intensity and enthusiasm that all who heard her were anxious to find the book. But she knew neither its title nor the name of the author. They asked her: " Where is the book? Where did you get it? When did you read it?" "Yesterday," she replied. "It must be somewhere about." She hesitated. She was begged to find it. And while she seemed to be reflecting helplessly, Judith said to her: "Perhaps you only dreamed it all." She cast down her eyes and crossed her arms over her bosom with an inimitable gesture and answered with a sense of guilt: "Yes, it seems to me that I did merely dream it all."

Christian asked Crammon: "Do you think that's mere affectation?"

"Not that," answered Crammon, "and yet a bit of feminine trickery. God has provided this sex with many dazzling weapons wherewith to overthrow us."

On the day of the festival Letitia wore a gown of white silk. It was a little dancing frock with many delicate pleats in the skirt and a dark blue sash about her hips. It looked like the foam of fresh milk. When she looked into the mirror she smiled excitedly as though she could not believe her eyes. The countess ran about behind her and said: "Darling, be careful of yourself!" But Letitia did not know what she meant.

There was a sense of intoxication in her when she spoke to the men and women and girls. She had always been fond of people; to-day they seemed irresistible to her. When she met Judith in front of the pavillion, which was bathed in light, she pressed her hands and whispered: "Could life be more beautiful? I am frightened to think this night must end."

XIV

On the meadow in front of the artificial water-fall Christian and some young girls were playing hide and seek after the manner of children. They all laughed as they played; young men formed a circle about them, and watched them half mockingly and half amused.

In the dark trees hung electric bulbs of green glass which were so well concealed that the sward seemed to glow with a light of its own.

Christian played the game with a carelessness that annoyed his partners. The girls wanted it to be taken more seriously, and it vexed them that, in spite of his inattention, he caught them with such ease. The young sister of Meerholz was among them, and Sidonie von Gröben, and the beautiful Fräulein von Einsiedel.

Letitia joined them. She went to the middle of the open space. She let Christian come quite near her. Then she eluded him more swiftly than he had thought possible. He turned to the others, but always Letitia fluttered in front of him. He sought to grasp her, but she was just beyond him. Once he drove her against the box-tree hedge, but she slipped into the foliage and was gone. Her movements, her running and turning, her merry passion had something fascinating; she called from the greenery with the little, laughing cries of a bird. Now he lay in wait for her, and the onlookers became curious.

When she reappeared he feigned not to see her, but suddenly he sped with incredible swiftness to the edge of the fountain's basin where she stood. But she was a shade swifter still and leapt upon the rock, since all the other ways were blocked, and jumped across the water lightly from stone to stone. Her frock with its delicate pleats and loose sleeves fluttered behind her, and, when Christian started in pursuit those below applauded.

Above it was dark. Letitia's shoes became wet and her foot slipped. But before Christian could grasp her she swung herself upon a huge boulder between two tall pines as though to defend herself there or else climb still farther. But her footing failed her on the damp moss and she uttered a little cry, for she knew that he had caught her now.

He had caught her, caught her as she fell, and now held her in his arms. She was very quiet and tried to calm her fluttering breath. Christian was breathing heavily too, and he wondered why the girl was so still and silent. He felt her lovely form and drew her a little closer with that suppressed laughter of his that sounded so cold and arrogant. The moonlight poured through the branches and made his face seem of an extraordinary beauty. Letitia saw his strong, white teeth gleam. She slipped from his arms, and put her own right arm about the trunk of one of the trees.

Here was all that she had dreamed of. Here was the breath of danger and the breath of desire, a wilderness and a moonlit night, distant music and a secret meeting. But her blood was quiet, for she was still a child.

Christian looked at the girl pliant against the tree; he saw her dishevelled hair, her dewy eyes and lips; his eyes followed the lines of her body and it seemed to him that he could taste the coolness of her skin and the sweetness of her innocent breath. He did not hesitate to take possession of his booty.

Swiftly he sought her hand, when suddenly he became aware of a toad that with loathsome sloth crept along Letitia's white frock, first across its hem, then upward toward her hip. He grew pale and turned away. " The others are waiting. We had better turn back," he said and began to climb downward.

Letitia followed his movements with staring eyes. The fiery emotion which had transformed her to her own vision into a fairy being, a Diana or Melusina, turned to pain and she began to weep. She did not know how to interpret what had happened, and her sorrow lasted until, by a fanciful but charming explanation, she had made it not more intelligible but more consoling in its character. Then she dried her tears and smiled again.

When Letitia arose the toad jumped into the moss. There was no sound.

XV

On the afternoon before the departure of Crammon and Christian there was a violent thunder storm. The two men paced up and down in the upper corridor of the château and discussed their plans. In a pause between two peals of thunder Crammon listened and said: " What a queer noise. Did you hear it? "

" Yes," Christian answered and they followed the direction of the sound.

At the end of the gallery was a mirrored hall, the doors of which were ajar. Crammon opened the door a little wider, peered in and laughed softly in his throat. Christian peered in too, above Crammon's head, and joined in the laughter.

On the brilliantly polished floor of the room, which contained no furniture except a few couches and armchairs ranged along the walls, Letitia stood in little blue slippers and a pale blue gown and played at ball. Her face had an expression of ecstasy. The all but uninterrupted lightning that turned the mirrors into yellow flame gave her play a ghostliness of aspect.

Now she would toss the ball straight up, now she would throw it against the wall between the mirrors and catch it as it rebounded. At times she let it fall on the floor and clapped her hands or spread out her arms until it leaped up to be -caught again. She turned and bent over and threw back her head, or advanced a step or whispered, always smiling and, utterly absorbed. After the two had watched her for a while, Crammon drew Christian away, for the lightning made him nervous. He hated an electrical storm and had chosen to walk in the gallery to escape it. He now lit his short pipe and asked peevishly: " Do you understand the girl? "

Christian made no answer. Something lured him back to the threshold of the hall in which Letitia was playing her solitary game. But he remembered the toad on her white dress, and a strange aversion arose in his heart. =

XVI

He did not love the memory of unpleasant events.

He did not like to speak of the past, whether it was pleasant or not. Nor did it please him to turn back upon a path. If ever it became necessary he soon grew weary.

He did not care for people whose faces showed the strain of intellectual labour, nor such as discoursed of books or of the sciences. Nor did he love the pale or the hectic or the over-eager or those who argued or insisted on the rightness of their opinions. If any one defended an opinion opposed to his own he smiled as courteously as though no difference existed. And it was painful to him to be asked concerning his opinion directly, and rather than bear the burden of a speech of explanation he did not hesitate to feign ignorance.

If in large cities he was forced to walk or ride through the quarters inhabited by the proletarian poor, he hastened as much as possible, compressed his lips, breathed sparingly, and his vexation would give his eyes a greenish glitter.

Once on the street a crippled beggar had caught hold of his great coat. He returned home and presented the coat to his valet. Even in his childhood he had refused to pass places where ragged people were to be seen, and if any one told of misery or need among men he had left the room, full of aversion for the speaker.

He hated to speak or to hear others speak of the functions or needs of the body—of sleep or hunger or thirst. The sight of a human being asleep was repulsive to him. He did not like emphatic leavetakings or the ceremonious greetings of those who had been absent long. He disliked church bells and people who prayed and all things that have to do with the exercise of piety. He was quite without understanding for even the very moderate Protestantism of his father.

He made no demand in words, but instinctively he chose to bear no company but that of well-clad, care-free, and clear-seeing people. Wherever he suspected secrets, hidden sorrows, a darkened soul, a brooding tendency, inner or outer conflicts, he became frosty and unapproachable and elusive. Therefore his mother said: " Christian is a child of the sun and can thrive only in the sunlight." She had made an early cult of keeping far from him all that is turbid, distorted, or touched with pain.

On her desk lay the marble copy of a plaster-cast of Christian's hand—a hand that was not small, but sinewy and delicately formed, capable of a strong grasp, but unused and quiet.

XVII

On the trip from Hanau to Frankfort the automobile accident occurred in which young Alfred Meerholz lost his life. Christian was driving, but, as in the old days when the great tree fell, he remained unharmed.

Crammon had accompanied Christian and Alfred as far as Hanau. There he wanted to visit Clementine von Westernach and then proceed to Frankfort by an evening train. Christian had sent the chauffeur ahead to Frankfort the day before in order to make certain purchases.

Christian at once drove at high speed, and toward evening, as the road stretched out before him empty and free of obstacles, he made the car fly. Alfred Meerholz urged him on, glowing in the intoxication of speed. Christian smiled and let the machine do its utmost.

The trees on both sides looked like leaping animals in a photograph; the white riband of the road rolled shimmering toward them and was devoured by the roaring car; the reddening sky and the hills on the horizon seemed to swing in circles; the air seethed in their ears; their bodies vibrated and yearned to be whirled still more swiftly over an earth that revealed all the allurement of its smoothness and rotundity.

Suddenly a black dot arose in the white glare of the road. Christian gave a signal with his horn. The dot quickly assumed human form. Again the signal shrieked. The figure did not yield. Christian grasped the steering wheel more firmly. Alfred Meerholz rose in his seat and shouted. It was too late for the brake. Christian reversed the wheel energetically; it went a trifle too far. There was a jolt, a concussion, a crash, the groan of a splintering tree, a hissing and crackling of flame, a clash and rattle of steel. It was over in a moment.

Christian lay stunned. Then he got up and felt his limbs and body. He could think and he could walk. "All's right," he said to himself.

Then he caught sight of the body of his friend. The young man lay under the twisted and misshapen chassis with a crushed skull. A little trickle of scarlet blood ran across the white dust of the road. A few paces to one side stood in surprised stupor the drunken man who had not made way.

People at once began gathering hurriedly from all directions. There was a hotel near by. Christian answered many questions briefly. The drunken man was taken in custody. A physician came and examined young Meerholz's body. It was placed on a stretcher and carried into the hotel. Christian telegraphed first to General Meerholz, then to Crammon.

His travelling bag had not been injured. While he was changing his clothes, police officers arrived, and took down his depositions concerning the accident. Then he went to the dining-room and ordered a meal and a bottle of wine.

He barely touched the food. The wine he gradually drank.

He saw himself standing in the dim hot-house awaiting Letitia. She had come animated by her excitement. Languishing and jesting she had whispered: "Well, my lord and master?" And he had said to her: "Have the image of a small toad made of gold, and wear the charm about your throat in order to avert the evil magic."

Her kiss seemed still to be burning on his lips.

At eleven o'clock that night came Crammon, the faithful. "I beg of you, my dear fellow, attend to all necessary arrangements for me," Christian said. "I don't want to pass the night here. Adda Castillo will be getting impatient." He handed Crammon his wallet.

Christian was thinking again of the romantic girl who, like all of her temper, gave without knowing what she gave or to whom, nor knew how long life is. But her kiss burned on his lips. He could not forget it.

Crammon returned. "Everything is settled," he said in a business like way. "The car will be ready in fifteen minutes. Now let us go and say farewell to our poor friend."

Christian followed him. A porter led them to a dim store-room in which the body had been placed until the morrow. A white cloth had been wrapped about the head. At the feet crouched a cat with spotted fur.

Silently Crammon folded his hands. Christian felt a cold breath on his cheeks, but there was no stirring in his breast. When they came out into the open he said: "We must buy a new car in Frankfort. We need not be back here before noon to-morrow. The general cannot possibly arrive until then."

Crammon nodded. But a surprised look sought the younger man, a look that seemed to ask: Of what stuff are you made?

About him, delicate, noble, proud, there was an icy air—the infinitely glassy clarity that rests on mountains before the dawn.

THE GLOBE ON THE FINGERTIPS OF
AN ELF

I

CRAMMON had been a true prophet. Ten months had sufficed to fix the eyes of the world upon the dancer, Eva Sorel. The great newspapers coupled her name with the celebrated ones of the earth; her art was regarded everywhere as the fine flower of its age.

All those to whose restless spiritual desires she had given form and body were at her feet. The leaders of sorely driven humanity drew a breath and looked up to her. The adorers of form and the proclaimers of new rhythms vied for a smile from her lips.

She remained calm and austere with herself. Sometimes the noise of plaudits wearied her. Hard beset by the vast promises of greedy managers, she felt not rarely a breath of horror. Her inner vision, fixed upon a far and ideal goal, grew dim at the stammered thanks of the easily contented. These, it seemed to her, would cheat her. Then she fled to Susan Rappard and was scolded for her pains.

"We wandered out to conquer the world," said Susan, "and the world has submitted almost without a struggle. Why don't you enjoy your triumph?"

"What my hands hold and my eyes grasp gives me no cause to feel very triumphant yet," Eva answered.

Susan lamented loudly. "You little fool, you've literally gone hungry. Take your fill now!"

"Be quiet," Eva replied, "what do you know of my hunger?"

People besieged her threshold, but she received only a few

46

and chose them carefully. She lived in a world of flowers.
Jean Cardillac had furnished her an exquisite house, the
garden terrace of which was like a tropical paradise. When
she reclined or sat there in the evening under the softened
light of the lamps, surrounded by her gently chatting friends,
whose most casual glance was an act of homage, she seemed
removed from the world of will and of the senses and to be
present in this realm of space only as a beautiful form.

Yet even those who thought her capable of any metamor-
phosis were astonished when a sudden one came upon her and
when its cause seemed to be an unknown and inconsiderable
person. Prince Alexis Wiguniewski had introduced the man,
and his name was Ivan Michailovitch Becker. He was short
and homely, with deep-set Sarmatian eyes, lips that looked
swollen, and a straggling beard about his chin and cheeks.
Susan was afraid of him.

It was on a December night when the snow was banked up
at the windows that Ivan Michailovitch Becker had talked
with Eva Sorel for eight hours in the little room spread with
Italian rugs. In the adjoining room Susan walked shivering
up and down, wondering when her mistress would call for
help. She had an old shawl about her shoulders. From time
to time she took an almond from her pocket, cracked it with
her teeth, and threw the shells into the fireplace.

But on this night Eva did not go to bed, not even when the
Russian had left her. She entered her sleeping chamber and
let her hair roll down unrestrained so that it hid her head and
body, and she sat on a low stool holding her fevered cheeks
in her hollow hands. Susan, who had come to help her undress,
crouched near her on the floor and waited for a word.

At last her young mistress spoke. "Read me the thirty-
third canto of the *Inferno*," she begged.

Susan brought two candles and the book. She placed the
candles on the floor and the volume on Eva's lap. Then she
read with a monotonous sound of lamentation. But toward

the end, especially where the poet speaks of petrified and frozen tears, her clear voice grew firmer and more eloquent.

> "Lo pianto stesso lì pianger non lascia;
> E il duol, che trova in sugli occhi rintoppo,
> Si volve in entro a far crescer l'ambascia:
> Chè le lagrime prime fanno groppo,
> E, sì come visiere di cristallo,
> Riempion sotto il ciglio tutto il coppo."[1]

When she had finished she was frightened by the gleaming moisture in Eva's eyes.

Eva arose and bent her head far backward and closed her eyes and said: "I shall dance all that—damnation in hell and then redemption!"

Then Susan embraced Eva's knees and pressed her cheek against the bronze coloured silk of the girl's garment and murmured: "You can do anything you wish."

From that night on Eva was filled with a more urgent passion, and her dancing had lines in which beauty hovered on the edge of pain. Ecstatic prophets asserted that she was dancing the new century, the sunset of old ideas, the revolution that is to come.

II

When Crammon saw her again she showed the exquisitely cultivated firmness of a great lady and forced his silent admiration. And again there began that restless burning in his heart.

He talked to her about Christian Wahnschaffe and one evening he brought him to her. In Christian's face there was something radiant. Adda Castillo had drenched it with her passion. Eva felt about him the breath of another woman and her face showed a mocking curiosity. For several seconds

---

[1] "The very weeping there allows them not to weep; and the grief, which finds impediment upon their eyes, turns inward to increase the agony: for their first tears form a knot, and, like crystal vizors, fill up all the cavity beneath their eye-brows."

the young man and the dancer faced each other like two statues on their pedestals.

Crammon wondered whether Christian would ever thank him for this service. He gave his arm to Susan, and the two walked to and fro in the picture gallery.

"I hope your blond German friend is a prince," said Susan with her air of worry.

"He's a prince travelling incognito in this vale of tears," Crammon answered. "You've made some stunning changes here," he added, gazing about him. "I'm satisfied with you both. You are wise and know the ways of the world."

Susan stopped and told him of what weighed upon her mind. Ivan Machailovitch Becker came from time to time, and he and Eva would talk together for many hours. Always after that Eva would pass a sleepless night and answer no questions and have a fevered gleaming in her eyes. And how was one to forbid the marvellous child her indulgence in this mood? Yet it might hold a danger for her. No stray pessimist with awkward hands should be permitted to drag down as with weights the delicate vibrations of her soul. "What do you advise us to do?" she asked.

Crammon rubbed his smooth chin. "I must think it over," he said, "I must think it over." He sat down in a corner and rested his head on his hands and pondered.

Eva chatted with Christian. Sometimes she laughed at his remarks, sometimes they seemed strange and astonishing to her. Yet even where she thought her own judgment the better, she was willing to hear and learn. She regarded his figure with pleasure and asked him to get her, from a table in the room, an onyx box filled with semi-precious stones. She wanted to see how he would walk and move, how he would stretch out his arm and hand after the box and give it to her. She poured the stones into her lap and played with them. She let them glide through her fingers, and said to Christian with a smile that he should have become a dancer.

He answered naïvely that he was not fond of dancing in
general, but that he would think it charming to dance with
her. His speech amused her, but she promised to dance with
him. The stones glittered in her hands; a quiver of her mouth
betrayed vexation and pride but also compassion.

When she laughed it embarrassed Christian, and when she.
was silent he was afraid of her thoughts. He had promised
to meet Adda Castillo at almost this hour. Yet he stayed
although he knew that she would be jealous and make a scene.
Eva seemed like an undiscovered country to him that lured
him on. Her tone, her gestures, her expression, her words, all
seemed utterly new. He could not tear himself away, and his
dark blue eyes clung to her with a kind of balked penetration.
Even when her · friends came—Cardillac, Wiguniewski,
d'Autichamps—he stayed on.

But Eva had found a name for him. She called him Eidolon.
She uttered that name and played with its sound even as she
played with the mani-coloured jewels in her lap.

III

One night Crammon entered a tavern in the outer boule-
vards. It was called " Le pauvre Job." He looked about him
for a while and then sat down near a table at which several
young men of foreign appearance were conversing softly in a
strange tongue.

It was a group of Russian political refugees whose meeting
place he had discovered. Their chief was Ivan Michailovitch
Becker. Crammon pretended to be reading a paper while he
observed his man, whom he recognized from a photograph
which Prince Wiguniewski had shown him. He had never seen
so fanatical a face. He compared it with a smouldering fire
that filled the air with heat and fumes.

· He had been told that Ivan Becker had suffered seven years
of imprisonment and five of Siberian exile and that many

thousands of the young men of his people were wholly devoted
to him and would risk any danger or sacrifice at his bidding.

"Here they live in the most brilliant spot of the habitable
earth," Crammon thought angrily, "and plan horrors."

Crammon was an enemy of violent overthrow. If it did not
interfere with his own comfort, he was rather glad to see
the poor get the better of the over-fed bourgeois. He was
a friend of the poor. He took a condescending and friendly
interest in the common people. But he respected high descent, opposed any breach of venerable law, and held his
monarch in honour. Every innovation in the life of the state
filled him with presentiments of evil, and he deprecated the
weakness of the governments that had permitted the wretched
parliaments to usurp their powers.

He knew that there was something threatening at the
periphery of his world. A stormwind from beyond blew out
lamps. What if they should all be blown out? Was not their
light and radiance the condition of a calm life?

He sat there in his seriousness and dignity, conscious of his
superiority and of his good deeds. As a representative of
order he had determined to appeal to the conscience of these
rebels if a suitable opportunity were to come. Yet what tormented him was less an anxiety over the throne of the Tsar
than one over Eva Sorel. It was necessary to free the dancer
from the snares of this man.

An accident favoured his enterprise. One man after another
left the neighbouring table and at last Ivan Becker was left
alone. Crammon took his glass of absinthe and went over.
He introduced himself, referring to his friendship with Prince
Wiguniewski.

Silently Becker pointed to a chair.

True to his kind and condescending impulses Crammon
assumed the part of an amiable man who can comprehend
every form of human aberration. He approached his aim
with innocent turns of speech. He scarcely touched the poison-

ous undergrowth of political contentions. He merely pointed out with the utmost delicacy that, in the West of Europe, the private liberty of certain lofty personages would have to remain untouched unless force were to be used to oppose force. Gentle as his speech was, it was an admonition. Ivan smiled indulgently.

"Though the whole sky were to flare with the conflagrations that devastate your Holy Russia," Crammon said with conscious eloquence, and the corners of his mouth seemed to bend in right angles toward his square chin, "we will know how to defend what is sacred to us. Caliban is an impressive beast. But if he were to lay his hands on Ariel he might regret it."

Again Ivan Michailovitch smiled. His expression was strangely mild and gentle, and gave his homely, large face an almost feminine aspect. He listened as though desiring to be instructed.

Crammon was encouraged. "What has Ariel to do with your misery? He looks behind him to see if men kiss the print of his feet. He demands joy and glory, not blood and force."

"Ariel's feet are dancing over open graves," Ivan Michailovitch said softly.

"Your dead are safe at peace," Crammon answered. "With the living we shall know how to deal."

"We are coming," said Ivan Michailovitch still more softly. "We are coming." It sounded mysterious.

Half fearfully, half contemptuously Crammon looked at the man. After a long pause he said as though casually, "At twelve paces I can hit the ace of hearts four times out of five."

Ivan Michailovitch nodded. "I can't," he said almost humbly, and showed his right hand, which he usually concealed skilfully. It was mutilated.

"What happened to your hand?" Crammon asked in pained surprise.

"When I lay in the subterranean prison at Kazan a keeper

forged the chain about me too hard," Ivan Michailovitch murmured.

Crammon was silent, but the other went on: " Perhaps you've noticed too that it's difficult for me to speak. I lived alone too long in the desert of snow, in a wooden hut, in the icy cold. I became unused to words. I suffered. But that is only a single word: suffering. How can one make its content clear? My body was but a naked scaffolding, a ruin. But my heart grew and expanded. How can I tell it? It grew to be so great, so blood red, so heavy that it became a burden to me in the fearful attempt at flight which I finally risked. But God protected me." And he repeated softly, " God protected me."

In Crammon's mind all ideas became confused. Was this man with his gentle voice and the timid eyes of a girl the murderous revolutionary and hero of possible barricades whom he had expected to meet? In his surprise and embarrassment he became silent.

"Let us go," said Ivan Michailovitch. " It is late." He arose and threw a coin on the table and stepped out into the street at Crammon's side. There he began again, hesitatingly and shyly: " I don't want to presume to judge, but I don't understand these people here. They are so certain of themselves and so reasonable. Yet that reasonableness is the completest madness. A beast of the field that feels the tremor of an earthquake and flees is wiser. And another thing: Ariel, the being whom you strive so eloquently to protect, has no moral responsibility. No one thinks of blaming it. What is it but form, gesture, beauty? But don't you think that the darker hue and deeper power that are born of the knowledge of superhuman suffering might raise art above the interests of idle sybarites? We need heralds who stand above the idioms of the peoples; but those are possibilities that one can only dream of with despair in one's heart." He nodded a brief good-night and went.

Crammon felt like a man who had merrily gone out in a

light spring suit but had been overtaken by a rainstorm and returns drenched and angry. The clocks were striking two. A lady of the Opéra Comique had been waiting for him since, midnight; the key to her apartment was in his pocket. But when he came to the bridge across the Seine he seized the key and, overcome by a violent fit of depression, flung it into the water.

"Sweet Ariel!" He spoke softly to himself. "I kiss the prints of your feet."

IV

Adda Castillo noticed that Christian was turning from her. She had not expected that, at least not so soon; and as she saw him grow cold, her love increased. But his indifference kept pace with her ardour, and so her passionate heart lost all repose.

She was accustomed to change and, in spite of her youth, had been greatly loved. She had never demanded fidelity before nor practised it. But this man was more to her than any other had been.

She knew who was robbing her of him; she had seen the dancer. When she called Christian to account he frankly admitted as a fact what she had mentioned only as a suspicion in the hope of having it denied. She instituted comparisons. She found that she was more beautiful than Eva Sorel, more harmoniously formed, racier and more impassioned. Her friends confirmed her in this opinion; and yet she felt that the other had some advantage to which she must yield. Neither she nor her flatterers could give it a name. But she felt herself the more deeply affronted.

She adorned her person, she practised all her arts, she unfolded all sides of her wild and entrancing temperament. It was in vain. Then she vowed vengeance and clenched her fists and stamped. Or else she begged and lay on her knees before him and sobbed. One method was as foolish as the other. He was surprised and asked calmly: "Why do you throw aside all dignity?"

One day he told her that they must separate. She turned very white and trembled. Suddenly she took a revolver from her pocket, aimed at him and fired twice. He heard the bullets whiz past his head, one on either side. They hit the mirror and smashed it, and the fragments clattered to the floor.

People rushed to the door. Christian went out and explained that the noise meant no harm and was due to mere carelessness. When he returned he found Adda Castillo lying on the sofa with her face buried in the pillows. He showed no fright and no sense of the danger that he had escaped. He thought merely how annoying such things were and how banal. He took his hat and stick and left the room.

It was long before Adda Castillo arose. She went to the mirror and shivered. There was but one fragment of it left in the frame. But by the help of this fragment she smoothed her coal-black hair.

A few days later she came to see Christian. On the card that she had sent in she begged for an interview of but five minutes. Her farewell performance in Paris was to take place that evening and she begged him to be present at the circus. He hesitated. The glowing eyes in the wax-white face were fixed on him in a mortal terror. It made him uncomfortable, but something like pity stirred within him and he agreed to come.

Crammon accompanied him. They entered just as Adda Castillo's act was about to begin. The cage with the lions was being drawn into the arena. Their seats were near the front. "They're getting to be a bit of a bore, these lions," Crammon grumbled and watched the audience through his glasses.

Adda Castillo in scarlet fleshings, her dark hair loose, her lips and cheeks heavily rouged, entered the cage of the lionness and her four cubs. Perhaps something in the woman's bearing irritated Teddy, the youngest lion. At all events he backed before her, roared and lifted his paw. Adda Castillo whistled and commanded him with a gesture to leave the mother animal. Teddy crouched and hissed.

At that moment Adda, instead of mastering the beast with her glance, turned to the public and searched the front rows with her sparkling eyes. Teddy leaped on her shoulder. She was down. One cry arose from many throats. The people jumped up. Many fled. Others grew pale but stared in evil fascination at the cage.

At that moment Trilby, the mother animal, came forward with a mighty leap, not to attack her mistress but to save her from the cubs. With powerful blows of her paw she thrust Teddy aside and stood protectingly over the girl who was bleeding from many wounds. But the cubs, greedy for blood, threw themselves on their mother and beat and bit her back and flanks, so that she retreated howling to a corner and left the girl to her fate.

The keepers had rushed up with long spears and hooks, but it was too late. The cubs had bitten their teeth deep into the body of Adda Castillo and torn her flesh to shreds. They did not let go until formaldehyde was sprinkled on her scattered remains.

The cries of pity and terror, the weeping and wringing of hands, the thronging at the gates and the noise of the circus men, the image of a clown who stood as though frozen on a drum, a horse that trotted in from the stables, the sight of the bloody, unspeakably mutilated body in its dripping shreds —none of all this penetrated in any connected or logical form the consciousness of Christian. It seemed to him mere confusion and ghostly whirl. He uttered no sound. Only his face was pale. His face was very pale.

In the motor car on their way to Jean Cardillac, with whom they were to dine, Crammon said: " By God, I wouldn't like to die between the jaws of a lion. It is a cruel death and an ignominious one." He sighed and surreptitiously looked at Christian.

Christian had the car stop and asked Crammon to present his excuses to Cardillac. "What are you going to do?" Crammon asked in his astonishment.

And Christian replied that he wanted to be alone, that he must be alone for a little.

Crammon could scarcely control himself. "Alone? You? What for?" But already Christian had disappeared in the crowd.

"He wants to be alone! What an insane notion!" Crammon growled. He shook his head and bade the chauffeur drive on. He drew up the collar of his greatcoat and dedicated a last thought to the unhappy Adda Castillo without assigning any guilt or blame to his friend.

V

"Eidolon is not as cheerful as usual," Eva said to Christian. "What has happened? Eidolon mustn't be sad."

He smiled and shook his head. But she had heard of the happening at the circus and also knew in what relation Adda Castillo had stood to Christian.

"I had a bad dream," he said and told her of it.

"I dreamed that I was in a railroad station and wanted to take a train. Many trains came in but roared and passed with indescribable swiftness. I wanted to ask after the meaning of this. But when I turned around I saw behind me in a semi-circle an innumerable throng. And all these people looked at me; but when I approached them, they all drew away slowly and silently with outstretched arms. All about in that monstrous circle they drew silently away from me. It was horrible."

She passed her hand over his forehead to chase the horror away. But she recognized the power of her touch and was frightened by her image in his eye.

When from the stage where she was bowing amid the flowers and the applause she perceived the touch of his glances she felt in them a threat of enslavement. When on his arm she approached a table and heard the delighted whisper of people at them both, she seemed to herself the victim of a conspiracy, and a hesitation crept into her bearing. When Crammon, practising a strange self-abnegation, spoke of Christian in extravagant terms, and Susan, even in their nocturnal talks, grew mythical concerning his high descent, when Cardillac grew restless and Cornelius Ermelang, the young German poet who adored her, asked questions with his timid eyes—when these things came to pass she feigned coldness and became unapproachable.

She scolded Susan, she made fun of Crammon, she laughed at Jean Cardillac, jestingly she bent her knee to the poet. She confused her entire court of painters, politicians, journalists, and dandies with her incomprehensible mimicry and flexibility, and said that Eidolon was only an illusion and a symbol.

Christian did not understand this—neither this nor her swift withdrawals from him, and then her turning back and luring him anew. A passionate gesture would arise and suddenly turn to reproof, and one of delight would turn into estrangement. It was useless to try to bind her by her own words. She would join the tips of her fingers and turn her head aside and look out of the corners of her eyes at the floor with a cool astuteness.

Once he had driven her into a corner, but she called Susan, leaned her head against the woman's shoulder and whispered in her ear.

Another time, in order to test her feeling, he spoke of his trip to England. With charmingly curved hands she gathered up her skirt and surveyed her feet.

Another time, in the light and cheerful tone they used to each other, he reproached her with making a fool of him. She crossed her arms and smiled mysteriously, wild and subdued at once. She looked as though she had stepped out of a Byzantine mosaic.

He knew the freedom of her life. But when he sought for the motives that guided her, he had no means of finding them.

He knew nothing of the intellectual fire of the dancer, but took her to be a woman like any other. He did not see that that which is, in other women, the highest stake and the highest form of life, needed to be in her life but a moment's inclination and a moment's gliding by. He did not grasp the form in her, but saw the contour melt in glimmering change. Coming from the sensual regions of one possessed like Adda Castillo, he breathed here an air purified of all sultriness, which intoxicated but also frightened him, which quickened the beat of the heart but sharpened the vision.

Everything was fraught with presages of fate: when she walked beside him; when they rode side by side in the Bois de Boulogne; when they sat in the twilight and he heard her clear and childlike voice; when in the palm garden she teased her little monkeys; when she listened to Susan at the piano and let the bright stones glide through her fingers.

One evening when he was leaving he met Jean Cardillac at the gate. They greeted each other. Then involuntarily Christian stopped and looked after the man, whose huge form threw a gigantic shadow on the steps. Invisible little slaves seemed to follow this shadow, all bearing treasures to be laid at Eva's feet.

An involuntary determination crystallized in him. It seemed important to measure his strength against this shadow's. He turned back and the servants let him pass. Cardillac and Eva were in the picture gallery. She was curled up on a sofa, rolled up almost like a snake. Not far from those two, on a low stool, sat Susan impassive but with burning eyes.

"You've promised to drive with me to the races at Long-champ, Eva," said Christian. He stood by the door to show that he desired nothing else.

"Yes, Eidolon. Why the reminder?" answered Eva without moving, but with a flush on her cheeks.

"Quite alone with me——?".

"Yes, Eidolon, quite alone."

"My dream suddenly came back to me, and I thought of that train that wouldn't stop."

She laughed at the naïve and amiable tone of his words. Her eyes grew gentle and she laid her head back on the pillows. Then she looked at Cardillac, who arose silently.

"Good-night," said Christian and went.

It was during these days that Denis Lay had arrived in Paris. Crammon had expected him and now welcomed him with ardour. "He is the one man living who is your equal and who competes with you in my heart," Crammon had said to Christian.

Denis was the second son of Lord Stainwood. He had had a brilliant career at Oxford, where his exploits had been the talk of the country. He had formed a new party amid the undergraduates, whose discussions and agitations had spared no time-honoured institutions. At twenty-two he was not only a marksman, hunter, fisherman, sailor, and boxer, but a learned philologist. He was handsome, wealthy, radiant with life, and surrounded by a legend of mad pranks and by a halo of distinction and elegance—the last and finest flower of his class and nation.

Christian recognized his qualities without envy and the two became friends at once. One evening he was entertaining Cardillac, Crammon, Wiguniewski, Denis Lay, the Duchess of Marivaux, and Eva Sorel. And it was on this occasion that Eva, in the presence of the whole company, lightly broke the promise that she had given him.

Denis had expressed the desire to take her to Longchamp in his car. Eva became aware of Christian's look. It was watchful, but still assured. She held a cluster of grapes in her hand. When she had placed the fruit back on the plate before her, she had betrayed him. Christian turned pale. He felt that she needed no reminder. She had chosen. It was for him to be quiet and withdraw.

Eva took up the cluster of grapes again. Lifting it on the palm of her hand she said with that smile of dreamy enthusiasm which seemed heartless to Christian now: "Beautiful fruit, I shall leave you until I am hungry for you."

Crammon raised his glass and cried: "Whoever wishes to do homage to the lady of our allegiance—drink! "

They all drank to Eva, but Christian did not lift his eyes.

VI

On the next night after her performance, Eva had invited several friends to her house. She had danced the chief rôle in the new pantomime called " The Dryads," and her triumph had been very great. She came home in a cloud of flowers. Later a footman brought in a basket heaped with cards and letters.

She sank into Susan's arms, happy and exhausted. Every pore of her glowed with life.

Crammon said: " There may be insensitive scoundrels in the world. But I think it's magnificent to watch a human being on the very heights of life."

For this saying Eva, with graceful reverence, gave him a red rose. And the burning in his breast became worse and worse.

It had been agreed that Christian and Denis were to have a fencing bout. Eva had begged for it. She hoped not only to enjoy the sight, but to learn something for her own art from the movements of the two young athletes.

The preparations had been completed. In the round hall hung with tapestries, Christian and Denis faced each other. Eva clapped her hands and they assumed their positions. For a while nothing was heard except their swift, muffled, and rhythmical steps and · the clash of their foils. Eva stood erect, all eye, drinking in their gestures. Christian's body was slenderer and more elastic than the Englishman's. The latter had more strength and freedom. They were like brothers of whom one had grown up in a harsh, the other in a mild climate; the one self-disciplined and upheld by a long tradition of breeding, the other cradled in tenderness and somewhat uncertain within. The one was all marrow, the other all radiance. In virility and passion they were equals.

Crammon was in the seventh heaven of enthusiasm.

When the combat was nearly at an end, Cornelius Ermelang appeared, and with him Ivan Michailovitch Becker. Eva had asked Ermelang to read a poem. He and Becker had known each other long, and when he had found the Russian walking to and fro near the gate he had simply brought him up. It was the first time that Ivan showed himself to Eva's other friends. Both were silent and sat down.

Christian and Denis had changed back to their usual garments, and now Ermelang was to read. Susan sat down near Becker and observed him attentively.

Cornelius Ermelang was a delicate creature and of a repulsive ugliness. He had a steep forehead, watery blue eyes with veiled glances, a pendulous nether lip, and a yellowish wisp of beard at the extreme end of his chin. His voice was extraordinarily gentle and soft, and had something of the singsong rhythm of a preacher's.

The name of the poem was " Saint Francis and Why Men Followed Him," and its content was in harmony with the traditions and the writings.

Once upon a time Saint Francis was tarrying in the convent of Portiuncula with Brother Masseo of Marignano, who was himself a very holy man and could speak beautifully and wisely concerning God. And for this reason Saint Francis loved him greatly. Now one day Saint Francis returned from the forest where he had been praying, and just as he emerged from the trees Brother Masseo came to meet him and said: " Why thee rather than another? Why thee? "

Saint Francis asked: "What is the meaning of thy words?"
Brother Masseo replied: "I ask why all the world follows thee,
and why every man would see thee and listen to thee and obey
thee. Thou art not goodly to look upon, nor learned, nor of
noble blood. Why is it that all the world follows thee?"
When Saint Francis heard this he was glad in his heart, and he
raised his face to Heaven and stood without moving for a long
space, because his spirit was lifted up to God. But when
he came to himself again, he threw himself upon his knees
and praised and thanked God, and full of a devout passion
turned to Brother Masseo and spoke: "Wouldst thou know
why they follow me, and me always, and me rather than another? This grace has been lent to me by the glance of
Almighty God Himself which rests on the good and the evil
everywhere. For His holy eyes saw among the sinners on
earth none who was more wretched than I, none who was less
wise and able, nor any who was a greater sinner. For the
miraculous work that He had it in His heart to bring about He
found no creature on earth so mean as I. And therefore did
He choose me to put to shame the world with its nobility and
its pride and its strength and its beauty and its wisdom, in
order that it might be known that all power and goodness
proceed from Him alone and from no created thing, and that no
one may boast before His face. But whoever boast, let him
boast in the Lord." And Brother Masseo was frightened at
this answer, which was so full of humility and spoken with
such fervour.

And the poem related how Brother Masseo went into the
forest out of which Saint Francis had come, and how tones as
of organ music came from the tops of the trees and formed
more and more clearly the question: Wouldst thou know why?
Wouldst thou know? And he cast himself upon the earth,
upon the roots and stones, and kissed the roots and stones and
cried out: "I know why! I know why!"

The stanzas had a sweetness and an inner ecstasy; their
music was muffled and infinitely fluid, with many but shy and
half-hidden rimes.

"It is beautiful," said Denis Lay, who understood German
perfectly.

And Crammon said: "It is like an old painting on glass."

"What I admire most," said Denis, "is that it brings the
figure of Saint Francis very close to one with that magical
quality of *cortesia* which he possessed above all other saints."

"*Cortesia?* What does it mean exactly?" Wiguniewski
asked. "Does it mean a humble and devout courtesy?"

Eva arose. "That is it," she said, "just that." And she
made an exquisite gesture with both hands. All looked at
her, and she added: "To give what is mine, and only to
appear to take what is another's, that is *cortesia.*"

During all this conversation Christian had withdrawn himself from the others. Aversion was written on his face. Even
during the reading he had hardly been able to keep his seat.
He did not know what it was that rebelled in him and irritated
him supremely. A spirit of mockery and scorn was in him
and fought for some expression. With assumed indifference
he called out to Denis Lay, and began to talk to him about
the stallion that Lay desired to sell and Christian to possess.
He had offered forty thousand francs for it. Now he offered
forty-five thousand, and his voice was so loud that all could
hear him. Crammon stepped to his side as though to guard
him.

"Eidolon!" Eva cried suddenly.

Christian looked at her with a consciousness of guilt. Their
eyes met. The others became silent in surprise.

"The beast is worth that anywhere," Christian murmured,
without taking his eyes from Eva.

"Come, Susan," Eva turned to the woman, and about her

mouth curled an expression of bitterness and scorn. "He knows how to fence and how to trade horses. Of *cortesia* he knows nothing. Good-night, gentlemen." She bowed and slipped through the green hangings.

In consternation the company scattered.

When she had reached her room Eva threw herself into a chair, and in bitterness of spirit hid her face in her hands. Susan crouched near her on the floor, waiting and wondering. When a quarter of an hour had passed she arose and took the clasps out of Eva's hair and began to comb it.

Eva was passive. She was thinking of her own master and of what he had taught her.

VIII

This is what her master had taught her: Train your body to fear and obey the spirit. What you grant the body beyond its necessity makes you its slave. Never be the one seduced. Seduce others, and your way will always be your own to see. Be a secret to others or you grow vulgar to yourself. Give yourself wholly only to your work. Passions of sense lay waste the heart. What one man truly receives of another is never the fullness of the hour or the soul, but lees and dregs that are fructified late and unconsciously.

She had been only twelve, when, persuaded by jugglers and answering the call of her fate, she had left her home in a remote little Franconian town. She was very far from her master then. But the way was pre-determined.

She never lost herself. She glided over difficulties and degradations as the chamois does over boulders and abysses. Whoever saw her amid the strolling jugglers held her to be the kidnapped child of distinguished parents. She was, as a matter of fact, the daughter of an obscure musician named Daniel Nothafft and of a servant girl. A dreamy feeling of pity and admiration united her to her father; her mother she had never known, and so discarded her ill-sounding name.

She was accustomed to pass the night in tents and barns. In towns by the sea she had often slept in the shelter of cliffs wrapped in a blanket. She knew the nocturnal sky with its clouds and stars. She had slept on straw amid the animals too, near asses and dogs, and on the rickety, over-burdened cart had ridden on the roadways through rain and snow. It was a romantic life that recalled another age.

She had had to sew her own costumes and to go through her daily and difficult exercises under the whip of the chief of the jugglers. But she learned the language of the country, and secretly bought at fairs in cities the books of the poets who had used it. Secretly she read, sometimes from pages torn out of the volumes and thus more easily concealed, Béranger, Musset, Victor Hugo, and Verlaine.

She walked the tight rope which, without any protective net below, was slung from gable to gable across the market-places of villages, and she walked as securely as on the ground. Or she acted as the partner of a dancing she-bear or with five poodles who turned somersaults. She was a trapeze artist too, and her greatest trick was to leap from one horse in full gallop to another. When she did that the hurdy-gurdy stopped its music so that the spectators might realize what a remarkable thing they were seeing. She carried the collection plate along the rope, and her glance persuaded many a one to dip into his pocket who had meant to slink away.

It was in villages and little towns lying along the Rhône that she first became aware among the spectators of a man who dragged himself about with difficulty on two crutches. He followed the troupe from place to place, and since his whole attention was fixed on Eva, it was evident that he did so for her sake.

It was after two years of this wandering life that in Lyons she was seized with typhoid fever. Her companions sent her to a hospital. They could not wait, but the chief juggler was to return after a period and fetch her. When he did return

she was just beginning to convalesce. Suddenly by her bed-
side she also saw the man with the crutches. He took the
juggler aside and one could see that they were talking about
money. From the pressure of her old master's hand Eva knew
that she saw him for the last time.

<h2 style="text-align:center">IX</h2>

The man with the crutches was named Lucas Anselmo Rappard. He saved Eva and awakened her. He taught her her
art. He took her under his care, and this care was tyrannical
enough. He did not set her free again until she had become all
that he had desired to make of her.

He had long lived in retirement at Toledo, because there were
three or four paintings in the Spanish city that rewarded him
for his isolation from the busy world. Also he found that the
sun of Spain warmed him through and through, and that he
liked the folk.

In spite of his crippled state he journeyed northward once a
year to be near the ocean. And like the men of old he went
slowly from place to place. His sister Susan was his unfailing companion. It was on one of his return journeys that he
had seen Eva quite by chance. The village fairs of this region
had long attracted him. And there he found unexpectedly
something that stimulated his creative impulse. It was a
sculptor's inspiration. He saw the form in his mind's eye.
Here was the material ready to his hand. The sight of Eva
relit an idea in him to which he had long despaired of giving
a creative embodiment.

First he called the whole matter a whim. Later, absorbed
in his task, he knew the passion of a Pygmalion.

He was forty at that time or a little more. His beardless face
was thick-boned, peasant-like, brutal. But on closer observa-
tion the intellect shone through the flesh. The greenish-grey
eyes, very deep-set in their hollows, had so compelling a glance
that they surprised and even frightened others.

This remarkable man had an origin and a fate no less remarkable. His father had been a Dutch singer, his mother a Dalmatian. They had drifted to Courland, where an epidemic killed both at almost the same time. The two children had been taken into the ballet school of the theatre at Riga. Lucas Anselmo justified the most brilliant hopes. His incomparable elasticity and lightness surpassed anything that had yet been seen in a young dancer. At seventeen he danced at the Scala in Milan, and roused the public to a rare exhibition of enthusiasm. But his success was out of its due time—too late or too early. His whole personality had something strange and 'curiously transplanted; and soon he became estranged from himself and from the inner forces of his life. At twenty a morbid melancholy seized him.

He happened at that time to be dancing in Petrograd.. A young but lately married lady of the court fell in love with him. She persuaded him to visit her on a certain night in a villa beyond the city. But her husband had been warned. He pleaded the necessity of going on a journey to make his wife the more secure. Then with his servants he broke into the lovers' chamber, had the lad beaten cruelly, then tied, and thrown naked into the snow. Here in the bitter cold the unhappy dancer lay for six hours.

A dangerous illness and a permanent crippling of his legs were the result of this violent adventure. Susan nursed him and never left him for an hour. She had always admired and loved him. Now she worshipped him. He had already earned a little fortune, and an inheritance from his mother's side increased it, so he was enabled to live independently.

A new man developed in him. His deformity gave to his mind the resilience and power that had been his body's. In a curious way he penetrated all the regions of modern life; and above pain, disappointment, and renunciation, he built a road from the senses to the mind. In his transformation from a dancer to a cripple he divined a deep significance. He now sought an idea and a law; and the harsh contrast between external calm and inner motion, of inner calm and outward rest-. lessness, seemed to nim important in any interpretation of mankind and of his age.

At twenty-two he set himself to study Latin, Greek, and Sanskrit. He became a thorough student, and took courses at the German universities. And this strange student, who dragged himself along on crutches, was often an object of curiosity. At the age of thirty he travelled with Susan to India, and lived for four years at Delhi and Benares. He associated with learned Brahmins and received their mystic teachings. Once he had sight of an almost legendary Thibetan priest, who had lived in a cave of the mountains for eighty years, and whom the eternal darkness had blinded, but whom the eternal loneliness had made a saint. The sight of the centenarian moved him, for the first time in his life, to tears. He now understood saintliness and believed in it. And this saint danced: he danced at dawn, turning his blinded eyes to the sun.

He saw the religious festivals in the temple cities on the Ganges, and felt the nothingness of life and the indifference of death when he saw those who had died of pestilence float by hundreds down the stream. He had himself carried into primeval forests and jungles, and saw everywhere in the inextricable coil of life and death each taking the other's form and impulse—decay becoming birth and putrefaction giving life. He was told of the marble-built city of a certain king, in which dwelled only dancing girls taught by priests. When their flesh faded and their limbs lost their agility, they were slain. They had vowed chastity, and none was permitted to survive the breaking of that vow. He approached the fabled city but could not gain admission. At night he saw the fires on its roofs, and heard the songs of its virginal dancers. Now and then it seemed to him that he heard a cry of death.

This night, with its fires and songs, its unseen dancers and uncertain cries, stored up new energies within his soul.

X

He took Eva with him to Toledo. He had rented a house there in which, men said, the painter El Greco had once dwelled.

The building was a grey cube, rather desolate within. Cats shared the dwelling, and owls, bats, and mice.

Several rooms were filled with books, and these books became Eva's silent friends in the years that came now, and during which she saw almost no one but Rappard and Susan.

In this house she learned to know loneliness and work and utter dedication to a task.

She entered the house full of fear of him who had forced her into it. His speech and behaviour intimidated her so that she had terror-stricken visions when she thought of him. But Susan did all in her power to soothe the girl.

Susan would relate stories concerning her brother at morning or in the evening hours, when Eva lay with her body desperately exhausted, too exhausted often to sleep. She had not been spoiled. The life with the troupe of jugglers had accustomed her to severe exertions. But the ceaseless drill, the monotonous misery of the first few months, in which everything seemed empty and painful, without allurement or brightness or intelligible purpose, made her ill and made her hate her own limbs.

It was Susan's hollow voice that besought her to be patient; it was Susan who massaged her arms and legs, who carried her to bed and read to her. And she described her brother, who in her eyes was a magician and an uncrowned king, and on whose eyes and breath she hung, described him through his past, which she retold in its scenes and words, at times too fully and confusedly, at others so concretely and glowingly

that Eva began to suspect something of the good fortune of
the coincidence that had brought her to his attention.

Finally came a day on which he spoke to her openly: "Do
you believe that you were born to be a dancer?" "I do believe it," she answered. Then he spoke to her concerning the
dance, and her wavering feeling grew firmer. Gradually she
felt her body growing lighter and lighter. When they parted
on that day, ambition was beginning to flame in her eyes.

He had taught her to stand with outstretched arms and to
let no muscle quiver; to stand on the tips of her toes so that
her crown touched a sharp arrow; to dance definite figures outlined by needles on the floor with her naked feet, and, when
each movement had passed into her very flesh, to brave the
needles blindfolded. He taught her to whirl about a taut
rope adjusted vertically, and to walk on high stilts without
using her arms.

She had had to forget how she had walked hitherto, how she
had stridden and run and stood, and she had to learn anew
how to walk and stride and run and stand. Everything, as he
said, had to become new. Her limbs and ankles and wrists
had to adjust themselves to new functions, even as a man who
has lain in the mire of the street puts on new garments. "To
dance," he would say, "means to be new, to be fresh at every
moment, as though one had just issued from the hand of God."

He inducted her into the meaning and law of every movement, into the inner structure and outer rhythm of every
gesture.

He created gestures with her. And about every gesture he
wove some experience. He showed her the nature of flight, of
pursuit, of parting, of salutation, of expectancy and triumph
and joy and terror; and there was no motion of a finger in
which the whole body did not have a part. The play of the
eyes and of facial expression entered this art so little that the
swathing of the face would not have diminished the effect that
was aimed at.

He drew the kernel from each husk; he demanded the quintessential only.

"Can you drink? Let me see you!" It was wrong. "Your gesture was a shopworn phrase. The man who had never seen another drink did not drink thus."

"Can you pray? Can you pluck flowers, swing a scythe, gather grain, bind a veil? Give me an image of each action! Represent it!" She could not. But he taught her.

Whenever she fell into a flat imitation of reality he foamed with rage. "Reality is a beast!" he roared, and hurled one of his crutches against the wall. "Reality is a murderer."

In the statues and paintings of great artists he pointed out to her the essential and noble lines, and illustrated how all that had been thus created and built merged harmoniously again with nature and her immediacy of truth.

He spoke of the help of music to her art. "You need no melody and scarcely tone. The only thing that matters is the division of time, the audibly created measure which leads and restrains the violence, wildness, and passion, or else the softness and sustained beauty of motion. A tambourine and a fife suffice. Everything beyond that is dishonesty and confusion. Beware of a poetry of effect that does not issue from your naked achievement."

At night he took her to wine rooms and taverns, where the girls of the people danced their artless and excited dances. He revealed to her the artistic kernel of each, and let her dance a bolero, a fandango, or a tarantella, which in this new embodiment had the effect of cut and polished jewels.

He reconstructed antique battle-dances for her, the Pyrrhic and the Karpaian; the dance of the Muses about the altar of Zeus on Helicon; the dance of Artemis and her companions; the dance of Delos, which imitated the path of Theseus through the labyrinth; the dance of the maidens in honour of Artemis, during which they wore a short chiton and a structure of willow on their heads; the vintners' dance preserved on the cup of Hiero, which includes all the motions used by the gatherers of the vine and the workers at the winepress. He showed her pictures of the vase of François, of the geometrical vase of Dipylon, of many reliefs and terracotta pieces, and made her study the figures that had an entrancing charm and incomparable rhythm of motion. And he procured her music for these dances, which Susan copied from old manuscripts, and which he adapted.

And from these creative exercises he led her on to a higher freedom. He now stimulated her to invent for herself, to feel with originality and give that feeling a creative form. He vivified her glance, that was so often in thrall to the technical or merely beautiful, liberated her senses, and gave her a clear vision of that deaf, blind swarm and throng whom her art would have to affect. He inspired her with love for the immortal works of man, armoured her heart against seduction by the vulgar, against a game but for the loftiest stakes, against action without restraint, being without poise.

But it was not until she left him that she understood him wholly.

When he thought her ripe for the glances of the world he gave her recommendations to smooth the way, and also Susan. He was willing to be a solitary. Susan had trained a young Castilian to give him the care he needed. He did not say whether he intended to stay in Toledo or choose some other place. Since they had left him, neither Eva nor Susan had heard from him: he had forbidden both letters and messages.

XI

Often in the night Susan would sit in some dark corner, and out of her deep brooding name her brother's name. Her thoughts turned about a reunion with him. Her service to Eva was but a violent interruption of the accustomed life at his side.

She loved Eva, but she loved her as Lucas Anselmo's work

and projection. If Eva gained fame it was for him, if she gathered treasure it was for him, if she grew in power it was for him. Those who approached Eva and felt her sway were his creatures, his serfs, and his messengers.

After the incident with Christian Wahnschaffe, as Susan crouched at Eva's feet and, as so often, embraced the girl's knees, she thought: Ah, he has breathed into her an irresistible soul, and made her beautiful and radiant.

But always she harboured a superstitious fear. She trembled in secret lest the irresistible soul should some day flee from Eva's body, and the radiance of her beauty be dulled, and nothing remain but a dead and empty husk. For that would be a sign to her that Lucas Anselmo was no more.

For this reason it delighted her when ecstasy and glee, glow and tumult reigned in Eva's life, and she was cast down and plagued by evil presentiments when the girl withdrew into quietness and remained silent and alone. So long as Eva danced and loved and was mobile and adorned her body, Susan dismissed all care concerning her brother. Therefore she would sit and fan the flame from which his spirit seemed to speak to her.

"Just because you've chosen the Englishman, you needn't send the German away," she said. "You may take the one and let the other languish a while longer. You can never tell how things will change. There are many men: they rise and fall. Cardillac is going down-hill now. I hear all kinds of rumours."

Eva, hiding her face in her hands, whispered: "Eidolon."

It vexed Susan. "First you mock him, then you sigh for him! What folly is this?"

Eva sprang up suddenly. "You shan't speak of him to me or praise him, wretched woman." Her cheeks glowed, and the brightly mocking tone in which she often spoke to Susan became menacing.

"*Golpes para besos,*" Susan murmured in Spanish. "Blows

for kisses." She arose in order to comb Eva's hair and braid it for the night.

The next day Crammon appeared. " I found you one whose laughter puts to shame the laughter of the muleteer of Cordova," he said with mock solemnity. " Why is he rejected? "

His heart bled. Yet he wooed her for his friend. Much as he loved and admired Denis Lay, yet Christian was closer to him. Christian was his discovery, of which he was vain, and his hero.

Eva looked at him with eyes that glittered, and replied: " It is true that he knows how to laugh like that muleteer of Cordova, but he has no more culture of the heart than that same fellow. And that, my dear man, is not enough."

" And what is to become of us? " sighed Crammon.

" You may follow us to England," Eva said, cheerfully. " I'm going to dance at His Majesty's Theatre. Eidolon can be my page. He can learn to practise reverence, and not to chaffer for horses when beautiful poems are being read to me. Tell him that."

Crammon sighed again. Then he took her hand, and devoutly kissed the tips of her fingers. " I shall deliver your message, sweet Ariel," he said.

XII

Cardillac and Eva fell out, and that robbed the man of his last support. The danger with which he was so rashly playing ensnared him; the abysses lured him on.

The external impetus to his downfall was furnished by a young engineer who had invented a hydraulic device. Cardillac had persuaded him with magnificent promises to let him engage in the practical exploitation of the invention. It was not long before the engineer discovered that he had been cheated of the profits of his labour. Quietly he accumulated evidence against the speculator, unveiled his dishonest dealings, and presented to the courts a series of annihilating charges. Although Cardillac finally offered him five hundred thousand francs if he would withdraw his charges, the outraged accuser remained firm.

Other untoward circumstances occurred. The catastrophe became inevitable. On a single forenoon the shares he had issued dropped to almost nothing. In forty-eight hours three hundred millions of francs had been lost. Innumerable well-established fortunes plunged like avalanches into nothingness, eighteen hundred mechanics and shop-keepers lost all they had in the world, twenty-seven. great firms went into bankruptcy, senators and deputies of the Republic were sucked down in the whirlpool, and under the attacks of the opposition the very administration shook.

Felix Imhof hurried to Paris to save whatever was possible out of the crash. Although he had suffered painful losses, he was ecstatic over the grandiose spectacle which Cardillac's downfall presented to the world.

Crammon laughed and rubbed his hands in satisfaction, and pointed to Imhof. " He wanted to seduce me, but I was as chaste as Joseph."

On the following evening Imhof went with his friends to visit Eva Sorel. She had left the palace which Cardillac had furnished for her, and had rented a handsome house in the Chaussée d'Antin.

Imhof spoke of the curious tragedy of these modern careers. As an example he related how three days before his collapse Cardillac had appeared at the headquarters of his bitterest enemies, the Bank of Paris. The directors were having a meeting. None was absent. With folded hands and tear-stained face the sorely beset man begged for a loan of twelve millions. It was a drastic symptom of his naïveté that he asked help of those whom he had fleeced on the exchange year in and year out, whose losses had glutted his wealth, and whom he wanted to fight with the very loan for which he begged.

Christian scarcely listened. He stood with Crammon beside

a Chinese screen. Opposite them sat Eva in a curiously dreamy mood, and not far from her was Denis Lay. Others were present too, but Christian gave them no attention.

Suddenly there was a commotion near the door. "Cardillac," some one whispered. All glances sought him.

It was indeed Cardillac who had entered. His boots were muddy, his collar and cravat in disorder. He seemed not to have changed his garments for a week. His fists were clenched; his restless eyes wandered from face to face.

Eva and Denis remained calmly as they were. Eva pressed her foot against the edge of a copper jar filled with white lilies. No one moved. Only Christian, quite involuntarily, approached Cardillac by a few paces.

Cardillac became aware of him, and drew him by the sleeve toward the door of the adjoining room. They had scarcely crossed the threshold when Cardillac whispered in an intense but subdued tone: "I must have two thousand francs or I'm done for! Advance me that much, monsieur, and save me. I have a wife and a child."

Christian was astonished. No one dreamed that the man had a family. And why turn precisely to him? Wiguniewski, d'Autichamps, many others knew him far better.

"I must be at the station in half an hour," he heard the man say, and his hand sought his purse.

Wife and child! The words flitted through his head, and there arose in him the violent aversion he always felt in the presence of beggars. What had he to do with it all? He took out the bank notes. Two thousand francs, he thought, and remembered the huge sums which one was accustomed to name in connection with the man who stood before him begging.

"I thank you." Cardillac's voice came to him as through a wall.

Then Cardillac passed him with bent head. But two men had in the meantime appeared in the other room. At the open folding-door the lackeys stood behind them with an embarrassed expression, for the men were police officials who were seeking Cardillac and had followed him here.

Cardillac, seeing them and guessing their errand, recoiled with a gurgling noise in his throat. His right hand disappeared in his coat-pocket, but instantly the two men leaped on him and pinioned his arms. There was a brief, silent struggle. Suddenly he was made fast.

Eva had arisen. Her guests crowded about her. She leaned against Susan's shoulder and turned her head a little aside, as though a touch of uncanny terror brushed her. But she still smiled, though now with pallid cheeks.

"He's magnificent, magnificent, even at this moment," Imhof whispered to Crammon.

Christian stared at Cardillac's huge back. It was, he couldn't help thinking, like the back of an ox dragged to slaughter. The two men between whom he stood hand-cuffed had greasy necks, and the hair on the back of their heads was dirty and ill-trimmed.

An unpleasant taste on his palate tormented Christian. He asked a servant for a glass of champagne.

Cardillac's words, "I have a wife and a child," would not leave his mind. On the contrary, they sounded ever more stridently within him. And suddenly a second, foolish, curious voice in him asked: How do you suppose they look—this wife, this child? Where are they? What will become of them?

It was as annoying and as painful as a toothache.

XIII

In Devon, south of Exeter, Denis Lay had his country seat. The manor stood in a park of immemorial trees, velvety swards, small lakes that mirrored the sky, and flowerbeds beautiful in the mildest climate of such a latitude on earth.

"We're quite near the Gulf Stream here," Crammon explained to Christian and Eva, who, like himself, were Lay's guests. And he had an expression as though with his own hands he had brought the warm current to the English coast from the Gulf of Mexico simply for the benefit of his friends.

With a gesture of sisterly tenderness Eva walked for hours among the beds of blossoming violets. Large surfaces were mildly and radiantly blue. It was March.

A company of English friends was expected, but not until two days later.

The four friends, going for a walk, had been overtaken by showers and came home drenched. When they had changed their clothes, they met for tea in the library. It was a great room with wainscoting of dark oak and mighty cross-beams, Halfway up there ran along the walls a gallery with carved balustrades, and at one end, between the pointed windows, appeared the gilded pipes of an organ.

The light was dim and the rain swished without. Eva held an album of Holbein drawings, and turned the pages slowly. Christian and Crammon were playing at chess. Denis watched them for a while. Then he sat down at the organ and began to play.

Eva looked up from the pictures and listened.

" I've lost the game," Christian said. He arose and mounted the steps to the gallery. He leaned over the balustrade and looked down. In an outward curve of the balustrade there lay, like an egg in its cup, a globe on a metal stand.

" What were you playing? " Eva asked, as Denis paused.

He turned around. " I've been trying to compose a passage from the Song of Songs," he answered. He played again and sang in an agreeable voice: " Arise, thou lovely one, for the winter is past."

The sound of the organ stirred a feeling of hatred in Christian. He gazed upon Eva's form. In a gown of sea-green, slim, far, estranged, she sat there. And as he looked at her there blended with his hatred of the music another feeling—one of oppression and of poignant pain, and his heart began to throb violently.

"Arise, thou lovely one, and come with me," Denis sang again, and Crammon softly hummed the air too. Eva looked up, and her glance met Christian's. In her face there was a mysterious expression of loftiness and love.

Christian took the globe from its stand and played with it. He let it roll back and forth between his hands on the flat balustrade like a rubber ball. The sphere suddenly slipped from him, fell and rolled along the floor to Eva's feet.

Denis and Crammon gathered about it; Christian came down from the gallery.

Eva picked up the globe and went toward Christian. He took it from her, but she at once held out her hands again. Then she held it daintily poised upon the fingertips of her right hand. Her left hand, with fingers spread out, she held close to it; her head was gently inclined, her lips half open.

"So this is the world," she said, "your world! The blue bits are the seas, and that soiled yellow the countries. How ugly the countries are, and how jagged! They look like a cheese at which mice have nibbled. O world, the things that creep about on you! The things that happen on you! I hold you now, world, and carry you! I like that!"

The three men smiled, but a psychical shudder passed through them. For they could no longer stand in human erectness on this little round earth. A breath of the dancer could blow them down into the immeasurable depths of the cosmos.

And Christian saw that Denis, fighting with an impulse, regarded him. Suddenly the Englishman came up to him and held out his hand. And Christian took the hand of his victorious rival, and knew in his secretest mind that an ultimate advantage was his. For between Eva's face and the smudged globe he seemed to see a ghostly little figure which charmed her with its glance and which was a tiny image of himself—Eidolon.

They planned that summer to return to the manor and hunt

the deer, as was the custom of the gentlemen of that region. But when summer came all things had changed, and Denis had glided from the smooth sphere of earth into the depth..

XIV

One day in London Crammon came to Christian, sat down affectionately beside him, and said: " I am leaving.".

" Where are you going? " Christian asked in surprise.

" North, to fish salmon," Crammon replied. " I'll join you later or you can join me."

" But why go at all? "

" Because I'll go straight to the dogs if I have to see this woman any longer without possessing her. That's all."

Christian looked at Crammon with a flame in his eyes, and checked a gesture of angry jealousy. Then his face assumed its expression of friendly mockery again.

So Crammon departed.

Eva Sorel became the undisputed queen of the London season. Her name was everywhere. The women wore hats à la Eva Sorel, the men cravats in her favourite colours. She threw into the shade the most sought-after celebrities of the day—including the Negro bruiser, Jackson. Fame came to her in full draughts, and gold by the pailfuls.

XV

May was very hot in London that year. Denis and Christian planned a night's pleasure on the Thames. They rented a steam yacht named " Aldebaran," ordered an exquisite meal on board, and Denis sent out invitations to his friends.

Fourteen members of his set joined the party. The yacht lay near the houses of Parliament, and shortly before midnight the guests appeared in evening dress. The son of the Russian ambassador was among them, the Honourable James Wheely, whose brother was in the ministry, Lord and Lady Westmoreland, Eva Sorel, Prince Wiguniewski, and others.

On the stroke of twelve the "Aldebaran" started out, and the small orchestra of well-chosen artists began to play.

When the yacht on its way upstream had reached the railway bridge of Battersea, there became visible on the left bank in the dim light of the street lamps an innumerable throng of men and women, close-packed, head by head, thousands upon thousands.

They were strikers from the docks. Why they stood here, so silent and so menacing in their silence, was known to no one on board. Perhaps it was a demonstration of some sort.

Denis, who had had a good deal of champagne, went to the railing, and in his recklessness shouted three cheers across the river. No sound answered him. The human mass stood like a wall, and in the sombre faces that turned toward the gleam of the yacht's light no muscle moved.

Then Denis said to Christian, who had joined him: "Let's swim across. Whoever reaches shore first is victor of the race, and must ask those people what they are waiting for and why they don't go home at this hour of the night."

"Swim over to *them?*" Christian shook his head. He was asked to touch slimy worms with his hands and pretend they were trophies.

"Then I'll do it alone!" Denis exclaimed, and threw his coat and waistcoat down on the deck.

He was known to be an admirable swimmer. The company therefore took his notion as one of the bizarre pranks for which he was known. Only Eva tried to restrain him. She approached him and laid her hand on his arm. In vain. He was quite ready to jump, when the captain grasped his shoulder and begged him to desist, since the river, despite its calm appearance, had a strong undercurrent. But Denis eluded him, ran to the promenade deck, and in another moment his slender body flew into the black water.

No one had a presentiment of disaster. The swimmer advanced with powerful strokes. The watchers on board were sure that he would easily reach the Chelsea shore. But suddenly, in the bright radiance of a searchlight from shore, they saw him throw up his arms above his head. At the same moment he cried piercingly for help. Without hesitation a member of the little orchestra, a cellist, sprang overboard in all his garments to help the drowning man. But the current caused by the ebbtide was very powerful, and both Denis and the musician were whirled onward by it, and disappeared in the inky waves.

Suddenly the confusion caused by these happenings lifted from Christian's mind, and before any could restrain him, he was in the water. He heard a cry, and knew that it came from Eva's lips. The ladies and gentlemen on board scurried helplessly to and fro.

Christian could no longer make out the forms of the other two. The water seemed to bank itself against him and hinder his movements. A sudden weakness took possession of him, but he felt no fear. Raising his head he saw the silent masses of the workers, men and women with such expressions as he had never seen. Although the glance which he directed toward them was but a momentary one, he felt almost sure that their sombre earnestness of gaze was fixed on him, and that these thousands and thousands were waiting for him, and for him alone. His weakness increased. It seemed to arise from his heart, which grew heavier and heavier. At that moment a life-boat reached him.

At three o'clock in the morning, in the earliest dawn, the bodies of Denis and the musician were found jammed between two beams near the arches of a bridge. Now they lay on deck and Christian could contemplate them. The guests had left the ship. Eva, too, had gone. She had been deeply shaken, and Prince Wiguniewski had accompanied her home.

The sailors had gone to their bunks. The deck was empty, and Christian sat alone with the two dead men.

The sun arose. The waters of the river began to glow. The

pavements of the desolate streets, the walls and the windows
of the houses flushed with the red of dawn. Sea-gulls circled
about the smokestack.

Christian sat alone with the dead men. He was huddled in
an old coat which the captain had thrown around his shoulders.
Steadily he gazed upon the faces of the dead. They were
swollen and ugly.

XVI

North of Loch Lomond, Christian and Crammon wandered
about shooting snipes and wild ducks. The land was rough
and wild; always within their hearing thundered the sea;
storm-harried masses of cloud raced across the sky.

"My father will be far from pleased," said Christian. "I've
spent two hundred and eighty thousand marks in the last ten
months."

"Your mother will persuade him to bear it," Crammon
answered. "Anyhow, you're of age. You can use several
times that much without any one hindering you."

Christian threw back his head, and drew the salty air deep
into his lungs. "I wonder what little Letitia is doing," he
said.

"I think of the child myself at times. She shouldn't be
left entirely to that old schemer," Crammon replied.

Her kiss no longer burned on Christian's lips, for other
flames had touched them since. Like laughing *putti* in a painting, the lovely faces fluttered about him. Many of them, to
be sure, were laughing now no more.

In a dark gown, emerging from between two white columns,
Eva had taken leave of him. He seemed to see her still—the
brunette pallor of her face, her inexpressibly slender hand, the
most eloquent hand in the world.

Jestingly and familiarly she had spoken to him in the
language of her German homeland, which seemed more piercingly sweet and melodious in her mouth than in any other's.

"Where are you going, Eidolon?" she had asked carelessly.

He had answered with a gesture of uncertainty. He evidently thought that his going or coming was indifferent to her.

"It isn't nice of you to go without asking leave," she said, and put her hands on his shoulders. "But perhaps it is just as well. You confuse me. I am beginning to think of you, and I don't want to do that."

"Why not?"

"Because I don't. Why do you need reasons?"

The dead and swollen face of Denis Lay rose up before them, and they both saw it in the empty air.

After a little he had dared to ask: "When shall we meet again?"

"It depends on you," she had answered. "Always let me know where you are, so that I can send for you. Of course, it's nonsense, and I won't. But it might just happen that in some whim I may want you and none other. Only you must learn——" She stopped and smiled.

"What, what must I learn?"

"Ask your friend Crammon. He'll teach you." After these words she had left him.

The sea roared like a herd of steers. Christian stopped and turned to Crammon. "Listen, Bernard, there's a matter that comes back curiously into my mind. When I last talked to Eva she said there was something I was to learn before I could see her again. And when I asked after her meaning, she said that you could give me a hint. What is it? What am I to learn?"

Crammon answered seriously: "You see, my boy, these things are rather complicated. Some people like their steak overdone, others almost raw, most people medium. Well, if you don't know a certain person's taste and serve the steak the way you yourself prefer it, you risk making a blunder and looking like a fool. People are far from simple."

"I don't understand you, Bernard."

"Doesn't matter a bit, old chap! Don't bother your handsome head about it. Let's go on. This damned country makes me melancholy."

They went on. But there was an unknown sadness in Christian's heart.

AN OWL ON EVERY POST

I

Letitia felt vague longings.

She accompanied her aunt, the countess, to the south of Switzerland, and loitered in wonder at the foot of blue glaciers; she lay on the shore of Lake Geneva, dreaming or reading poetry. When she appeared smiling on the promenade, admiring glances were all about her. Enthusiastically conscious of her youth and of her emotional wealth, she enjoyed the day and the evening as each came, pictures and books, fragrances and tones. But her longings did not cease.

Many came and spoke to her of love—some frankly and some by implication. And she too was full of love—not for him who spoke, but for his words, expressions, presages. If a delighted glance met hers, it delighted her. And she lent her ear with equal patience to wooers of twenty or of sixty.

But her yearnings were not assuaged.

Her aunt, the countess, said: "Have nothing to do with aristocrats, my dear. They are uncultivated and full of false pride. They don't know the difference between a woman and a horse. They would nail your young heart to a family tree, and if you don't appreciate that favour sufficiently, they stamp you as déclassée for life. If they have no money they are too stupid to earn any; if they have it they don't know how to spend it sensibly. Have no dealings with them. They're not quite human."

The countess' experiences with the aristocracy had been very bitter. "You can imagine, my dear," she said, "that I was hard pressed in my time to be forced to say these things now."

Letitia sat on the edge of her bed and regarded her silk stocking, which had a little hole in it, and still felt the same longing.

Judith wrote her: "We expect you and the countess so soon as we are settled in our new house near Frankfort. It's a kind of fairy palace that papa has built us, and it's to be the family seat hereafter. It's situated in the forest of Schwanheim, and is only ten minutes by motor from the city. Everybody who has seen it is mad about it. Felix Imhof says it reminds him of the palace of the Minotaur. There are thirty-four guest-rooms, a gallery fifty metres long with niches and columns, and a library that's been modelled after the cupola of St. Peter's at Rome. There are twenty thousand perfectly new books in it. Who's to read them all?"

"I love the thought of them," said Letitia, and pressed her hand against her heart.

She had had a golden charm made in the likeness of a tiny toad. She did not wear it about her neck, but kept it in a little leathern case, from which she often took it, and brooded over it lovingly.

In Schwetzingen she had met a young Argentinian of German descent. He was studying law at Heidelberg, but he confessed to her frankly that he had come to Europe to get him a German wife. He gave her this information at noon. At night he gave her to understand that in her he had met his goal.

His name was Stephen Gunderam. His skin was olive, his eyes glowing, his hair coal black and parted in the middle. Letitia was fascinated by his person, the countess by the rumours of his wealth. She made inquiries, and discovered that the rumours had not been exaggerated. The lands of the Gunderams on the Rio Plata were more extensive than the Duchy of Baden.

"Now, sweetheart, there's a husband for you!" said the countess. But when she considered that she would have to part with Letitia, she began to cry, and lost her appetite for a whole forenoon.

Stephen Gunderam told them about his far, strange country, about his parents, brothers, servants, herds, houses. He declared that the bride he brought home would be a queen. He was so strong that he could bend a horse-shoe. But he was afraid of spiders, believed in evil omens, and suffered from frequent headaches. At such times he would lie in bed, and drink warm beer mixed with milk and the yolk of eggs. This was a remedy which an old mulatto woman had once given him.

Letitia barely listened. She was reading:

> "And have you seen an inmost dream
> Fled from you and denied?
> Then gaze into the flowing stream,
> Where all things change and glide."

"You really must hurry, darling," the countess admonished her again.

But Letitia was so full of longing.

II

In a city on the Rhine, Christian and Crammon were delayed by an accident. Something had happened to the motor of their car, and the chauffeur needed a whole day for repairs.

It was a beautiful evening of September, so they left the city streets and wandered quietly along the bank of the river. When darkness fell, they drifted by chance into a beer-garden near the water. The tables and benches, rammed firmly into the earth, stood among trees full of foliage, and were occupied by several hundred people—tradesmen, workingmen, and students.

"Let us rest a while and watch the people," said Crammon. And near the entrance they found a table with two vacant seats. A bar-maid placed two pitchers of beer before them.

Under the trees the air had something subterranean about it, for it was filled with the odour of the exudations of so many people. The few lamps had iridescent rings of smoke about them. At the adjoining table sat students with their red caps and other fraternity insignia. They had fat, puffed-out faces and insolent voices. One of them hit the table three times with his stick. Then they began to sing.

Crammon opened his eyes very wide, and his lips twitched mockingly. He said: "That's my notion of the way wild Indians act—Sioux or Iroquois." Christian did not answer. He kept his arms quite close to his body, and his shoulders drawn up a little. There was a good deal of noise at all the tables, and, after a while, Christian said: "Do let us go. I'm not comfortable here."

"Ah, but my dear boy, this is the great common people!" Crammon instructed him with a mixture of arrogance and mockery. "Thus do they sing and drink and—smell. 'And calmly flows the Rhine.' Your health, your Highness!" He always called Christian that among strangers, and was delighted when those who overheard showed a respectful curiosity. As a matter of fact, several of the men at their table looked at them in some consternation, and then whispered among themselves.

A young girl with blond braids of hair wreathed about her head had entered the garden. She stopped near the entrance, and looked searchingly from table to table. The students laughed, and one called out to her. She hesitated shyly. Yet she went up to him. "Whom are you looking for, pretty maiden?" a freshman asked. The girl did not answer. "Hide in the pitcher for your forwardness," a senior cried. "It is for me to ask." The freshman grinned, and took a long draught of beer. "What do you desire, little maiden?" the senior asked in a beery voice. "Have you come to fetch your father, who clings too lovingly to his jug?" The girl blushed and nodded. She was asked to give her name, and said it was Katherine Zöllner. Her father, she said, was a boatman. She spoke softly, yet so that Christian and Crammon understood what she said. Her father was due to join his ship for Cologne at three o'clock in the morning. "For Cologne," the senior growled. "Give me a kiss, and I'll find your father for you."

The girl trembled and recoiled. But the fraternity approved of the demand, and roared applause. "Don't pretend!" the senior said. He got up, put his arms roughly about her waist, and, despite her resistance and fright, he kissed her.

"Me, too! Me, too!" The cries arose from the others. The girl had already been passed on to a second, a third snatched her, then a fourth, fifth, sixth. She could not cry out. She could scarcely breathe. Her resistance grew feebler, the roaring and the laughter louder. The fellows at the neighbouring table grew envious. A fat man with warts on his face called out: "Now you come to us!" His comrades brayed with laughter. When the last student let her go, it was this man who grasped her, kissed her and threw her toward his neighbour. More and more men arose, stretched out their arms, and demanded the defenceless victim. Nothing happened except that they kissed her. Yet there spread through the crowd a wildness of lust, so that even the women screeched and cried out. The students, in the meantime, proud of their little game, raised their rough voices and sang a foolish song.

The body of the girl, now an unresisting and almost lifeless thing, was whirled from arm to arm. Christian and Crammon had arisen. They gazed into the quivering throng under the trees, heard the shrieks, the cries, the laughter, saw the girl, now far away, and the hands stretched out after her, and her face with eyes that were now closed, now open again in horror. At last one was found who had compassion. He was a young workingman, and he hit the man who was just kissing the girl square between the eyes. Two others then attacked him, and there ensued a rough fight, while the girl with her little remaining strength reeled toward the fence where the ground was grassy. Her hair fell loose, her blue bodice was torn and showed her naked bosom, her face was covered with ugly bruises. She tried to keep erect, groped about, but fell. A few thoughtful people now came up, helped her, and asked each other what was to be done.

Christian and Crammon followed the shore of the river back to the city. The students had begun a new ditty, that sounded discordantly through the night, until the distance gradually silenced it.

III

In the middle of the night Christian left his couch, slipped into a silk dressing gown and entered Crammon's room. He lit a candle, sat down by the side of Crammon's bed, and shook his sleeping friend by the shoulder. Crammon battled with sleep itself, and Christian turned his head away in order not to see the struggling, primitive face.

At last, after much grunting and groaning, Crammon opened his eyes. "What do you want? " he asked angrily. "Are you practising to play a ghost? "

"I would like to ask you something, Bernard," Christian said.

This enraged Crammon all the more. "It is crazy to rob a man of his well-deserved rest. Are you moonstruck, or have you a bellyache? Ask what you want to ask, but hurry! "

"Do you believe I do right to live as I do? " asked Christian. "Be quite honest for once, and answer me."

"There is no doubt that he's moonstruck! " Crammon was truly horrified. "His mind is wandering. We must summon a physician." He half-rose, and fumbled for the electric button.

"Don't do that! " Christian restrained him mildly, and smiled a vexed smile. "Try to consider what I've said. Rub your eyes if you aren't quite awake yet. There's time enough for sleep. But I am asking you, Bernard, for your quite sin-, cere opinion: Do you think I am right in living as I do? ”

“ My dear Christian Wahnschaffe, if you can tell me by what process this craze has——”

“ Don’t jest, Bernard,” Christian interrupted him, frown-ing. “ This is no time for a jest. Do you think that I should have remained with Eva? ”

“ Nonsense,” said Crammon. “ She would have betrayed you; she would have betrayed me. She would betray the emperor, and yet stand guiltless in the sight of God. You can’t reckon with her, you can’t really be yourself with her. She was fashioned for the eye alone. Even that little story of the muleteer of Cordova was a trick. Be content, and let me sleep.”

Christian replied thoughtfully. “ I don’t understand what you say, and you don’t understand what I mean. Since I left her I feel sometimes as though I had grown hunchbacked. Jesting aside, Bernard, I get up sometimes and a terror comes over me. I stretch myself out. I know that I’m straight, and yet I feel as though I were hunchbacked.”

“ Completely out of his head,” Crammon murmured.

“ And now tell me another thing, Bernard,” Christian con-tinued, undeflected by his friend, and his clear, open face assumed an icy expression. “ Should we not have helped the boatman’s daughter, you and I? Or should I not have done so, if you did not care to take the trouble? Tell me that! ”

“ The devil take it! What boatman’s daughter? ”

“ Are you so forgetful? The girl in the beer-garden. She even gave her name—Katherine Zöllner. Don’t you remem-ber? And how those ruffians treated her? ”

“ Was I to risk my skin for a boatman’s daughter? ” Cram-mon asked, enraged. “ People of that sort may take their pleasures in their own fashion. What is it to you or to me? Did you try to hold back the paws of the wild beasts that tore up Adda Castillo? And that was a good deal worse than being kissed by a hundred greasy snouts. Don't be an idiot, my dear fellow, and let me sleep! "

" I am curious," said Christian.

" Curious? What about? "

" I'm going to the house where she lives and see how she is. I want you to go along. Get up."

Crammon opened his mouth very wide in his astonishment. " Go now? " he stammered, " at night? Are you quite crazy? "

" I knew you'd scold," Christian said softly and with a dreamy smile. " But that curiosity torments me so that I've simply been turning from side to side in bed." And in truth his face had an expression of expectation and of subtle desire that was new to Crammon. He went on: " I want to see what she is doing, what her life is like, what her room looks like. One should know about all that. We are hopelessly ignorant about people of that kind. Do please come on, Bernard." His tone was almost cajoling.

Crammon sighed. He waxed indignant. He protested the frailty of his health and the necessity of sleep for his wearied mind. Since Christian, however, opposed to all these objections an insensitive silence, and since Crammon did not want to see him visit a dangerous and disreputable quarter of the city alone by night, he finally submitted, and, grumbling still, arosé from his bed.

Christian bathed and dressed with his accustomed care. Before leaving the hotel they consulted a directory, and found the address of the boatman. They hired a cab. It was half-past four in the morning when their cab reached the hut beside the river bank. There was light in the windows.

Crammon was still at a loss to comprehend. With the rusty bell-pull in his hand, his confused and questioning eyes sought Christian once more. But the latter paid no attention to his friend. A care-worn, under-nourished woman appeared at the door. Crammon was forced to speak, and, with inner vexa-

tion, said that they had come to ask after her daughter. The
woman, who immediately imagined that her daughter had had
secret affairs with rich gentlemen, stepped aside and let the two
pass her.

IV

What Crammon saw and what Christian saw was not the
same thing.

Crammon saw a dimly lit room, with old chests of drawers
that were smoke-stained, with a bed and the girl Katherine on
it covered by the coarse, red-checked linen, with a cradle in
which lay a whining baby. He saw clothes drying by the
oven, the boatman sitting and eating potato soup, a bench on
which a lad was sleeping, and many other unclean, ugly things.

To Christian it was like a strange dream of falling. He,
too, saw the boatman and the poor woman and the girl, whose
glassy eyes and convulsed features brought home to him at
once the reason for his visit. But he saw these things as one
sees pictures while gliding down a shaft, pictures that recur
at intervals, but are displaced by others that slip in between
them.

Thus he saw Eva Sorel feeding a walnut to one of her little
monkeys.

The boatman got up and took off his cap. And suddenly
Christian saw Denis Lay and Lord Westmoreland giving each
other their white-gloved hands. It was an insignificant thing;
but his vision of it was glaring and incisive.

Now the lad on the bench awakened, stretched himself, sat
up with a start, and gave a sombre stare of astonishment at
the strangers. The girl, ill from her horrible experience, turned
her head away, and pulled the coverlet up to her chin. And
suddenly Christian saw the charming vision of Letitia, playing at ball in the great room crossed by the gleams of lightning; and each thing that he saw had a relation to some other
thing in that other world.

The curiosity that had brought him hither still kept that unwonted smile on his face. But he looked helplessly at Crammon now, and he was sensitive to, the indecency of his silent, stupid presence there, the purposelessness and folly of the whole nocturnal excursion. It seemed almost intolerable to him now to stay longer in this low-ceiled room, amid the odour of ill-washed bodies, and clothing that had been worn for years.

Up to the last moment he had imagined that he would talk to the girl. But it was precisely this that he found it impossible to do. He did not even dare to turn his head to where she lay. Yet he was acutely conscious of her as he had seen her out there, reeling from the tables with loose hair and torn bodice.

When he thought over the words that he might say to her, each seemed strikingly superfluous and vulgar.

The boatman looked at him, the woman looked at him. The lad stared with malevolently squinting eyes, as though he planned a personal attack. And now there emerged also an old man from behind a partition where potatoes were stored, and regarded him with dim glances. In the embarrassment caused him by all these eyes, he advanced a few steps toward Katherine's bed. She had turned her face to the wall, and did not move. In his sudden angry despair he put his hands into pocket after pocket, found nothing, hardly knew indeed what he sought, felt the diamond ring on his finger which was a gift of his mother, hastily drew it off, and threw it on the bed, into the very hands of the girl. It was the act of one who desired to buy absolution.

Katherine moved her head, saw the magnificent ring, and contempt and astonishment, delight and fear, struggled in her face. She looked up, and then down again, and grew pale. Her face was not beautiful, and it was disfigured by the emotions she had experienced during the past hours. An impulse that was utterly mysterious to himself caused Christian suddenly to laugh cheerfully and heartily. At the same time he turned with a commanding gesture to Crammon, demanding that they go.

Crammon had meantime determined to ease the painfulness of the situation in a practical way. He addressed a few words to the boatman, who answered in the dialect of Cologne. Then he drew forth two bank notes and laid them on the table. The boatman looked at the money; the hands of the woman were stretched out after it. Crammon walked to the door.

Five minutes after they had entered the house, they left it again. And they left it swiftly, like men fleeing.

While the cab drove over the rough stones of the street, Crammon said peevishly: " You owe your paymaster a hundred marks. I won't charge you for anything except the money. You can't, I suppose, give me back my lost sleep."

" I shall give you for it the Chinese apple of amber-coloured ivory about which you were so enthusiastic at Amsterdam," Christian replied.

" Do that, my son," Crammon said, " and do it quickly, or my rage over this whole business will make me ill."

When he got up at noon thoroughly rested, Crammon reflected on the incident with that philosophic mildness of which, under the right circumstances, he was capable. After they had had a delightful breakfast, he filled his short pipe, and discoursed: " Such extravagances in the style of Haroun al Rashid get you nowhere, my dear boy. You can't fathom those sombre depths. Why hunt in unknown lands, when the familiar ones still have so many charms? Even your humble servant who sits opposite you is still a very treasure of riddles and mysteries. That is what a wise poet has strikingly expressed:

"What know we of the stars, of water or of wind?
What of the dead, to whom the earth is kind?
Of father and mother, or of child and wife?
Our hearts are hungry, but our eyes are blind."

Christian smiled coolly. Verses, he thought contemptuously, verses. . . .

V

When they reached the magnificent structure in the forest of Schwanheim, they found a great restlessness there and a crowd of guests. Letitia had not yet arrived; Felix Imhof was expected hourly; purveyors and postmen came and went uninterruptedly. The place hummed like a hive.

Frau Wahnschaffe greeted Christian with restraint and dignity, although her joy gave her eyes a phosphorescent gleam. Judith looked exhausted, and paid little attention to her brother. But one evening she suddenly rushed into his arms, with a strange wild cry that betrayed the impatience and the hidden desires that had so long preyed on the cold and ambitious girl.

Christian felt the cry like a discord, and disengaged himself.

He and Crammon went hunting or took trips to the neighbouring cities. Nothing held Christian anywhere. He wanted always to go farther or elsewhere. His very eyes became restless. When they walked through the streets, he glanced surreptitiously into the windows of apartments and into the halls of houses.

One night they sat in a wine cellar at Mainz, drinking a vintage that was thirty years old and had a rare bouquet. Crammon, who was a connoisseur through and through, kept filling his glass with an enchanted air. "It's sublime," he said, and began eating his caviare sandwich, "simply sublime. These are the realities of life. Here are my altars, my books of devotion, my relics, the scenes of my silent prayers. The immortal soul is at rest, and the lofty and unapproachable lies in the dust behind me."

"Talk like a decent man," said Christian.

But Crammon, who felt the ecstasy of wine, was not to be deflected. "I have drunk the draught of earthly delight. I have done it, O friend and brother, in huts and palaces, North and South, on sea and land. Only the final fulfilment was denied me. O Ariel, why did you cast me forth?"

He sighed, and drew from his inner pocket a tiny album in a precious binding. He always had it with him, for it contained twelve exquisite photographs of the dancer, Eva Sorel. "She is like a boy," he said, wholly absorbed in the pictures, "a slender, swift, unapproachable boy. She stands on the mystic boundary line of the sexes; she is that equivocal and twofold thing that maddens men if they but think of flesh and blood. Elusive she is as a lizard, and chill in love as an Amazon. Do you not feel a touch of horror, Christian? Does not a cold ichor trickle through your veins, when you imagine her in your arms, breast to breast? I feel that horror! For there would be something of the perverse in it—something of an unnatural violation. He who has touched her lips is lost. We saw that for ourselves."

Christian suddenly felt a yearning to be alone in a forest, in a dark and silent forest. He did feel a sense of horror, but in a way utterly alien to Crammon's thought. He looked at the older man, and it was hard for him to comprehend that there, opposite him, sat his familiar friend, whose face and form he had seen a thousand times unreflectively.

Crammon, contemplating the photograph on which Eva appeared dancing with a basket of grapes, began again: "Sweetest Ariel, they are all harlots; all, all, all, whether shameless and wild or fearful and secretive: you alone are pure—a vestal, a half-ghost, a weaver of silk, like the spider, who conquers the air upon her half-spun web. Let us drink, O friend! We are made of dirt, and must be medicined by fire!"

He drained his glass, rested his head upon his hand, and sank into melancholy contemplation.

Suddenly Christian said: "Bernard, I believe that we must part."

Crammon stared at him, as though he had not heard right.

"I believe that we must part," Christian repeated softly and with an indistinct smile. "I fear that we are no longer suited to each other. You must go your ways, and I shall go mine."

Crammon's face became dark red with astonishment and rage. He brought his fist down on the table and gritted his teeth. "What do you mean? Do you think you can send me packing as though I were a servant? Me?" He arose, took his hat and coat, and went.

Christian sat there for long with his thoughts. The indistinct smile remained on his lips.

When Christian, on awakening next day, rang for his valet, Crammon entered the room in the man's stead and made a deep bow. Over his left arm he had Christian's garments, in his right hand his boots. He said good-morning quite in the valet's tone, laid the clothes on a chair, set the boots on the floor, asked whether the bath was to be prepared at once, and what Herr Wahnschaffe desired for breakfast. And he did all this with complete seriousness, with an almost melancholy seriousness, and with a certain charm within the rôle he was assuming that could not fail to be pleasing.

Christian was forced to laugh. He held out his hand to Crammon. But the latter, refusing to abandon his acting, drew back, and bowed in embarrassment. He pulled the curtains aside, opened the windows, spread the fresh shirt, the socks, the cravat, and went, only to return a little later with the breakfast tray. After he had set the table and put the plates and cups in order, he stood with heels touching and head gently inclined forward. Finally, when Christian laughed again, the expression of his features altered, and he asked half-mockingly, half-defiantly: "Are you still prepared to assert that you can get along without me?"

"It's impossible to close accounts with you, dear Bernard," Christian answered.

"It is not one of my habits to leave the table when only

the soup has been served," Crammon said. "When my time comes I trundle myself off without urging. But I don't permit myself to be sent away."

"Stay, Bernard," Christian answered. He was shamed by his friend. "Only stay!" And their hands clasped.

But it almost seemed to Christian that his friend had really in a sense become a servant, that he was one now, at all events, toward whom one no longer had the duty of intimate openness, with whom no inner bond united one—a companion merely.

From that time on, jests and superficial persiflage were dominant in their conversations, and Crammon either did not see or failed very intentionally to observe that his relations with Christian had undergone a fundamental change.

VI

The arrival of the Argentinian caused a commotion among the guests of the house of Wahnschaffe. He had exotic habits. He pressed the hands of the ladies to whom he was presented with such vigour that they suppressed a cry of pain. Whenever he came down the stairs he stopped a few steps from the bottom, swung himself over the balustrade like an acrobat, and went on as though this were the most natural thing in the world. He had presented the countess with a Pekingese dog, and whenever he met the animal he tweaked its ear so that it howled horribly. And he did not do that merrily or with a smile, but in a dry, businesslike manner.

Among the numerous trunks that he brought with him, one was arranged in the form of a travelling pharmacy. Screwed down tightly in neat compartments there were all possible mixtures, powders, and medicaments; there were little boxes, tubes, jars, and glasses. If any one complained of indisposition, he at once pointed out the appropriate remedy in his trunk, and recommended it urgently.

Felix Imhof had taken an enthusiastic fancy to him. Whenever he could get hold of him, he took him aside, and questioned him regarding his country, his plans and undertakings, his outer and his inner life.

Judith, who was jealous, resented this bitterly. She made scenes for the benefit of Felix, and reproached Letitia for her failure to absorb Stephen Gunderam's attention.

Letitia was astonished, and her eyes grew large. With innocent coquetry she asked: " What can I do about it? "

Judith's answer was cynical. " One must study to please the men."

She hated the Argentinian. Yet when she was alone with him she sought to ensnare him. Had it been possible to alienate him from Letitia, she would have done so out of sheer insatiableness.

Her eyes glittered with a constant and secret desire. She went to the theatre with Imhof, Letitia, and Stephen to see Edgar Lorm in " The Jewess of Toledo." The applause which was so richly given to the actor stirred the very depth of her soul and filled it with more piercing desire. But whether she desired the man or the artist, his art or his fame, she was herself unable to tell.

She waited impatiently for Crammon, of whose friendship with Lorm she had heard. He was to bring the actor to the house with him. She was accustomed to have all men come after whom she cast her hook. They usually bit, were served up, and then enjoyed in proportion to their excellence of flavour. The household consumption of people was large.

But Crammon and Christian did not return until Lorm's visit to Frankfort was over. So Judith fell into an evil mood, and tormented all about her without reason. Had her wish been fulfilled, her flickering soul, that needed ever new nourishment, might have been calmed. Now she buried herself stubbornly in the thought of what had passed by her.

VII

Crammon and Christian had been spending a week with Clementine and Franz Lothar von Westernach in Styria. Clementine had summoned Crammon for the sake of her brother, who had recently returned from a stay in Hungary with a deeply shaken mind.

Crammon and Franz Lothar were very old friends. The latter's profession of diplomacy had made the frank and flexible man reserved and difficult. He took his profession seriously, although he did not love it. A hypochondriacal state of the nerves had developed in him, even in his youth.

Christian's sympathy went out to him in his present state. He felt tempted to question the man who sat so still and with a dim stare in his eyes. Clementine, in her empty chattering manner, gave Crammon directions for his behaviour, at which he shrugged his shoulders.

She said that she had written to her cousin, Baron Ebergeny, on whose estate in Syrmia Franz had been a guest. But the baron, who was half a peasant, had been able to give her no explanation of any real import. He had merely pointed out that he and Franz Lothar, on one of the last days of the latter's presence, had witnessed the burning of a barn at Orasje, a neighbouring village, during which many people had lost their lives.

No information was to be obtained from Franz Lothar himself. He was steadily silent. His sister redoubled her care, but his sombre reticence only increased. Perhaps Crammon was capable of some tone, some glance, that pierced and melted his petrified soul. One evening, at all events, the unexpected happened. Crammon learnt that the burning of the barn was the real cause of his morbid melancholy.

According to her custom, Clementine had gone to bed early. Christian, Crammon, and Franz Lothar sat silently together. Suddenly—without any external impetus—Franz covered his

face with his hands, and deep sobs came from his breast.
Crammon sought to soothe him. He stroked his hair and
grasped his hands. In vain. The sobbing became a convulsion that shook the man's body violently.

Christian sat without moving. A bitterness rose in his
throat, for there came to him with unexpected power a sense
of the essential reality of the spiritual pain that was being
uttered here.

The convulsion ceased as suddenly as it had begun. Franz
Lothar arose, walked up and down with dragging footsteps,
and said: "You shall hear how it was." Thereupon he sat
down and told them.

In the village of Orasje a dance had been planned. No hall
was available, and so the large, well-boarded barn of a peasant
was prepared. Numerous lamps were hung up, and the wooden
walls adorned with flowers and foliage. According to a local
custom, the magnates on all the neighbouring estates and their
families received invitations to attend the festivity. A mounted
messenger delivered these solemnly by word of mouth.

Franz Lothar begged his brother to take him to the peasants'
ball. He had long heard stories in praise of the picturesque-
ness of these feasts: the snow-white garments of the men, the
strong and varied colours of the women's, the national dances,
the primitive music. There was a promise in all these, both
of pleasure and of a knowledge of new folk-ways.

They intended to drive over at a late hour when the dancing had already begun. Two young countesses and the latters'
brother, all members of their circle, planned to join them. But
in the end the others went first, for the young ladies did not
want to miss any of the dancing. Franz Lothar had long
and cordially admired the Countess Irene, who was the older
of the two.

Several days before the ball, however, a quarrel had broken
out between the youths and maidens of Orasje. On the way to
chuch, a lad, whom a seventeen-year-old beauty had given too

rude an evidence of her dislike, had put a live mouse on her
naked shoulder. The girl ran crying to her companions, and
they sent an envoy to the youths, demanding that the guilty
one apologize.

The demand was refused. There was laughter and teasing.
But they insisted on this punishment, although they were
repeated their demand in a more drastic form. When it was
refused a second time they determined to invite to their ball
the young men of Gradiste, between whom and those of Orasje
there was a feud of many years' standing. They knew the
insult they were inflicting on the youths of their own village.
But they insisted on this punishment, although they were
warned even by their fathers and mothers, and by loud and
silent threats which should have inspired them with fear.

The youths of Gradiste were, of course, loudly triumphant
over their cheap victory. On the evening of the dance they
appeared without exception, handsomely dressed, and accompanied by their own village band. Of the youths of Orasje
not one was to be seen. In the twilight they passed in ghostly
procession through the streets of ,the village, and were then
seen no more.

The elders and the married folk of.Orasje sat at tables in
their yards and gardens, and chatted. But they were not as
care-free as on other festive evenings, for they felt the vengeful mood of their sons, and feared it. They drank their wine
and listened to the music. In the barn over three hundred
young people were assembled. The air was sultry, and the
dancers were bathed in sweat. Suddenly, while they were
dancing a Czarda, the two great doors of the barn were simul-
taneously slammed to from without. Those who saw it and
heard it ceased dancing. And now a powerful and disturbing
noise broke in upon the loud and jubilant sound of the instruments. It was the sound of hammers, and a sharp and terror-
shaken voice called out: " They are nailing up the doors."

The music stopped. In a moment the atmosphere had.

become suffocating. As though turned to stone, they all stared at the doors. Their blood seemed to congeal under the terrible blows of the hammers. Loud and mingled voices came to them from without. The older people there raised their protesting voices. The voices grew loud and wild, and then rose to desperate shrieks and howls. Then it began to crackle and hiss. The blows of the hammers had shaken down a lamp. The petroleum had caught on fire, and the dry boarding of the floor flared like tinder that could no longer be extinguished.

All reason and all human restraints fled. In the twinkling of an eye the three hundred became like wild beasts. With the violence of mania the youths hurled themselves against the locked doors; but these had been built of heavy oak, and resisted all exertions. The girls shrieked madly; and since the smoke and the fumes did not all float out through the cracks in the walls and through the small, star-shaped window-holes, the girls drew up their skirts about their heads. Others threw themselves moaning to the floor; and when they were trodden on by the others, who surged so madly to and fro, they writhed convulsively, and stretched out their arms. Soon the dry woodwork had become a mass of flame. The heat was intolerable. Many tore off their garments, both youths and maidens, and in the terror and the torment of death, united in the wild embraces of a sombre ecstasy, and wrung from their doomed lives an ultimate sting of delight.

These embracing couples Franz Lothar saw later with his own eyes as lumps of cinders amid the smoking ruins. He arrived with his cousin, when the whole horror had already taken place. They had seen the reflection of the flames in the sky from afar, and whipped up their horses. From the neighbouring villages streamed masses of people. But they came too late to help. The barn had been burned down within five minutes, and all within, except five or six, had found their death.

Among the victims was also the Countess Irene, her sister

and brother. Terrible as this was, it added but little to the unspeakable horror of the whole catastrophe. The image of that place of ruins; the sight of the smouldering corpses; their odour and the odour of blood and burned hair and garments; the pied, short-haired village dogs, who crept with greedy growls about this vast hearth of cooked flesh; the distorted faces of the suffocated, whose bodies lay untouched amid the other burned and blackened ones; the loud or silent grief of mothers, fathers, brothers; the Syrmian night, fume-filled to the starry sky,—these things rained blow on blow upon the spirit of Franz Lothar, and caused a black despair to creep into the inmost convolutions of his brain.

It eased him that he had at last found the release of speech. He sat by the window, and looked out into the dark.

Crammon, a sinister cloud upon his lined forehead, said: "Only with a whip can the mob be held in leash. What I regret is the abolition of torture. The devil take all humanitarian twaddle! " Then he went out and put his arms about Lothar and kissed him.

But Christian felt a sense of icy chill and rigidness steal over him.

Their departure was set for the next morning. Crammon entered the room of Christian, who was so lost in thoughts that he did not reply to the greeting of his friend. " Look here, what's wrong with you? " Crammon exclaimed, as he examined him. " Have you looked in the glass? "

Christian had dispensed with his valet on this trip, or the slight accident could not have happened. The colours of his suit and his cravat presented an obvious discord.

" I'm rather absent-minded to-day," Christian said, half-smiling. He took off the cravat, and replaced it by another. It took him three times as long as usual. Crammon walked impatiently up and down.

VIII

Confusion seized upon Christian whenever he sought to think about the condition in which he found himself.

In his breast there was an emptiness which nothing could fill from without, and about him was a rigid armour that hindered all freedom of movement. He yearned to fill the emptiness and to burst the armour.

His mother became anxious, and said: " You look peaked, Christian. Is anything wrong with you? " He assured her that there was nothing. But she knew better, and inquired of Crammon: " What ails Christian? He is so still and pale."

Crammon answered: " Dear lady, that is his style of personality. Experiences carve his face. Has it not grown nobler and prouder? You need fear nothing. He follows his road firmly and unwaveringly. And so long as I am with him, nothing evil can happen to him."

Frau Wahnschaffe was moved in her faint way, though still in doubt, and gave him her hand.

Crammon said to Christian: " The countess has made a great catch—a person from overseas. Quite fitting."

" Do you like the man? " Christian asked, uncertainly.

" God forbid that I should think evil of him," Crammon replied, hypocritically. " He is from so far away, and will go so far away again, that I cannot but find him congenial. If he takes that child Letitia with him, he shall be accompanied by my blessings. Whether it will mean her happiness, that is a matter I refuse to be anxious about. Such remote distances have, at all events, something calming. The Argentine, the Rio de la Plata! Dear me, it might just as well be the moon! "

Christian laughed. Yet the figure of Crammon, as it stood there before him, seemed to dissolve into a mist, and he suppressed what he still had to say.

Twenty-three of the guest rooms were occupied. People

arrived and left. Scarcely did one begin to recognize a face, when it disappeared again. Men and women, who had met but yesterday, associated quite intimately to-day, and said an eternal farewell to-morrow. A 'certain Herr von Wedderkampf, a business associate of the elder Wahnschaffe, had brought his four daughters. Fräulein von Einsiedel arranged to settle down for the winter, for her parents were in process of being divorced. Wolfgang, who was spending his vacation at home, had brought with him three student friends. All these people were in a slightly exalted mood, made elaborate plans for their amusement, wrote letters and received them, dined, flirted, played music, were excited and curious, witty and avid for pleasure, continued to carry on their worldly affairs from here, and assumed an appearance of friendliness, innocence, and freedom from care.

Liveried servants ran up and down the stairs, electric bells trilled, motor car horns tooted, tables were laid, lamps shone, jewels glittered. Behind one door they flirted, behind another they brewed a scandal. In the hall with the fair marble columns sat smiling couples. It was a world thoroughly differentiated from those quite accidental modern groupings at places where one pays. It was full of a common will to oblige, of secret understandings, and of social charm.

Letitia had gone with her aunt to spend a week in Munich. She did not return until the third day after Christian's arrival. Christian was glad to see her. Yet he could not bring himself to enter into conversation with her.

IX

One morning he sat at breakfast with his father. He marvelled how strange to him was this gentleman with the white, parted hair, with the elegantly clipped and divided beard and the rosy complexion.

Herr Wahnschaffe treated him with very great courtesy. He inquired after the social relations that Christian had formed in England, and commented upon his son's frugal answers with instructive remarks concerning men and things. "It is well for Germans to gain ground there—useful and necessary."

He discussed the threatening clouds in the political sky, and expressed his disapproval of Germany's attitude during the Moroccan crisis. But Christian remained silent, through want of interest and through ignorance, and his father became visibly cooler, took up his paper, and began to read.

What a stranger he is to me, Christian thought, and searched for a pretext that would let him rise and leave. At that moment Wolfgang came to the table, and talked about the results of the races at Baden-Baden. His voice annoyed Christian, and he escaped.

It happened that Judith was sitting in the library and teased him about Letitia. Then Letitia herself and Crammon entered chatting. Felix Imhof soon joined them. Letitia took a book, and carefully avoided, as was clear, looking in Christian's direction. Then those three left the room again, and Judith listened with pallor to their retreating voices, for she had heard Felix pay Letitia a compliment. "Perhaps she is committing a great folly," she said. Then she turned to her brother. "Why are you so silent?" She wrinkled her forehead, and rested her folded hands on his shoulder. "We are all merry and light hearted here, and you are so changed. Don't you like to be among us? Isn't it lovely here at home? And if you don't like it, can't you go at any time? Why are you so moody?"

"I hardly know; I am not moody," Christian replied. "One cannot always be laughing."

"You'll stay until my wedding, won't you?" Judith continued, and raised her brows. "I'll never forgive you if you don't." Christian nodded, and then she said with a friendly urgency, "Why don't you ever talk to me, you bear? Ask me something!"

Christian smiled. " Very well, I'll ask you something," he said. " Are you contented, Judith? Is your heart at peace? "

Judith laughed. " That's asking too much at once! You used not to be so forthright." Then she leaned forward, with her elbows on her knees, and spread out her hands. " We Wahnschaffes can never be contented. All that we have is too little, for there is always so much that one has not. I'm afraid I shall be like the fisherman's wife in the fairy tale. Or, rather, I'm not afraid but glad at the thought that I'll send my fisherman back to the fish in the sea again and again. Then I shall know, at least, what he is willing to risk."

Christian regarded his beautiful sister, and heard the temerity of her words. There was an audacity about her gestures, her words, her bright, clear voice, and the glow of her eyes. He remembered how he had sat one evening with Eva Sorel; and she had been as near him as Judith was now. In silent ecstasy he had looked at Eva's hands, and she had raised her left hand and held it against the lamp, and though the radiance outlined only the more definitely the noble form of the rosy translucence of her flesh, the dark shadow of the bony structure had been plainly visible. And Eva had said: " Ah, Eidolon, the kernel knows nothing of beauty."

Christian arose and asked almost sadly: " You will know what he risks. But will that teach you to know what you gain? "

Judith looked up at him in surprise, and her face darkened.

X

One day he entered the sitting-room of his mother, but she was not there. He approached the door that led to her bedroom, and knocked. When he received no answer, he opened it. She was not in this room either. Looking about, he became aware of a brown silk dress trimmed with lace that belonged to his mother and that had been put on a form. And for a second he seemed to see her before him, but without a head. He fell to thinking, and the same thought came to him that he had had in his father's presence: What a stranger she is to me! And the dress, that hid only the wicker form, became an image of his mother, more recognizable to him than her living body.

For there was about her something impenetrable and inexplicable—the rigid attitude, the hopeless mien, the dull eye, the rough voice that had no resonance, her whole joyless character. She, in whose house all made merry, and whose whole activity and being seemed dedicated to give others the opportunity of delight, was herself utterly barren of joy.

But she had the most magnificent pearls in Europe. And all men knew this and esteemed her for it and boasted of it.

Christian's self-deception went so far, that he was about to talk to that hollow form more intimately than he would have done to his living mother. A question leaped to his lips, a tender and cheerful word. Then he heard her footsteps, and was startled. He turned around, and seemed to see her double.

She was not surprised at meeting him here. She was rarely surprised at anything. She sat down on a chair and her eyes were empty.

She discussed Imhof, who had introduced a Jewish friend of his to the house. She deprecated association with Jews as a practice. She added that Wahnschaffe—she always called her husband so—agreed with her.

She expressed her disapproval of Judith's engagement. "Wahnschaffe is really opposed to this marriage too," she said, "but it was difficult to find a pretext to refuse. If Judith sets her heart on anything! Well, you know her! I am afraid her chief ambition was to get ahead of her friend Letitia."

Christian looked up in amazement. His mother did not observe it, and continued: "With all his good qualities Imhof does not seem reliable. He is a plunger, and restless and changeable as a weather vane. Of the ten millions which his foster father left him, five or six are already lost through speculation and extravagance. What is your judgment of him? "

"I haven't really thought about it," Christian answered. This conversation was beginning to weary him.

"Then, too, his origin is obscure. He was a foundling. Old Martin Imhof, whom Wahnschaffe knew, by the way, and who belonged to one of the first patrician families of Düsseldorf, is said to have adopted him under peculiar circumstances. He was an old bachelor, and had a reputation for misanthropy. At last he was quite alone in the world, and absolutely adored this strange child. Hadn't you heard about that? "

"Some rumour, yes," Christian said.

"Well, now tell me something about yourself, my son," Frau Wahnschaffe asked, with a changed expression and with a smile of suffering.

But Christian had no answer. His world and his mother's world—he saw no bridge between the two. And as the knowledge came to him, another matter also became clear. And it was this, that there was likewise no bridge between the world of his conscious life and another that lay far behind it, misty and menacing, luring and terrible at once, which he did not understand, nor know, of which he had not even a definite presage, but which had come to him only as a vision through flashes of lightning, or as a dream or in a swift touch of horror.

He kissed his mother's hand, and hastened out.

XI

In spite of a gently persistent rain, he walked with Letitia through the twilit park. Many times they wandered up and down the path from the hot-houses to the pavillion, and heard the sound of a piano from the house. Fräulein von Einsiedel was playing.

At first their conversation was marked by long pauses. Something in Letitia was beseeching: Take me, take me!

Christian understood. He wore his arrogant smile, but he did not dare to look at her. " I love music heard from afar," Letitia said. " Don't you, Christian? "

He drew his raincoat tighter about him, and replied: " I care little about music."

" Then you have a bad heart, or at least a hard one."

" It may be that I have a bad heart; it is certainly hard."

Letitia flushed, and asked: " What do you love? I mean what things. What? " The archness of her expression did not entirely conceal the seriousness of her question.

" What things I love? " he repeated lingeringly, " I don't know. Does one have to love things? One uses them. That is all."

" Oh, no! " Letitia cried, and her deep voice brought a peculiar warmth to Christian. " Oh, no! Things exist to be loved. Flowers, for instance, and stars. One loves them. If I hear a beautiful song or see a beautiful picture, at once something cries within me: That is mine, mine! "

" And do you feel that too when a bird suddenly drops down and dies, as you have seen it happen? Or when a wounded deer dies before you when you are hunting? " Christian asked, hesitatingly.

Letitia was silent, and looked at him with a touch of fear. The glance of her eyes was inexpressibly grateful to him. Take me, take me, that silent voice pleaded with him again. " But those are not things," she said softly, " they are living beings."

His voice was gentler than hitherto when he spoke again: " All things that are fragrant and glowing, that serve adornment and delight are yours indeed, Letitia. But what are mine?" He stood still, and asked again with a look of inner distress which shook Letitia's soul. Never had she expected such words or such a tone of him.

Her glance reminded him: you kissed me once! Think of it—you kissed me once!

"When is your wedding going to be?," he asked, and his lids twitched a little.

"I don't know exactly. We're not even formally engaged at present," Letitia answered, laughing. "He has declared that I must be his wife and won't be contradicted. Christmas my mother is coming to Heidelberg, and then, I suppose, the wedding will take place. What I do look forward to is the voyage overseas and the strange country." And in her radiant eyes flamed up the impassioned plea: Oh, take me, take me! My yearning is so great! But with a coquettish turn of the head, she asked: "How do you like Stephen?"

He did not answer her question, but said softly: "Some one is watching us from the house."

Letitia whispered: "He is jealous of the very earth and air." It began to rain harder, and so they turned their steps toward the house. And Christian felt that he loved her.

An hour later he entered the smoking room. Imhof, Crammon, Wolfgang, and Stephen Gunderam sat about a round table, and played poker. The demeanour of each accorded with his character: Imhof was superior and talkative, Crammon absent-minded and sombre, Wolfgang distrustful and excited. Stephen Gunderam's face was stonily impassive. He was as utterly dedicated to his occupation as a somnambulist. He has been winning uninterruptedly, and a little mountain of bank notes and gold was rising in front of him. Crammon and Imhof moved aside to make room for Christian. At that moment Stephen jumped up. Holding his cards in his hand, he stared at Christian with eyes full of hatred.

Christian regarded him with amazement. But when the other three, rather surprised, also moved to get up, Stephen Gunderam sank back into his chair, and said with sombre harshness: "Let us play on. May I ask for four cards?"

Christian left the neighbourhood of the table. He felt that he loved Letitia. His whole heart loved her, tenderly and with longing.

XII

A discharged workman had lain in wait one evening for the automobile of Herr Albrecht Wahnschaffe. When the car slowed up and approached the gate of the park, the assassin, hidden by the bushes, had stealthily shot at his former employer.

The bullet only grazed its victim's arms. The wound was slight, but Albrecht Wahnschaffe had to remain in bed for several days. After his deed the criminal had escaped under cover of darkness. It was not until next morning that the police succeeded in catching him.

This happening, inconsiderable as were its consequences, had disturbed for a little the merry life in the house of Wahnschaffe. Several persons left. Among these was Herr von Wedderkampf, who told his daughters that the ground here was getting too hot for his feet.

But on the third evening every one was dancing again.

It surprised Christian. He did not understand such swift forgetfulness. He was surprised at the equanimity of his mother, the care-free mood of his sister and brother.

He wished to learn the name of that workingman, but no one knew. He was told that the man's name was Müller. Also that it was Schmidt. He was surprised. Nor did any one seem to know exactly what motive impelled the man to his deed. One said that it had been mere vengefulness, the result of the flame of class hatred systematically fanned. Another said that only a lunatic could be capable of such a deed.

Whatever it was, this shot fired from ambush by an unknown man for an unknown cause was not quite the same to Christian as it was to all the others who lived about him and sought their pleasure in their various ways. It forced him to meditation. His meditation was aimless and fruitless enough. But it was serious, and caused him strange suffering.

He would have liked to see the man. He would have liked to look into his face.

Crammon said: "Another case that makes it clear as day that the discarding of torture has simply made the canaille more insolent. What admirable inventions for furthering discipline and humanity were the stocks and the pillory!"

Christian visited his father, who sat in an armchair with his arm in a sling. A highly conservative newspaper was spread out before him. Herr Wahnschaffe said: "I trust that you and your friends are not practising any undue restraint. I could not endure the thought of darkening the mood of my guests by so much as a breath."

Christian was astonished at this courtesy, this distinction and temperance, this amiable considerateness.

XIII

Deep in the woods, amid ruins, Stephen Gunderam demanded of Letitia that she decide his fate.

A picnic in very grand style had been arranged; Letitia and Stephen had remained behind here; and thus it had happened.

Around them arose the ancient tree-trunks and the immemorial walls. Above the tree-tops extended the pallid blue of the autumnal sky. His knees upon the dry foliage, a man, using sublime and unmeasured words, asserted his eternal love. Letitia could not withstand the scene and him.

Stephen Gunderam said: "If you refuse me nothing is left me but to put a bullet through my head. I have had it in readiness for long. I swear to you by the life of my father that I speak truly."

Could a girl as gentle and as easily persuaded as Letitia assume the responsibility for such blood-guiltiness? And she gave her consent. She did not think of any fetter, nor of the finality of such a decision, nor of time nor of its consequences, nor of him to whom her soul was to belong. She thought only of this moment, and that there was one here who had spoken to her these sublime and unmeasured words.

Stephen Gunderam leaped up, folded her in his arms and cried: " From now on you belong to me through all eternity —every breath, every thought, every dream of yours is mine and mine only! Never forget that—never! "

" Let me go, you terrible man! " Letitia said, but with a shiver of delight. She felt herself carried voluptuously upon a wave of romance. Her nerves began to vibrate, her glance shimmered and broke. For the first time she felt the stir of the flesh. With a soft cry she glided from his grasp.

Even on the way home they received congratulations. Crammon slunk quietly away. When Christian came and gave Letitia his hand, there was in her eyes a restless expectation, a fantastic joy that he could not understand at all. He could not fathom what she hid behind this expression. He could not guess that even at this moment she was faithlessly withdrawing herself from him to whom she had just entrusted her life, its every breath and thought and dream, and that in her innocent but foolish way she desired to convey to Christian a sense of this fact.

He loved her. From hour to hour his love grew. He felt it to be almost an inner law that he must love her—a command which said to him: This is she to whom you must turn; a message whose burden was: In her shall you find yourself.

He seemed to be hearing the voice of Eva: Your path was from me to her. I taught you to feel. · Now give that feeling to a waiting heart. You can shape it and mould it and yourself. Let it not be extinguished nor flicker out and die.

Thus the inner voice seemed to speak.

XIV

Crammon, the thrice hardened, had a dream wherein some one reproved him for standing by idly, while his flesh and blood was being sold to an Argentinian ranchman. So he went to the countess, and asked her if she indeed intended to send the tender child into a land of savages. "Don't you feel any dread at the thought of her utter isolation in these regions of the farthest South?" he asked her, and rolled his hands in and out, which gave him the appearance of an elderly usurer.

"What are you thinking of, Herr von Crammon?" The countess was indignant. "What right have you to question me? Or do you happen to know a better man for her, a wealthier, more distinguished, more presentable one? Do you imagine one can be happy only in Europe? I've had a look at a good many people. They ran after us by the dozen at Interlaken, Aix-les-Bains, at Geneva and Zürich and Baden-Baden—old and young, Frenchmen and Russians, Germans and Englishmen, counts and millionaires. We didn't start out with any particular craze for the exotic. Your friend Christian can bear witness to that! But he, I dare say, thought himself too good for us. It's bad enough that I have to let my darling go across the ocean, without your coming to me and making my heart heavier than ever!"

But Crammon was not to be talked down. "Consider the matter very carefully once more," he said. "The responsibility is tremendous. Do you realize that venomous snakes exist in those regions whose bite kills within five seconds? I have read of storms that uproot the most powerful trees and overturn houses nine stories high. So far as I have been informed, certain tribes native to Terra del Fuego still practise cannibalism. Furthermore, there are species of ants that attack human beings and devour them bodily. The heat of summer is said to be insufferable, and equally so the cold of winter. It is an inhospitable region, countess, and a dirty one with dangerous inhabitants. I want you to consider the whole matter carefully once more."

The countess was rather overcome. Delighted with the effect of his words, Crammon left her with head erect.

That evening, when Letitia was already in bed, the countess, with arms crossed on her bosom, walked up and down in the girl's room. Her conscience was heavy, but she hardly knew how to begin a discussion. All afternoon she had been writing letters and addressing announcements of the engagement, and now she was tired. The little dog, Puck, meanwhile sat on a silken pillow in the adjoining room, and barked shrilly and without cause from time to time.

Letitia stared into the dim space above her with eyes that gleamed softly with the mystery of dreams. So rapt was she that if one had pressed a pin into her flesh she would not have noticed it.

At last the countess conquered herself sufficiently. She sat down near the bed, and took Letitia's hands into her own. "Is it true, sweetheart," she began, "and did Stephen tell you about all these things that Herr von Crammon speaks of— venomous snakes and cannibals and tornadoes and wild ants and frightful heat and cold in this terrible country that you're going to? If all this is true, I want to beseech you to reconsider very thoroughly this step that you're about to take."

Letitia laughed a deep and hearty laugh. "Are you beginning to get frightened now, auntie?" she cried, "just as I've been dreaming about the future! Crammon has played an ill-timed prank. That is all. Stephen never lies, and according to his description the Argentine is a veritable earthly paradise. Do listen, auntie!" She said this with an air of mystery, moved to the edge of her bed, and regarded the countess full of confidence and delight. "The land is full of peaches as large as a child's head and of the most exquisite flavour. They are so plentiful that those that cannot be eaten or sold are piled up in great heaps and burned. They have game of all sorts, which they prepare in wonderful ways quite unknown in Europe, and fishes and fowl and honey, the rarest vegetables, and everything that the heart can desire."

The countess' face brightened. She petted Letitia's arm,

and said: "Well, of course, in that case, and if it is really so . . ."

But Letitia went on: "When I've become thoroughly acclimated and familiar with everything, I'll ask you, dear aunt, to come out to us. You'll have a house of your own, a charming villa all overgrown with flowers. Your pantries shall be filled afresh daily and you shall have a marble bath next to your bedroom. You'll be able to get into it as often as you like, and you will have Negro women to wait on you."

"That is right, my darling," the countess answered, and her face was transfigured with delight. "Whether it's a paradise or not, I am pretty sure that it will be dirty. And dirt, as you know, is something I hate almost as much as poisonous serpents or cannibals."

"Don't be afraid, auntie," said Letitia, "we'll lead a wonderful life there."

The countess was calmed, and embraced Letitia with overwhelming gratitude.

xv

In order to escape from the confusion at Wahnschaffe Castle, as the new house was known, Christian and Crammon retired for several days to Christian's Rest. Scarcely had they settled down, when they were joined by Judith and her companion, by Letitia and Fräulein von Einsiedel.

The countess and Stephen Gunderam had gone to Heidelberg, where they were expecting Frau von Febronius. Letitia was to follow them a week later. Felix had been summoned to Leipzig, where he was to join in the founding of a great new publishing house. After his return to the castle, his and Judith's wedding was to take place.

Judith announced that she intended to enjoy the last days of her liberty. It had not needed much persuasion to bring Letitia with her. The companion and Fräulein von Einsiedel were regarded as chaperones, and so with laughter and merriment these four surprised Christian and Crammon suddenly.

The weather was beautiful, though somewhat cold. They passed most of their time out of doors, walking in the woods, playing golf, arranging picnics. The evenings flew by in cheerful talk. Once Crammon read to them Goethe's "Torquato Tasso," and imitated the intonation and the rhythms of Edgar Lorm so deceptively that Judith grew excited and could not hear enough. She was attracted by the very imitation that he practised; to Letitia the verses were like wine; Fräulein von Einsiedel, who had been mourning a lost love for years, struggled with her tears at many passages. Judith, on the other hand, saw an adored image in a magic mirror, and when the reading was over, turned the conversation to Lorm, and besought Crammon to tell her about him.

Crammon did as she desired. He told her of the actor's romantic friendship with a king, of his first marriage to a fair-haired Jewess. He had loved her madly, and she had left him suddenly and fled to America. He had followed her thither, and tracked her from place to place, but all his efforts to win her back had been in vain. He had returned in grave danger of losing himself and wasting his talent. Lonely and divided in his soul, he had tried to settle in various places. He had broken his contracts, been outlawed by the managers, and barely tolerated by the public as a dangerous will o' the wisp. At last, however, his genius had fought down all unfortunate circumstances as well as the weaknesses of his own nature, and he was now the most radiant star in the heaven of his art.

When Crammon had ended, Judith came up to him and stroked his cheeks. "That was charming, Crammon. I want you to be rewarded."

Crammon laughed in his deepest bass voice, and answered: "Then I ask as my reward that you four ladies return to-morrow morning to the castle, and leave my friend Christian and me to each other's silence. Isn't it true, Christian, dear boy? We like to brood over the mysteries of the world."

"The brute!" they cried out, "the traitor! The base intriguer!" But it was only a jesting indignation. Their return had really been set for the next day.

Christian arose and said: "Bernard is not wrong when he says we desire silence. It is lovely to be surrounded by loveliness. But you girls are too restless and unquiet." He had spoken in jest. But as he passed his hand over his forehead, one could see the deep seriousness in his heart.

They all looked at him. There was something strangely proud about his appearance. Letitia's heart beat. When he looked at her, her eyes fell and she blushed deeply. She loved all that he was, all that lay behind him, all that he had experienced, all women he had loved, all men from whom he came or to whom he went.

Suddenly she remembered the little golden toad. She had brought it with her and she determined to give it to him to-day. But to do that she wanted to be alone with him.

XVI

It was her wish that their meeting be at night, and she gave him a sign. Unnoticed by the others, she succeeded in whispering to him that she would come to him that night with a gift. He was to wait for her.

He looked at her without a word. When she glided away, his lips throbbed.

After midnight, when all were asleep in the house, she left her chamber, and mounted to the upper floor where Christian had his rooms. She went softly but without especial fear. Bending her head forward, she held in her hands the folds of the white silken over-garment that she wore. Its transparent texture was more like a white shimmer, a pearly gleam upon her flesh than a garment. It was doubled only about her waist and bosom, and her steps were impeded by a satin riband about her knees. Thus, while her pulses throbbed, she had to trip, to her own amusement, like the Geisha girls she had seen in a theatre.

When Christian had locked the door behind her, she leaned against it in sudden weakness.

Gently he took her wrists, and breathed a kiss upon her forehead, smiled, and asked: ".What did you want to bring to me, Letitia? I long to know."

Suddenly she was aware that she had forgotten the golden toy. Shortly before she had left her room, she had laid it in readiness; and yet she had forgotten it. " How stupid of me! " The words slipped out, and she gazed in shame at her little shoes of black velvet. " How stupid of me! There was a little toad made of gold that I meant to bring to you."

It startled him. Then he recalled the words that he had spoken so many months ago. The intervening time seemed thrice its natural length. He wondered now how he could ever have been frightened of a toad. He could, to be sure, hear his own words again: " Have a little toad made of gold, that the evil magic may disappear." But the monition had no validity to-day. The spell had been broken without a talisman.

And as he saw the girl stand before him, quivering and intoxicated, the trembling and the ecstasy seized him too. Many others had come to him—none so innocent and yet so guilty, none so determined and so deluded at once. He knew those gestures, that silent yearning, the eye that flamed and smouldered, the half-denial and the half-assent, the clinging and repulsing, the sighs and the magical tears that tasted like warm and salty dew. He knew! And his senses urged him with all their power to experience and to taste it all again.

But there were things that stood between him and his desire. There was a pallid brunette face whose eyes were upon him with unimaginable clearness. There was a blood-soaked face to which the black hair clung. There was a face that had once been beautiful, swollen by the waters of the

Thames. And there was a face full of hatred and shame against the coarse linen of a bed, and another in the storeroom of a hotel which was swathed in a white cloth. There were other faces—faces of men and women, thousands upon thousands, on the shore of a river, and still others that were stamped upon and charred, which he had seen as though they were concrete realities through the eyes of another. All these things stood between him and his desire.

And his heart opposed it too. And the love that he felt for Letitia.

He grew a little paler, and a chill crept into his finger-tips. He took Letitia by the hand, and led her to the middle of the room. She looked about her timidly, but every glance was his who filled her whole being. She asked him concerning the pictures that hung on the wall, and admired a picture of himself which was among them. She asked after the meaning of a little sculptured group which he had bought in Paris: a man and a woman emerging from the earth of which they were made, contending with primitive power.

Her deep voice had a more sensuous note than ever. And as he answered her, the temptation assailed him anew to touch with his lips the warm, rosy, throbbing curve of her shoulder, which was like a ripe fruit. But an inescapable voice within him cried: Resist once! Resist but this single time!

It was difficult, but he obeyed.

Letitia did not know what was happening to her. She shivered, and begged him to close the window. But when he had done so, her chill increased. She looked at him furtively. His face seemed arrogant and alien. They had sat down on a divan, and silence had fallen upon them. Why did I forget the little toad? Letitia thought. My folly is to blame for everything. And instinctively she moved away from him a little.

"Letitia," he said, and arose, "perhaps you will understand it all some day." Then he kneeled on the floor at her feet, and took her cool hands and laid them against his cheeks.

"No, I don't understand," Letitia whispered, and her eyes were wet, although she smiled, "and I shall never understand."

"You will! Some day you will!"

"Never," she asserted passionately, "never!" All things were confused within her. She thought of flowers and stars, of dreams and images. She thought of birds that fell dead out of the air, as he had described them once, and a deer dying at the hunter's feet. She thought of paths upon which she would go, of far sea-faring, and of jewels and costly garments. But none of these images held her. They were formed and dissolved. A chain broke in her soul, and she felt a need to lie down and weep for a while. Not for long. And it was possible that, when the weeping was over, she might look forward with delight once more to the coming day and to Stephen Gunderam and to their wedding.

"Good-night, Christian," she said, and gave him her hand as after a simple chat. And all the objects in the room had changed their appearance. On the table stood a cut-glass bowl full of meadow-saffron, and their white stalks were like the antennæ of a polypus. The night outside was no longer the same night. One seemed quite free now in a peculiar way—in a defiant and vengeful way.

Christian was amazed by her gesture and posture. He had not touched her; yet it was a girl who had come to him, and it was a woman who went. "I will think about it," she said, and nodded to him with a great, dark look. "I will learn to understand it."

So she went—went on into her rich, poverty-stricken, adventurous, difficult, trifling life.

Christian listened to the dying echo of her tread beyond the door. He stood without moving, and his head was bent. To him, too, the night had changed into another. Despite his obedience to the inner voice, a doubt gnawed at his soul whether what he had done was right or wrong, good or evil.

One day Christian received a letter that bore the signature of Ivan Michailovitch Becker. Becker informed him that he was staying for a short time in Frankfort, and that a woman, a mutual friend, had insisted that he should visit Christian Wahnschaffe. But this he would not do for well-considered reasons. If, however, Christian Wahnschaffe's state of mind was such as their friend seemed to assume, he would be glad to see him on some evening.

Eva's name was not mentioned. But twice he spoke of that woman who was their mutual friend—twice. And Becker had added the street where he lived and the number of the house.

Christian's first impulse was to ignore the invitation. He told himself that there was nothing in common between him and Becker. The Russian had not been congenial to him. He had disapproved and arrogantly overlooked the man's friendship with Eva. Whenever he thought of his ugly face, his dragging gait, his sombre, silent presence, a sense of discomfort seized upon him. What did the man want? Why this summons in which there was a shadow of menace?

After he had tried in vain to keep from brooding over this incident, he showed the letter to Crammon, in the secret hope that his friend would warn him against any response. Crammon read the letter, but shrugged his shoulders and said nothing. Crammon was in a bad humour; Crammon was hurt. He had felt for some time that Christian excluded him from his confidence. In addition he was thinking far more of Eva Sorel than was good for the peace of his soul. He paid ardent attention to Fräulein von Einsiedel, nor was that lady unresponsive. But this triumph could not restore the equilibrium of his mind, and Becker's letter opened his old wound anew.

Christian put an end to his vacillation by a sudden decision, and started out to find Becker. The house was in the suburbs, and he had to climb the four flights of stairs of a common tenement. He was careful to come in contact with neither the walls nor the balustrades. When he had reached the door and pulled the bell, he was pale with embarrassment and disgust.

When Christian had entered the shabbily furnished room and sat opposite Becker, what impressed him most was the stamp of suffering on the Russian's face. He asked himself whether this was new or whether he had merely not perceived it before. When Becker spoke to him, his answers were shy and awkward.

"Madame Sorel is going to Petrograd in the spring," Ivan Michailovitch told him. "She has signed a three-months' contract with the Imperial Theatre there."

Christian expressed his pleasure at this information. "Are you going to stay here long?" he asked, courteously.

"I don't know," was the answer. "I'm waiting for a message here. Afterwards I shall join my friends in Switzerland."

"My last conversation with Madame Sorel," he continued, "was exclusively about you." He watched Christian attentively out of his deep-set eyes.

"About me? Ah . . ." Christian forced himself to a conventional smile.

"She insisted on my remaining in communication with you. She said that it meant much to her, but gave no reason. She never does give reasons, though. She insisted likewise that I send her a report. Yet she did not even give me a message for you. But she kept repeating: 'It means something to me, and it may mean very much to him.' So you see that I am only her instrument. But I hope that you are not angry with me for annoying you."

"Not in the least," Christian asserted, although he felt oppressed. "Only I can't imagine what is in her mind." He sat there wondering, and added: "She has her very personal ways!"

Ivan Becker smiled, and the moisture of his thick lips became unpleasantly visible. " It is very true. She is an enthusiastic creature, and a woman of great gifts. She has power over others, and is determined to use that power."

· A pause ensued.

" Can I be of assistance to you? " Christian asked conventionally.

Becker regarded him coldly. " No," he said, " not of the least." He turned his eyes to the window, from which one could see the chimneys of the factories, the smoke, and the sinister snow-fraught air. Since the room was unheated, he had a travelling rug spread across his knees, and under it he hid his crippled hand. A movement of his limbs shifted the rug, and the hand became visible. Christian knew the story of it. Crammon had told him at the time in Paris of his meeting and his talk with Becker. He had heard it with indifference, and had avoided looking at the hand.

Now he regarded it. Then he got up, and with a gesture of freedom and assurance, which astonished even Becker, despite the Russian's superficial knowledge of him, he held out his own hand. Ivan Michailovitch gave him his left hand, which Christian held long and pressed cordially. Then he left without speaking another word.

XVIII

But on the following day he returned.

Ivan Michailovitch told him the story of his life. He offered him a simple hospitality, made tea, and even had the room heated. He spoke rather disconnectedly, with half-closed eyes and a morbid, suffering smile. Now he would relate episodes of his youth, now of his later years. The burden was always the same: oppression, need, persecution, suffering—suffering without measure. Wherever one went, one saw crushed hearts, happiness stamped out, and personalities destroyed. His parents had gone under in poverty, his brothers

and sisters had drifted away. and were lost, his friends had
fallen in wars or died in exile. It was a life without centre or
light or hope—a world of hate and malevolence, cruelty and
darkness.

Christian sat there and listened until late into the night.

Next they met in a coffee house, an ugly place which
Christian would once not have endured, and sat until far into
the night. Often they sat in silence; and this silence tormented
Christian, and kept him in a state of unbearable tension. But
his expression was a gentle one.

They took walks along the river, or through the streets and
parks in the snow. Ivan Michailovitch spoke of Pushkin and
Byelinsky, of Bakunin and Herzen, of Alexander I and the legend of his translation to heaven, and of the peasants—the
poor, dark folk. He spoke of the innumerable martyrs of forgotten names, men and women whose actions and sufferings
beat at the heart of mankind, and whose blood, as he said, was
the red dawn of the sunrise of a new and other age.

So Christian kept disappearing from his home, and no one
knew where he went.

Once Ivan Michailovitch said: "I am told that a workingman made a murderous assault on your father. The man was
condemned to seven years in the penitentiary yesterday."

"Yes, it is true," Christian replied. "What was his name?
I have forgotten it."

It turned out that the man's name was neither Schmidt nor
Müller, but Roderick Kroll. Ivan Michailovitch knew it.
"There's a wife and five little children left in extreme distress,"
he said. "Have you ever tried for a moment to grasp imagina-
tively what that means—real distress? Is your imagination
powerful enough to realize it? Have you ever seen the countenance of a human being that suffered hunger? There is this
woman. She bore five children, and loves these children just
as your mother loves hers. Very well. The drawers are empty,
the hearth is cold, the bedding is in pawn, their clothes and

shoes are in rags. These children are human, each one, just
as you and I are. They have the same instinctive expectation
of content, bread, quiet sleep, and pure air, that you have or
Herr von Crammon or countless others, who never realize re-
·flectively that all these things are theirs. Very well. Now
the world does not only feign to know nothing of all this, not
only resents being reminded of it, but actually demands of
these beings that they are to be silent, that they accept and
endure hunger, nakedness, cold, disease, the theft of their
natural rights, and the insolent injustice of it all, as something
quite natural and inevitable. Have you ever thought about
that? "

"It seems to me," Christian replied, softly, "that I have
never thought at all."

"This man," Ivan Michailovitch continued, "this Roderick
Kroll, so far as I have been able to learn, was systematically
exasperated to the very quick. He was an enthusiastic social-
ist, but somewhat of an annoyance even to his own party on
account of his extreme views and his violent propaganda.
The masters dug the ground from under his feet. They embittered him by the constant sting of small intrigues, and
drove him to despair. The intention was to render him harmless and to force him to silence. But tell me this: is there an
extreme on the side of the oppressed that is so unfair, so insolent, so damnable as the extreme on the other side—the arrogance, luxury, revelling, the hardness of heart, and the in-
sensate extravagance of every day and every hour? You did
not even know the name of that man! "

Christian stood still. The wind blew the snow into his
face, and wet his forehead and ·cheeks. "What shall I do,
Ivan Michailovitch? " he asked, slowly.

Ivan Michailovitch stopped too. "What shall I do? " he
cried. "That is what they all ask. That is what Prince
Jakovlev Grusin asked, one of our chief magnates and marshal
of the nobility in the province of Novgorod. After he had

starved his peasants, plundered his tenants, sent his officials
to Siberia, violated girls, seduced women, driven his own sons
to despair, spent his life in gluttony, drunkenness, and whor-
ing, and heaped crime upon crime—he went into a monastery in
the seventy-fourth year of his age, and day after day kneeled in
his cell and cried: 'What shall I do? My Lord and Saviour,
what shall I do?' And no one, naturally, had an answer for
him. I have heard the question asked softly by another, whose
soul was clean and white. He was going to his death, and his
age was seventeen. Nine men with their rifles stood by the
trench of the fortress. He approached, reeling a little, and his
guiltless soul asked: 'Father in Heaven, what shall I do?
What shall I do?'"

Ivan Michailovitch walked on, and Christian followed him.
"And we poor men, we terribly poor men," Ivan Becker said,
"what shall *we* do?"

XIX

Judith's wedding was to be celebrated with great magnificence.

Even to the preliminary festival more than two hundred
guests had been invited. There was no end to the line of
motor cars and carriages.

The coal and iron barons of the whole province appeared,
military and civil officials of high rank with their ladies, the
chief patricians and financiers of Frankfort, members of the
Court circles of Darmstadt and Karlsruhe, and friends from
afar. A tenor from Berlin, a famous lyric singer, a Viennese
comedian, a magician, and a juggler had been engaged to
furnish the guests with amusement.

The great horse-shoe table in the dining-hall, radiant with
gold, silver, and cut glass, had three hundred and thirty covers.

The festive throng surged up and down in the marble gallery
and the adjoining rooms. Yellow and rose predominated in the
toilettes of the ladies; the young girls were mostly in white.

Bare shoulders were agleam with diamonds and pearls. The severe black and white of the men effectually softened the gorgeousness of the colour scheme.

Christian was walking up and down with Randolph von Stettner, a young lieutenant of hussars, stationed at Bonn. They had been friends since their boyhood, had not seen each other for several years, and were exchanging reminiscences. Randolph von Stettner said that he was not very happy in his profession; he would much rather have taken a university degree. He had a strong taste for the study of chemistry, and felt out of place as a soldier. " But it is futile to kick against the pricks," he ended, sighing; " a man must merely take the bit between his teeth and keep still."

Christian happened to observe Letitia, who stood in the centre of a circle of men. Upon her forehead was forgetfulness; she knew nothing of yesterday and nothing of to-morrow. There was no one else so absorbed by the passing hour as she.

A footman approached Christian and gave him a card. The footman frowned doubtfully, for the card was not quite clean. On it Christian read these pencilled words: " I. M. Becker must speak with you at once." Hurriedly he excused himself and went out.

Ivan Michailovitch stood perfectly still in the outer hall. Newly arrived guests, who gave the footmen their hats and coats, passed by without noticing him. The men took mincing steps, the ladies sought the mirror for a final look with their excited eyes.

Ivan Michailovitch wore a long grey coat, shabby and wet. The black-bearded face was pale as wax. Christian drew him into an empty corner of the hall, where they were undisturbed.

" I beg you to forgive me for throwing a shadow on all this festivity," Ivan Michailovitch began, " but I had no choice. I received a notification of expulsion from the police this afternoon. I must leave the city and the country within twelve hours. The simple favour I ask of you is to take this note-

book into your keeping, until I myself or some properly identi-
fied friend asks it back." He glanced swiftly about him, took
a thin, blue notebook out of his pocket, and gave it to
Christian, who slid it swiftly and unobtrusively into a pocket
of his evening coat.

"It contains memoranda in Russian," Ivan continued,
"which have no value to any one but myself, but which must
not be found on me. Since I am being expelled there is little
doubt but that my person and effects will be searched."

"Won't you come and rest in my room?" Christian asked,
timidly. "Won't you eat or drink something?"

Ivan Michailovitch shook his head. From the hall floated
the sound of the violins, playing an ingratiating air by Puccini.

"Won't you at least dry your coat?" Christian asked again.
The strains of the music, the splendour there within, the merriment and laughter, the fullness of beauty and happiness, all
this presented so sharp a contrast to the appearance of this
man in a wet coat, with wax-like face and morbidly flaming
eyes, that Christian could no longer endure his apparently un-
feeling position between these two worlds, of whose utter and
terrible alienation from each other he was acutely aware.

Ivan Michailovitch smiled. "It is kind of you to think of
my coat. But you can't do any good. It will only get wet
again."

"I'd like to take you, just as you are," said Christian, and
he smiled too, "and go in there with you."

Ivan Michailovitch shrugged his shoulders, and his face grew
dark.

"I don't know why I should like to do that," Christian
murmured. "I don't know why it tempts me. I stand before
you, and you put me in the wrong. Whether I speak or am
silent does not matter. By merely being I am in the wrong.
We should not be conversing here in the servants' corner. You
are making some demand of me, Ivan Michailovitch, are you
not? What is it that you demand?"

The words bore witness to a confusion of the emotions that
went to the very core of his being. They throbbed with the
yearning to become and to be another man. Ivan Michailovitch, in a sudden flash of intuition, saw and understood. At
first he had suspected that here was but a lordly whim, or that it
was at best but the foolish and thoughtless defiance of a too
swiftly ardent proselyte that urged this proud and handsome
man to his words. He recognized his error now. He understood that he heard a cry for help, and that it came from the
depth of one of those decisive moments of which life holds
but few.

" What is it that I am to demand of you, Christian Wahnschaffe? " he asked, earnestly. " Surely not that you drag me
in there to your friends, and ask me to regard that as a definite
deed and as a triumph over yourself? "

" It would not be that," Christian said, with lowered
eyes, " but a simple confession of my friendship and my
faith."

" But consider what a figure I would cut in my blouse, taken
so unwillingly and emphatically, to use the Russian proverb,
into the realm of the spheres. You would be forgiven. You
would be accused of an eccentricity, and laughed at; but it
would be overlooked. But what would happen to me? You
could guard me from obvious insult. The profound humiliation
of my position would still be the same. And what purpose
would such a boastful action serve? Do you see any promise
of good in it—for myself, or you, or the others? I could accuse
no one, persuade no one, convince no one. Nor would you
yourself be convinced."

He was silent for a few seconds, and then regarded Christian
with a kind and virile glance. Then he continued. " Had I
appeared in evening clothes, this whole conversation would be
without meaning. That shows how trivial it is. Why,
Christian Wahnschaffe, should I exhibit my blouse and coat
amid the garb of your friends? Do you go with me to a place

where your coat is a blasphemy and a stain, and where my rough, wet one is a thing of pride and advantage. I know such a house. Go with me! "

Christian, without answering a word, summoned a footman, took his fur-coat, and followed Ivan Becker into the open. The lackey hurried to the garage. In a few minutes the car appeared. Christian permitted Ivan Michailovitch to precede him into it, asked for the address, and sat down beside him. The car started.

XX

Twice before this had Ivan Michailovitch visited the family of the imprisoned workman, Roderick Kroll. His interest in these people was not an immediate one. It had been evoked by the interest he took in Christian Wahnschaffe. There was something in Christian that moved him deeply. After their first conversation he had at once reflected long concerning his personality and his great charm, as well as concerning the circumstances of his life and the social soil from which he had sprung. And since the name of the industrial baron Wahnschaffe had been so closely connected with the trial of Roderick Kroll, and since that trial had made quite a stir in the world, his attention had naturally been drawn in this direction. It is possible that he had already weighed the step he was now taking. For he was immovably convinced that many men would be better, and deal more justly, if they could but be brought to see, or given an opportunity to see, the realities of the world.

Frau Kroll and her five children had found refuge in a mere hole of a garret at the top of a populous tenement on the extreme edge of the city. Before that she had inhabited one of the numerous cottages for workingmen that Albrecht Wahnschaffe had built near his factories. But she had been driven from this home, and had moved to the city.

The room she now had gave shelter not only to herself and

her children, the oldest of whom was twelve, but to three
lodgers: a rag-picker, a hurdy-gurdy man, and a chronically
drunken vagabond.   The room had a floor-space of sixty
square feet; the lodgers slept on dirty straw sacks, the children
on two ragged mattresses pushed close together, Frau Kroll
on a shawl and a bundle of old clothes' in the corner where
the slanting ceiling met the floor.

On this particular day the agent of the landlord had appeared three times to demand the rent.   The third time, since
no money was forthcoming, he had threatened to evict them
all that night.   Fifteen minutes before the arrival of Ivan
Becker and Christian he had appeared with the janitor and
another helper in the dim, evil-smelling room, and had proceeded to make good his threat.   His face had an expression
of good nature rather than of harshness.   He was proud of the
touch of humour which he brought to the execution of his
duties.   Cries and lamentations did not disturb him in the
least.   He said: " Hurry, children!   Come on there! "   Or
else: " Shoulder your guns and march!   Let's have no scenes!
Don't get excited!   No use getting on your knees!   Time is
money!   Quick work is good work! "

As was usual on such occasions, a commotion stirred all the
neighbours, and they assembled in the hall.   There was a
yellow-haired woman in her shift; there was one in a scarlet
dressing gown; there was a cripple without legs, an old man
with a long beard, children who were fighting one another, a
painted woman with a hat as large as a cart-wheel, another
with a burning candle in her hand, while a man who had just
come in from the street in her company sought to hide in the
darkness near the roof.

What one heard was the wailing of the Kroll children, and
the hard beseeching voice of the woman, who looked on with
desperate eyes as the agent and his men heaped up her poor
possessions.   The vagabond cursed, the hurdy-gurdy man
dragged his straw sack toward the door, the agent snapped his

fingers and said: "Hurry, good people, hurry! Let's have no
tender scenes! My supper is getting cold!"

XXI

Christian and Ivan Becker entered. They forced their way
through the staring crowd. Christian had on his costly fur-
coat. The agent stood still and his jaw dropped. His men
instinctively touched their caps. Ivan Michailovitch wanted to
close the door, but the woman in the big hat stood on the
threshold and would not stir. "The door should be closed,"
he said to the agent, who went forward and closed it, simply
thrusting the woman roughly back. Ivan asked whether the
woman and her children were to be evicted. The agent declared that she was unable to pay her rent, that one extension
of time after another had been granted her, but that to continue would be to create disorder and institute a bad example.
Ivan Michailovitch answered that he understood the situation.
Then he turned to Christian, and repeated the words as though
he needed to translate them into another tongue: "She cannot
pay her rent." A whistle sounded from without, and a woman
screeched. The agent opened the door, cried out a command,
and slammed it again. Silence ensued.

Frau Kroll was crouching among her children, her elbows
dug into her lap. She had a robust figure, and a bony face
that was pale as dough and deeply furrowed. It looked like
the head of a corpse. The children looked at her in terror:
two were mother naked, and one of these had the itch. The
agent, assuming a benevolent tone, asked Ivan Becker whether
something was to be done for these people; he evidently did not
dare to address Christian. "I think we shall be able to do
something for them," Ivan answered, and turned to Christian.

Christian heard and saw. He nodded rapidly, and gave an
impression of timidity and passionate zeal.

Christian's attention somehow became fixed on a water jug
with a broken handle. The jug was stamped with a greenish

pattern and the banal arabesques bit into his mind. The snow-edged, slanting window in the roof troubled him, and the sight of a single muddy boot. Next a sad fascination came to him from a rope that dangled from the roof, and from a little coal-oil lamp with a smoky chimney. His mere bodily vision clung to these things. But they passed into his soul, and he merged into oneness with them. He himself was that broken jug with its green figures, the snow-edged window, the muddy boot, the dangling rope, the smoky lamp. He was being transformed as in a melting furnace, shape glided into shape; and although he was objectively aware of what was taking place and also of the people—the beggar, the woman, the children, Ivan Michailovitch, the agent, and those who waited outside —yet it cost him a passionate effort to keep them outside of himself for yet a little while, until they should plunge down upon his soul with their torment, despair, cruelty, and madness, like wild dogs throwing themselves upon a bone.

A sigh escaped him; a disturbed and fleeting smile hovered about his lips. One of the children, a boy of four, clad in a shapeless rag, came to him, and gazed up at him as though he were a tower. At once the eyes of the others were fixed on him too. At least, he felt them. His breast seemed a fiery crucible upborne and held high by the boy's emaciated arms. In a moment he had filled his hand with gold pieces, and by a gesture encouraged the child to hold out its hands. He poured the gold into them. But they could grasp only a few. The coins rolled on the floor, and the people there watched them in dumb amazement.

He drew out his wallet, took from it with trembling fingers every bank note it held, looked about, and approached the cowering woman. Then suddenly there seized him a strange contempt for his own erectness while she crouched on the floor. And so he kneeled, kneeled down beside her, and let the notes slip into her lap. He did not know how much money there was. But it was found later that the sum was four thousand six hundred marks. He arose and took Ivan's arm, and the latter understood his glance.

There was a breathless silence when they left. The agent and his men, the lodgers, the children—all seemed turned to stone. The woman stared at the wealth in her lap. Then she uttered a loud cry and lost consciousness. The little boy played with the pieces of gold, and they clinked as only gold can, faintly sweet and without hardness.

Below, in the street, Ivan Michailovitch said to Christian: " That you kneeled down before her—that was it, and that alone! The gift—there was something fateful in it to me and something bitter! But that you kneeled down beside her— ah, that was it! " And with a sudden gesture he lifted himself on his toes, and took Christian's head between his hands, and kissed him with a kiss that was a breath upon the forehead. Then he murmured a word of farewell, and hurried down the street without looking at the waiting car.

Christian ordered the chauffeur to drive out to Christian's Rest. Two hours later he was there, in deep quietude, the quietude that he needed. He telephoned his family that unforeseen events had prevented him from staying to the end of the evening's festivities, but that he would be present at the ceremony of Judith's marriage without fail. Then he retired to the farthest room of his house, and held vigil all night.

XXII

Letitia married six weeks after Judith. At Stephen Gunderam's desire, however, the wedding was a quiet one. There was a simple meal in a hotel at Heidelberg, and those present were Frau von Febronius, the countess, their two nephews Ottomar and Reinhold, and an Argentinian friend of Stephen's —a raw-boned giant who had been sent to Germany for a year to acquire polish.

Ottomar recited an original poem in praise of his pretty

cousin, and Reinhold had composed an address in the style of Luther's table-talk. Stephen Gunderam showed small appreciation of the literary culture of his new kinsman.

Frau von Febronius was silent even at the moment of farewell. The countess wept very copiously. She provided Letitia with all manner of rules and admonitions, but the most difficult of all she had delayed, out of sheer cowardice to the very last. She drew Letitia into her own room and, blushing and paling by turns, attempted to give the girl some notion of the physiology of marriage. But her courage failed her even now, and whenever she approached the real crux of her subject, she began to stammer and grow confused. It amused Letitia immensely.

Stephen Gunderam wanted to depart in haste, like some one anxious to secure his booty.

Frau von Febronius said to her sister: " I have evil presentiments in regard to this marriage, even though the child seems quite happy. It is only her own nature that protects her against unhappiness. It is her only dowry, but a wonderful one." Then the countess folded her hands, and shed tears, and said: " If I have sinned, I pray God to forgive me."

The voyage proved Letitia to be an excellent sailor. For a few days she and her husband stopped in Buenos Ayres and met many people. Stephen's acquaintances regarded her with sympathetic curiosity; and everything was strange and fascinating to her—the people, the houses, animals, plants, the very earth and sky. But most fascinating and strange to her was still the jealous tyranny of the man she had married, although at times the fascination held a touch of fear. But when that assailed her, she jested even with herself, and drove it away.

Early one morning there drew up a firmly built, heavy little coach, with two small, swift horses, to carry them the thirty miles to the Gunderam estate. Generously provisioned they left the city. After a few hours the road ended as a brook is lost in sands, and before them stretched to the very horizon the pathless plain of the pampas.

Yet they were not unguided. On either side of the way which the horses had to travel, poles had been driven into the grassy earth. These poles were of about human height, and stood at intervals of about twenty yards. Thus the horses pursued their way calmly. The Negro on the box had no need to urge them on. The safe and monotonous journey permitted him to sleep.

There were no settlements at all. When the horses needed food or came upon water, a halt was made under the open sky. No house, no tree, no human being appeared from sun to sun, and a dread stole upon Letitia. She had long given up talking, and Stephen had long given up encouraging her. He slept like his coachman.

When the sun had sunk behind a veil of whitish clouds, Letitia stood up, and gazed searchingly over the endless plain of grass. The high wooden posts still projected with unwearying regularity at both sides of the uncut road.

But suddenly she saw on one of the posts a greyish-brown bird, moveless and bent, with huge, round, glowing eyes.

"What kind of a bird is that?" she asked.

Stephen Gunderam started from his slumber. "It's an owl," he answered. "Have you never seen one? Every evening, when darkness falls, they sit on the posts. Look, it is starting: there is one on each."

Letitia looked and saw that it was true. On every post and on either side, far as one's sight could reach, sat with its great, circular, glowing eyes a heavy, slothful, solemn owl.

OR EVER·THE SILVER CORD·BE LOOSED

I

FRAULEIN VON EINSIEDEL took Crammon's tender trifling quite seriously. When Crammon observed this, he grew cold, and planned at once to rid himself of the threatened complication.

She sent him urgent little notes by her maid; he left them unanswered. She begged him for a meeting; he promised to come but did not. She reproached him and inquired after the reason. He cast down his eyes and answered sadly: " I was mistaken in the hour, dear friend. For some time my mind has been wandering. I sometimes wake in the morning and fancy that it is still evening. I sit down at table and forget to eat. I need treatment and shall consult a physician. You must be indulgent, Elise."

But Elise did not want to understand. According to Crammon's words of regretful deprecation, she belonged to the sort of woman who makes a kiss or a tender meeting an excuse for drawing all sorts of tiresome and impossible inferences.

He said to himself: " You must be robust of soul, Bernard, and not permit your innate delicacy to make a weakling of you. Here is a little trap for mice, and you can smell the cheese from afar. She is pretty and good, but alas, quite blind and deluded. As though a brief pleasure were not to be preferred to a long wretchedness! "

To be prepared for any event, he packed his belongings.

II

Crammon had discovered where and in whose company Christian had been on the night of the festival preceding

Judith's wedding. The chauffeur had been indiscreet. Then Crammon, in his brotherly concern, had made inquiries, and the rumours that had reached the castle had all been confirmed.

One morning, when they were both at Christian's Rest, Crammon entered his friend's room and said: " I can't hold in any longer. The sorrow of it gnaws at me. You ought to be ashamed, Christian, especially of your secretiveness. You join fugitive disturbers of the peace and hurlers of·bombs, and then you confuse the innocent poor by your brainless generosity. What is it to lead to? "

Christian smiled, and did not answer.

" How can you expose yourself in that fashion," Crammon cried; "yourself and your family and your friends? I shall tell you this in confidence, dearest boy: If you imagine that you have really helped the woman to whom that Russian desperado dragged you, you are badly mistaken. Fortunately I can rob you of that illusion."

" Did you hear anything about her? " Christian asked, with a surprising indifference in his tone and expression.

Crammon seemed to expand, and told his tale with breadth and unction: " Certainly I have. I have even had dealings with the police and saved you annoyance. The woman was to have been arrested and the money confiscated. Luckily I was able to prevent that. I believe that the State should keep order, but I don't think it desirable that the government should interfere in our private affairs. Its duty is to safeguard us; there its function ends. So much for that! Concerning your protégée I have nothing pleasant to report. The rain of gold simply distracted the crowd in that house. They stuck to her and begged, and several of them stole. Naturally there was a fight, and some one plunged a knife into some one else's bowels, and the maddened woman·beat them both with a coal shovel. The police had to interfere. Then the woman moved into other quarters, and bought all sorts of trash—

furniture, beds, clothing, kitchen utensils, and even a cuckoo clock. You have seen those little horrors. A cuckoo comes out of the clock and screams. I was once staying with people who had three of them. Whenever I went to sleep another cuckoo screeched; it was enough to drive one mad. In other respects my friends were charming.

" As for the Kroll woman—your gift robbed her of every vestige of common sense. She keeps the money in a little box, which she carries about and won't let out of her sight by night or day. She buys lottery tickets, penny dreadfuls; the children are as dirty as ever and the household as demoralized. Only that dreadful cuckoo clock roars. So what have you accomplished? Where is the blessing? Common people cannot endure sudden accessions of fortune. You do not know their nature in the slightest degree, and the best thing you can do is to leave them in peace."

Christian's eyes wandered out to the cloudy sky. Then he turned to Crammon. He saw, as though he had never seen it before, that Crammon's cheeks were rather fat, and that his chin was bedded in soft flesh and had a dimple. He could not make up his mind to answer. He smiled, and crossed his legs!

What shapely legs, Crammon thought and sighed, what superb legs!

III

A few days later Crammon appeared again with the intention of testing Christian.

" I don't like your condition, my dear boy," he began, " and I won't pretend to you that I do. It's just a week to-day that we've been perishing of boredom here. I grant you it's a delightful place in spring and summer with agreeable companions, when one can have picnics in the open and think of the dull and seething cities. But now in the midst of winter, without orgies or movement or women—what is the use of it?

Why do you hide yourself? Why do you act depressed? What
are you waiting for? What have you in mind? ".

"You ask so many questions, Bernard," Christian replied.
"You should not do that. It is as well here as elsewhere.
Can you tell me any place where it is better? "

The last question aroused Crammon's hopes. In the
expectation of common pleasures his face grew cheerful.
"A better place? My dearest boy, any compartment in
a train is better. The greasy reception room of Madame
Simchowitz in Mannheim is better. However, we shall
be able to agree. Here is an admirable plan. Palermo,
Conca d'Oro, Monte Pellegrino, and Sicilian girls with
avid glances behind their virtuous veils. From there
we shall take a flying trip to Naples to see my sweet little
friend Yvonne. She has the blackest hair, the whitest teeth,
and the most exquisite little feet in Europe. The regions
between are—sublime. Then we can send a telegram to Prosper Madruzzi, who is nursing his spleen in his Venetian villa,
and let him introduce us into the most inaccessible circles of
Roman society. There one has dealings exclusively with
contessas, marchesas, and principessas. The striking characters of all five continents swarm there as in a fascinating mad-
house; cold-blooded American women commit indiscretions
with passionate lazzaroni, who have magical names and impossible silk socks; every kennel there can claim to be a curiosity,
every heap of stones adds to your culture, at every step you
stumble over some masterpiece of art."

Christian shook his head. "It doesn't tempt me," he said.

"Then I'll propose something else," Crammon said. "Go
with me to Vienna. It is a city worthy of your interest. Have
you ever heard of the Messiah? The Messiah is a person at
whose coming the Jews believe time will come to an end, and
whom they expect to welcome with the sound of shawms and
cymbals. It is thus that every distinguished stranger is greeted
in Vienna. If you cultivate an air of mystery, and are not

too stingy in the matter of tipping, and occasionally snub some one who is unduly familiar—all Viennese society will be at your feet. A pleasant moral slackness rules the city. Everything that is forbidden is permitted. The women are simply *hors concours;* the broiled meat at Sacher is incomparable; the waltzes which you hear whenever a musician takes up a fiddle are thrilling; a trip to the Little House of Delight—name to be taken literally, please—is a dream. I yearn for it all myself—the ingratiating air, the roast chicken, the apple-pudding with whipped cream, and my own little hut full of furniture of the age of Maria Theresa, and my two dear, old ladies. Pull yourself together, and come with me."

Christian shook his head. "It is nothing for me," he said.

A flush of indignation spread over Crammon's face. "Nothing for you? Very well. I cannot place the harem of the Sultan at your disposal, nor the gardens promised by the Prophet. I shall leave you to your fate, and wander out into the world."

Christian laughed, for he did not believe him. On the next day, however, Crammon said farewell with every sign of deep grief, and departed.

IV

Christian remained at his country house. A heavy snow-fall came, and the year drew toward its end.

He received no visitors. He answered neither the letters nor the invitations of his friends. He was to have spent Christmas with his parents at the castle, but he begged them to excuse him.

Since he was of age, Christian's Rest had now passed fully into his possession, and all his objects of art were gathered here—statuary, pictures, miniatures, and his collection of snuff-boxes. He loved these little boxes very much.

The dealers sent him their catalogues. He had a trusted agent at every notable auction sale. To this man he would telegraph his orders, and the things would arrive—a beaker of mountain crystal, a set of Dresden porcelains, a charcoal sketch by Van Gogh. But when he looked at his purchases, he was disappointed. They seemed neither as rare nor as precious as he had hoped.

He bought a sixteenth century Bible, printed on parchment, with mani-coloured initials and a cover with silver clasps. It had cost him fourteen thousand marks, and contained the book-plate of the Elector Augustus of Saxony. Curiously he turned the pages without regarding the words, which were alien and meaningless to him. Nothing delighted him but his consciousness of the rarity and preciousness of the volume. But he desired other things even rarer and more precious.

Every morning he fed the birds. With a little basket of bread crumbs he would issue from the door, and the birds would fly to him from all directions, for they had come to know both him and the hour. They were hungry, and he watched them busy at their little meal. And doing this he forgot his desires.

Once he donned his shooting suit, and went out and shot a hare. When the animal lay before him, and he saw its dying eyes, he could not bear to touch it. He who had hunted and killed many animals could no longer endure this sport, and left his booty a prey to the ravens.

Most of his walks led him through the village, which was but fifteen minutes from his park. At the end of the village, on the high-road, stood the forester's house. Several times he had noticed at one of its windows the face of a young man, whose features he seemed to recall. He thought it must be Amadeus Voss, the forester's son. When he was but six he had often visited that house. Christian's Rest had not been built until later, and in those early years his father had rented the game preserve here and had often lodged for some days at the forester's. And Amadeus had been Christian's playmate.

The face, which recalled his childhood to him, was pallid and
hollow-cheeked. The lips were thin and straight, and the
head covered with simple very light blond hair. The reflection
of the light's rays in the powerful lenses of spectacles made
the face seem eyeless.

It amazed Christian that this young man should sit there
for hours, day after day, without moving, and gaze through the
window-panes into the street. The secret he felt here stirred
him, and a power from some depth seemed to reach out for
him.

One day Christian met the mayor of the village at the
gate of his park. Christian stopped him. " Tell me," he said,
" is the forester Voss still alive? "

"No, he died three years ago," the man answered. " But
his widow still lives in the house. The present forester is
unmarried, and lets her have a few rooms. I suppose you are
asking on account of Amadeus, who has suddenly turned up
for some strange reason—"

" Tell me about him," Christian asked.

" He was to have been a priest, and was sent to the seminary
at Bamberg. One heard nothing but good of him there, and
his teachers praised him to the sky. He got stipends and schol-
arships, and every one expected him to do well for himself.
Last winter his superiors got him a position as tutor to
the boys of the bank president, Privy Councillor Ribbeck.
You're familiar with the name. Very big man. The two boys
whose education Voss was to supervise lived at Halbertsroda,
an estate in Upper Franconia, and the parents didn't visit them
very often. They say the marriage isn't a happy one. Well,
everything seemed turning out well. Considering his gifts and
the patron he had now, Amadeus couldn't have wanted for
anything. Suddenly he drops down on us here, doesn't budge
from the house, pays no attention to any one, becomes a burden
to his poor old mother, and growls like a dog at any one who
talks to him. There must have been crazy doings at Halberts-

roda. No one knows any details, you know. But every now and then the pot seethes over, and then you get the rumour that there was something between him and the Privy Councillor's wife."

The man was very talkative, and Christian interrupted him at last. "Didn't the forester have another son?" A faint memory of some experience of his childhood arose in him.

"Quite right," said the mayor. "There was another son. His name was Dietrich, and he was a deaf-mute."

"Yes, I remember now," Christian said.

"He died at fourteen," the mayor went on. "His death was never properly explained. There was a celebration of the anniversary of the battle of Sedan, and he went out in the evening to look at the bonfires. Next morning they found his body in the fish-pond."

"Did he drown?"

"He must have," answered the mayor.

Christian nodded farewell, and went slowly through the gate toward his house.

V

Letitia and her husband were in the opera house at Buenos Ayres. The operetta of the evening was as shallow as a puddle left by the rain in the pampas.

In the box next to theirs sat a young man, and Letitia yielded now and then to the temptation of observing his glances of admiration. Suddenly she felt her arm roughly grasped. It was Stephen who commanded her silently to follow him.

In the dim corridor he brought his bluish-white face close to her ear, and hissed: "If you look at that fool once more, I'll plunge my dagger into your heart. I give you this warning. In this country one doesn't shilly-shally."

They returned to their box. Stephen smiled with a smile as glittering as a torero's, and put a piece of chocolate into his mouth. Letitia looked at him sidewise, and wondered whether he really had a dagger in his possession.

That night, when they drove home, he almost smothered her with his caresses. She repulsed him gently, and begged: "Show me the dagger, Stephen. Give it to me! I want so much to see it."

"What dagger, silly child?" he asked, in astonishment.

"The dagger you were going to plunge into my heart."

"Let that be," he answered, in hollow tones. "This is no time to speak of daggers and death."

But Letitia was stubborn. She insisted that she wanted to see it. He took his hands from her, and fell into sombre silence.

The incident taught Letitia that she could play with him. She no longer feared that sombre stillness of his, nor his great skull on his powerful neck, nor the thin mouth, nor the paling face, nor the great strength of his extraordinary small hands. She knew that she could play with him.

Great fire-flies flew through the air, and settled in the grass about them. When the carriage stopped at the villa, Letitia looked around with a cry of delight. Sparks seemed to be falling in a golden rain. The gleaming insects whirred about the windows, the roof, the flowery creepers on the walls. They penetrated into the hall.

Letitia stopped at the dark foot of the stairs, looked at the phosphorescent glimmer, and asked fearfully and with an almost imperceptible self-mockery in her deep voice: "Tell me, Stephen, couldn't they set the house on fire?"

The Negro Scipio, who appeared with a lamp at the door, heard her words and grinned.

VI

Around Twelfth Night Randolph von Stettner with several friends came to Christian's Rest. The young men had called up Christian by telephone, and he had been alone so long

that he was glad to receive them and be their host. He was
always glad to see Randolph. The latter brought with him
two comrades, a Baron Forbach and a Captain von Griesingén,
and also another friend, a young university teacher, who was
fulfilling his required military service at Bonn and was therefore also in uniform. Christian had met him before at a celebration of the Borussia fraternity.

A delicious meal was served, followed by excellent cigars
and liqueurs.

"It is consoling to see that you still don't despise the comforts of the flesh," Randolph von Stettner said to Christian.

Captain von Griesingen sighed: "How should one despise
them? They torment us and they flit temptingly about us!
Think of all that is desirable in the world—women, horses,
wine, power, fame, money, love! There is a dealer of jewels
in Frankfort, named David Markuse, who has a diamond
that is said to be worth half a million. I have no desire for
that special object. But the world is full of things that are
possessed and give delight."

"It is the diamond known as Ignifer," Dr. Leonrod remarked, "a sort of adventurer among precious stones."

"Ignifer is an appropriate name for a diamond," said Randolph. "But why do you speak of it so gravely? What, except
its price, makes it differ from other stones? Has it had so
strange a fate?"

"Undoubtedly," said Dr. Leonrod, "most strange. I happen to know the details because, as a professional mineralogist,
I take a certain interest in precious stones, too."

"Do tell us about it!" the young officers cried.

"Whoever buys Ignifer," Dr. Leonrod began, "will show no
little courage. The jewel is a tragic thing. It has been proved
that its first owner was Madame de Montespan. No sooner
did it come into her possession than the king dismissed her.
Marie Antoinette owned it next. It weighed ninety-five carats
at that time. But during the Revolution it was stolen and

divided, and did not reappear until fifty years later. The
recovered stone weighed sixty carats. An Englishman, named
Thomas Horst, bought it, and was soon murdered. The heirs
sold it to an American. ˙ The lady who wore it, a Mrs. Malm-
cote, was throttled by a madman at a ball. Then Prince
Alexander Tshernitsheff brought it to Russia, and gave it to
an actress who was his mistress. Another lover shot and killed
her on the stage. The prince was blown to pieces by a nihilist.
Then the stone was brought to Paris, and purchased by the
Sultan Abdul Hamid for his favourite wife. The woman was
poisoned, and you all know what happened to the Sultan.
After the Turkish Revolution Ignifer drifted West again, and
then back to the Orient. For its new owner, Tavernier,
took a voyage to India, and was shipwrecked and drowned.
For a time it was thought that the diamond was lost. But
that was an error; it had been deposited in a safety vault in
a Calcutta bank. Now it is back in Europe, and for sale."

"The stone must harbour an evil spirit," said Randolph.
"I confess that I have no desire for it. I am very little
inclined to superstition; but when the facts are as compelling
as in this case, the most enlightened scepticism seems rebuked."

"What does all that matter if the stone is beautiful, if it
really is incomparably lovely? " Christian cried, with a defiant
look, that yet seemed turned inward upon his soul. After this
he said little, even when the conversation drifted to other
subjects.

Next day at noon he ordered his car and drove in to Frankfort to the shop of the jeweller David Markuse.

VII

Herr Markuse knew Christian.

Ignifer was kept in the safe of a fire-proof and burglar-proof
vault. Herr Markuse lifted the stone out of its case, laid it
upon the green cloth of a table, stepped aside, and looked at
Christian.

Christian looked silently at the concentrated radiance of the stone. His thought was: This is the rarest and costliest thing in the world; nothing can surpass it. And it was immediately clear to him that he must own the jewel.

The diamond had the faintest tinge of yellow. It had been cut so that it had many rich facets. A little groove had been cut into it near one end, so that a woman could wear it around her neck by a thin chain or a silken cord.

Herr Markuse lifted it upon a sheet of white paper and breathed upon it. "It is not of the first water," he said, "but it has neither rust nor knots. There is no trace of veins or cracks, no cloudiness or nodules. Not a flaw. The stone is one of nature's miracles."

The price was five hundred and fifty thousand marks. Christian offered the half million. Herr Markuse consulted his watch. "I promised a lady that I would hold it," he declared. "But the promised hour is past." They agreed upon five hundred and twenty thousand marks. Half was to be paid in cash, the other in two notes running for different periods. "The name of Wahnschaffe is sufficient guarantee," the merchant said.

Christian weighed the diamond in his hand, and laid it down again.

David Markuse smiled. "In my business one learns how to judge people," he said without any familiarity. "You are making this purchase with a deeper intention than you yourself are probably conscious of. The soul of the diamond has lured you on. For the diamond has a soul."

"Do you really mean that?" Christian was surprised.

"I know it. There are people who lose all shame when they see a beautiful jewel. Their nostrils quiver, their cheeks grow pale, their hands tremble uncertainly, their pupils expand, and they betray themselves by every motion. Others are intimidated, or bereft of their senses, or saddened. You gain

curious insights into human nature. /The masks drop. Diamonds make people transparent."

The indiscreet turn of the conversation irritated Christian.
But he had often before become aware of the fact that something in him seemed to invite the communicativeness and confidence of others. He arose, and promised to return that
evening.

"The lady of whom I was speaking," Markuse continued,
as he accompanied him to the door, " and who was here yesterday, is a very wonderful lady. When she came in, I thought:
is it possible for mere walking to be so beautiful? Well, I soon
found out that she is a famous dancer. She is stopping at the
Palace Hotel for a day, on her way from Paris to Russia,
merely in order to see Ignifer. I showed her the stone. She
stood looking at it for at least five minutes. She did not move,
and the expression of her face! Well, if the jewel didn't represent a large part of all I have in the world, I would have begged
her simply to keep it. Such moments are not exactly frequent
in my business. She was to have returned to-day, but, as I
have told you, she didn't keep her engagement."

"And you don't know her name? " Christian asked, shyly.

"Oh, yes. Her name is Eva Sorel. Did you ever hear of
her? "

The blood came into Christian's face. He let go the knob
of the door. "Eva Sorel is here? " he murmured. He pulled
himself together, and opened the door to an empty room
that was carpeted in red, and the walls of which were hidden
by ebony cases. Almost at the same moment the opposite door
was thrown open; and, followed by four gentlemen, Eva Sorel
crossed the threshold.

Christian stood perfectly still.

" Eidolon! " Eva cried, and she folded her hands in that
inimitably enthusiastic and happy gesture of hers.

VIII

Christian did not know the gentlemen who were with her. Their features and garments showed them to be foreigners. Accustomed to surprising events in Eva's daily life, they regarded Christian with cool curiosity.

Eva's whole form was wrapped in a grey mole-skin coat. Her fur cap was trimmed with an aigrette of herons' feathers, held by a marvellous ruby clasp. From under the cap her honey-coloured hair struggled forth. The wintry air had given her skin an exquisite delicate tinge of pink.

With a few steps she came stormily to Christian, and her white gloved hands sought both of his. Her great and flaming looks drove his conscious joy and his perceptions of her presence back upon his soul, and fear appeared upon his features. He found himself as defenceless as a ball flung by another's hand. He awaited his goal.

"Did you buy Ignifer?" That was her first question. Since he was silent, she turned with raised brows to David Markuse.

The merchant bowed and said: "I thought that I could no longer count on you, Madame. I am sorry with all my heart."

"You are right. I hesitated too long." Eva spoke her melodious German, with its slightly foreign intonation. Turning to Christian she went on: "Perhaps it makes no difference, Eidolon, whether you have it or I. It is like a heart that ambition has turned to crystal. But you are not ambitious. If you were, we should have met here like two birds swept by a storm into the same cave. The preciousness of the stone almost makes it ghostly to me, and I would permit no one to give it to me who was not conscious of its significance. And who is there? What do they give one? Wares from a shop, that is all."

David Markuse looked at her in admiration, and nodded.

"It is said to bring misfortune to its possessors," Christian almost whispered.

"Do you intend to test yourself, Eidolon, and put it to the proof? Will you challenge the demon to prevail against you? Ah, that is what allured me, too. Its name made me envious. As I held it, it seemed like the navel of Buddha, from which one cannot divert one's thought, if one has once seen it."

She noticed that the people about them seemed to make Christian hesitate, so she took his arm, and drew him behind the curtains of a window-niche.

"That it brings misfortune to people is certain," Christian repeated mechanically. "How can I keep it, Eva, since you desired it?"

"Keep it and break the evil spell," Eva answered, and laughed. But his seriousness remained unchanged; and she apologized for her laughter by a gesture, as though she were throwing aside the undue lightness of her mood. She watched him silently. In the sharp light reflected from the snow, her eyes were green as malachite. "What are you doing with yourself?" she asked. "Your eyes look lonesome."

"I have been living rather alone for some time," answered Christian. His utterances were dry and precise. "Crammon too has left me."

"Ivan Becker wrote me about you," Eva said in muffled tones. "I kissed the letter. I carried it in my bosom, and said the words of it over to myself. Is there such a thing as an awakening? Can the soul emerge from the darkness, as a flower does from the bulb? But there you stand in your pride, and do not move. Speak! Our time is short."

"Why speak at all?"

Although his eyes seemed so unseeing, it did not escape him that Eva's face had changed. A new severity was on it, and a heightened will controlled its nerves, even to the raising and lowering of her long lashes. Experience of men and things had lent it an austere radiance, and her unbounded mastery over them a breath of grandeur.

"I had not forgotten that this is the city where you dwell," she said, "but in these driven hours there was no place for you. They count my steps, and lie in wait for the end of my sleeping. What I should have is either a prison or a friend unselfish enough to force me to be more frugal of myself. In Lisbon the queen gave me a beautiful big dog, who was so devoted to me that I felt it in my very body. A week later he was found poisoned at the gate of the garden. I could have put on mourning for him. How silent and watchful he was, and how he could love! " She raised her shoulders with a little shiver, dropped them again, and continued with hurry in her voice. " I shall summon you some day. Will you come? Will you be ready? "

" I shall come," Christian answered very simply, but his heart throbbed.

" Is your feeling for me the same—changeless and unchangeable? " In her look there was an indescribably lyrical lift, and her body, moved by its spirit, seemed to emerge from veils.

He only bowed his head.

" And how is it in the matter of *cortesia?* " She came nearer to him, so that he felt her breath on his lips. " He smiles," she exclaimed, and her lips opened, showing her teeth, " instead of just once throwing himself on his knees in rage or jubilation —he smiles. Take care, you with your smile, that I am not tempted to extinguish your smiling some day." She stripped the glove from her right hand, and gave the naked hand to Christian, who touched it with his lips. "It is a compact, Eidolon," she said serenely now, and with an air of seduction, " and you will be ready." Emerging from the niche, she turned to the gentlemen who had come with her, and who had been holding whispered conversations: " Messieurs, nous sommes bien pressés."

She inclined her head to the jeweller, and the heron feathers trembled. The four gentlemen let her precede them swiftly, and followed her silently and reverently.

IX

When next Christian went through the village and saw Amadeus Voss at the window, he stopped.

Voss got up suddenly and opened the window, and thereupon Christian approached.

It was a time of thaw. The water dripped from the roofs and gutters. Christian felt the moist air swept by tepid winds as something that gives pain.

Behind the powerful lenses the eyes of Amadeus Voss had a yellowish glitter. "We must be old acquaintances," he said, "although it is very long ago since we hunted blackberries among the hedges. Very long." He laughed a little weakly.

Christian had determined to lead the conversation to the dead brother of Amadeus. There was that event in the mist of the past concerning which he could gain no clearness, much as he might reflect.

"I suppose everybody is wondering about me," Voss said, in the tone of one who would like to know what people are saying. "I seem to be a stumbling-block to them. Don't you think so?"

"I mustn't presume to judge," Christian said, guardedly.

"With what an expression you say that!" Voss murmured, and looked Christian all over. "How proud you are. Yet it must have been curiosity that made you stop."

Christian shrugged his shoulders. "Do you remember an incident that took place when I stayed here with my father?" he asked gently and courteously.

"What kind of an incident? I don't know. Or—but wait! Do you mean that affair of the pig? When they killed the pig over there in the inn, and I——"

"Quite right. That was it," Christian said with a faint smile. He had scarcely spoken when the scene and the incident appeared with unwonted clarity before his mind.

He and Amadeus and the deaf and dumb Dietrich had been

standing at the gate. And the pig had begun to scream. At that moment Amadeus had stretched out his arms, and held them convulsively trembling in the air. The long, loud, and piercing cry of the beast's death agony had been something new and dreadful to Christian too, and had drawn him running to the spot whence it came. He saw the gleaming knife, the uplifted and then descending arm of the butcher, the struggle of the short, bristly legs, and the quivering and writhing of the victim's body. The lips of Amadeus, who had reeled after him, had been flecked with foam, and he pointed and moaned: " Blood, blood! " And Christian had seen the blood on the earth, on the knife, on the white apron of the man. He did not know what happened next. But Amadeus knew.

He said: " When the pig screamed, a convulsive rigour fell upon me. For many hours I lay stiff as a log. My parents were badly frightened, for I had never had any such attacks before. What you remember is probably how they tried to cheer me or shame me out of my collapse. They walked into the puddle of blood and stamped about in it so that the blood spurted. My dumb brother noticed that this only increased my excitement. He made noises in his throat, and raised his hands beseechingly, while my mother was hastening from the house. At that moment you struck him in the face with your fist." ,

" It is true. I struck him," said Christian, and his face became very pale.

" And why? Why did you do that? We haven't met since that day, and we've only seen each other from afar. That is, I've seen you. You were far too proud and too busy with your friends to see me. But why did you strike Dietrich that day? He had a sort of silent adoration of you. He followed you about everywhere. Don't you remember? We often laughed about it. But from that day on he was changed—markedly so."

" I believe I hated him at that moment," Christian said,

reflectively. " I hated him because he could neither hear nor speak. It struck me as a sort of malevolent stubbornness."

" Strange! It's strange that you should have felt so."

They both became silent. Christian started to leave. Voss rested his arms on the window ledge and leaned far out. " There's a paragraph in the paper saying that you've bought a diamond for half a million. Is that true? "

" It is true," Christian replied.

" A single diamond for over half a million? I thought it was merely a newspaper yarn. Is the diamond to be seen? Would you show it to me? " In his face there was something of horrified revolt, of panting desire, but also of mockery. Christian was startled.

" With pleasure, if you'll come to see me," he answered, but determined to have himself denied to Voss if the latter really came.

For a secret stirred him again, a depth opened at his feet, an arm was stretched out after him.

x

On a certain night Letitia awoke and heard dragging, running steps, the breathing of pursuers and pursued, whispers and hoarse curses, now nearer, now farther. She sat up and listened. Her bed-chamber opened upon gardens. Its doors led to the verandah that surrounded the entire house.

Then the hurrying steps approached; she saw forms that detached themselves in black from the greenish night and flitted by: one, and then another, and then a third, and after a little while a fourth. She was frightened, but she hated to call for help. To rouse Stephen, who slept in the adjoining room, was a risk for her, as it was for every one. At such times he would roar like a steer, and strike out wildly.

Letitia laughed and shuddered at the thought.

She fought her fear, got up, threw on a dressing gown, and stepped determinedly on the verandah. At that moment thick clouds parted and revealed the moon. Surprised by the unexpected light, the four forms stopped suddenly, collided against each other, and stood panting and staring.

What Letitia saw was old Gottlieb Gunderam and his three sons, Riccardo, Paolo, and Demetrios, the brothers of her husband. There was an unquenchable distrust between this father and his sons. They watched and lay in wait for each other. If there was cash in the house, the old man did not dare go to bed, and each of the brothers accused the rest of wanting to rob their father. Letitia knew that much. But it was new to her that in their dumb rage and malice they went so far as to chase each other at night, each pursuer and pursued at once, each full of hatred of the one in front and full of terror of the one behind him. She laughed and shuddered.

The old man was the first to slink away. He dragged himself to his room, and threw himself on the bed in his clothes. Beside the bed stood two huge travelling boxes, packed and locked. They had stood thus for twenty years. Daily, during all that period, he had determined at least once to flee to the house in Buenos Ayres, or even to the United States, whenever the conflict, first with his wife and later with his sons, became too much for him. He had never started on that flight; but the boxes stood in readiness.

Silently and secretively the brothers also disappeared. While Letitia stood on the verandah and looked at the moon, she heard the rattle of a phonograph. Riccardo had recently bought it in the city, and it often happened that he set it to playing at night.

Letitia stepped a little farther, and peered into the room in which the three brothers sat with sombre faces and played poker. The phonograph roared a vulgar waltz out of its brazen throat.

Then Letitia laughed and shuddered.

XI.

Christian wondered whether Amadeus would come. Two days passed in slightly depressing suspense.

He had really intended to go to Waldleiningen to look after his horses. Sometimes he could actually see their spirited yet gentle eyes, their velvet coats, and that fine nervousness that vibrated between dignity and restiveness. He recalled with pleasure the very odour of the stables.

The pure bred Scotch horse which he had bought of Denis Lay was to run in the spring races. His grooms told him that the beautiful animal had been in poor form for some weeks, and he thought that perhaps it missed his tender hand. Nevertheless he did not go to Waldleiningen.

On the third day Amadeus Voss sent a gardener to ask whether he might call that evening. Instead Christian went down to the forester's house that afternoon at four, and knocked at the door.

Voss looked at him suspiciously. With the instinct of the oppressed classes he divined the fact that Christian wanted to keep him from his house. But Christian was far from being as clear about his own motives as Amadeus suspected. He scented a danger. Some magic in it drew him on half-consciously to go forth to meet it.

Looking about in the plain but clean and orderly room Christian saw on the tinted wall above the bed white slips of paper on which verses of Scripture had been copied in a large hand. One was this: " He was led as a sheep to the slaughter; and like a lamb dumb before his shearer, so opened he not his mouth." And another was this: " For it is a day of trouble, and of treading down, and of perplexity by the Lord God of hosts in the valley of vision, breaking down the walls, and of crying to the mountains." And this other: " The Lord said unto me, Within a year, within the years of an hireling, and all the glory of Kedar shall fail." And finally there was this:

"I know thy works, that thou art neither cold nor hot; I would thou were cold or hot. So then because thou art lukewarm, and neither cold or hot, I will spue thee out of my mouth."

Christian looked at Amadeus Voss long and curiously. Then he asked, in a very careful voice, and yet not without an inevitable tinge of worldly mockery: "Are you very religious?"

Amadeus frowned and answered: "Whether I answer one way or the other it will mean equally little to you. Did you come to cross-question me? Have we anything in common that an answer to that question could reveal? Amadeus Voss and Christian Wahnschaffe—are those not the names of sundered poles? What image is there that could express the differences that divide us? Your faith and mine! And such things are possible on the same earth!"

"Was your youth especially hard?" Christian asked, innocently.

Voss gave a short laugh, and looked at Christian sidewise. "D'you know what meal days are? Of course you don't. Well, on such days you get your meals at strangers' houses who feed you out of charity. Each day of the week you're with another family. Each week repeats the last. Not to be thought ungrateful you must be obedient and modest. Even if your stomach revolts at some dish, you must pretend it's a delicacy. If the grandfather laughs, you must laugh too; if an uncle thinks he's a wit, you must grin. If the daughter of the house chooses to be insolent, you must be silent. If they respond to your greeting, it's a great favour; the worn overcoat with ragged lining they gave you when winter came binds you in eternal gratitude. You come to know all the black moods of all these people with whom you sit at table, all their shop-worn opinions, their phrases and hypocritical expressions; and for the necessary hour of each day you must learn to practise its special kind of dissembling. That is the meaning of meal days."

He got up, walked to and fro, and resumed his seat. "The devil appeared to me early," he said in a hollow voice. "Perhaps I took a certain experience of my childhood more grievously to heart than others, perhaps the poison of it filtered deeper into me. But you cannot forget. It is graven upon my soul that my drunken father beat my mother. He did it every Saturday night with religious regularity. That image is not to be obliterated."

Christian did not take his eyes from the face of Amadeus.

Softly, and with a rigid glance, Voss continued: "One night before Easter, when I was eight years old, he beat her again. I rushed into the yard, and cried out to the neighbours for help. Then I looked up at the window, and I saw my mother stand there wringing her hands in despair. And she was naked." And his voice almost died into silence as he added: "Who is it that dare see his own mother naked?"

Again he arose and wandered about the room. He was so full of himself that his speech seemed indeed addressed to himself alone. "Two things there are that made me reflect and wonder even in my childhood. First, the very many poor creatures, whom my father reported because they stole a little wood, and who were put in prison. I often heard some poor, little old woman or some ragged half-starved lad beg for mercy. There was no mercy here. My father was the forester, and had to do his duty. Secondly, there were the many rich people who live in this part of the country in their castles, on their estates, in their hunting-lodges, and to whom nothing is denied that their wildest impulses demand. Between the two one stands as between two great revolving cylinders of steel. One is sure to be crushed to bits in the end."

For a while he gazed into emptiness. "What is your opinion of an informer?" he asked, suddenly.

Christian answered with a forced smile: "It's not a good one."

"Listen to me. In the seminary I had a fellow-student named Dippel. His gifts were moderate, but he was a decent chap and a hard worker. His father was a signalman on the railroad—one of the very poor, and his son was his one hope and pride. Dippel happened to be acquainted with a painter in whose studio he came across an album of photographs displaying the female form in plastic poses. The adolescent boy gazed at them again and again, and finally begged the painter to lend him the album. Dippel slept in my dormitory. I was monitor, and I soon observed the crowding and the sensuous atmosphere about Dippel, who had shown the pictures to a few friends. It was like a spreading wound. I went into the matter and ruthlessly confiscated the pictures. I informed the faculty. Dippel was summoned, sternly examined, and expelled. Next day we found him swinging dead from the apple tree."

Christian's face flushed hotly. The tone of equanimity with which it was recited was more repulsive than the story itself.

Amadeus Voss continued: "You think that was a contemptible action. But according to the principles that had been impressed on us I was merely doing my duty. I was sixteen; and I seemed to be, and was, in a dark hole. I needed to get out to the air and light. I was like one squeezed in by a great throng, who cannot see what happens beyond. The fumes of impatience throttled me, and everything in me cried out for space and light. It was like living on the eternally dark side of the moon. I was afraid of the might of evil; and all that I heard of men was more or less evil. The scales rose and fell in my breast. There are hours in which one can either become a murderer or die on the cross. I yearned for the world. Yet I prayed much in those days, and read many books of devotion, and practised cruel penances. Late at night, when all others slept, a priest found me absorbed in prayer with the hair-shirt about my body. During mass or choral singing an incomparable and passionate devotion streamed through me. But then again I saw flags in the streets of the city, or well-dressed women, or I· stood in the railway station, and ·a train of luxurious cars seemed to mock me. Or I saw.a man who had hurled himself out of a window and whose brains spattered the pavement, and he seemed to cry out to me: Brother, brother! Then the evil one arose in bodily form and I desired to clutch him. Yes, evil has bodily form and only evil—injustice, _ stupidity, lying, all the things that are repulsive to one to the very core, but which one must embrace and be, if one has not been born with a silver spoon in one's mouth. To save a ray of light for myself, I learned to play the organ. It helped little. What does music matter, or poems or beautiful pictures, or noble buildings, or books of philosophy, or the whole magnificent world without? I cannot reach myself. Between me and that real self there is something—what is it? A wall of red-hot glass. Some are accursed from the beginning. If I ask: how could the curse be broken? there is but one answer: the monstrous would need to come to pass, the unimaginable! Thus it is with me."

Christian was shocked. " What do you mean by that? " ·

" One would have to gain a new experience," answered Amadeus Voss, " to know a being truly human—in the highest and deepest sense." In the gathering dusk his face had the hue of stone. It was a well-shaped face—long, narrow, intelligent, full of impassioned suffering. The lenses in front of his eyes sparkled in the last light of day, and on his fair hair· was a glimmer as upon jewels.

" Are you going to stay in the village? " Christian inquired, not from a desire to know, but out of the distress which he felt in the heavy silence. " You were employed by Councillor Ribbeck. Will you return to him? "

Voss's nerves twitched. " Return? There is no return," he murmured. " Do you know Ribbeck? Well, I hardly know

him myself. I saw him just twice. The first time was when
he came to the seminary to engage a tutor for his sons. When
I think of him I have the image of something fat and frozen.
I was picked out at once. My superiors approved of me highly
and desired to smooth my path. Yes. And I saw him for the
second time one night in December, when he appeared at
Halbertsroda with a commissary of police to put me out. You
needn't look at me that way. There were no further consequences. It wouldn't have done to permit any."

He fell silent. Christian got up. Voss did not urge him to
stay longer, but accompanied him to the door. There he said
in a changed voice: "What kind of a man are you? One sits
before you and pours out one's soul, and you sit there in silence.
How does it happen? "

"If you regret it I shall forget all you have said," Christian
answered in his flexible, courteous way, that always had a
touch of the equivocal.

Voss let his head droop. "Come in again when you are passing," he begged gently. "Perhaps then I'll tell you about what
happened there! " He pointed with his thumb across his
shoulder.

"I shall come," said Christian.

XII

Albrecht Wahnschaffe came into his wife's bedroom. She
was in bed. It was a magnificent curtained bed with carved
posters. On both sides of the wall hung costly tapestries
representing mythological scenes. A coverlet of blue damask
concealed Frau Wahnschaffe's majestic form.

Gallantly he kissed the hand which she held out toward him
with a weary gesture, and glided into an armchair. "I want
to talk to you about Christian," he said. "For some time
his doings have worried me. He drifts and drifts. The latest
thing is his purchase of that diamond. There is a challenge
in such an action. It annoys me."

Frau Wahnschaffe wrinkled her forehead, and answered: "I see no need to worry. Many sons of wealthy houses pass their time as Christian does. They are like noble plants that need adornment. They seem to me to represent a high degree of human development. They regard themselves quite rightly as excellent within themselves. By birth and wealth they are freed from the necessity of effort. Their very being is in their aristocratic aloofness and inviolability."

Albrecht Wahnschaffe bowed. He played with his slender white fingers that bore no sign of age. He said: "I'm sorry that I cannot quite share your opinion. It seems to me that in the social organism each member should exercise a function that serves the whole. I was brought up with this view, and I cannot deny it in favour of Christian. I am not inclined to quarrel with his mere expenditure of money, though he has exceeded his budget considerably during the last few months. The house of Wahnschaffe cannot be touched even by such costly pranks. What annoys me is the aimlessness of such a life, its exceedingly obvious lack of any inner ambition."

From under her wearily half-closed lids Frau Wahnschaffe regarded her husband coolly. It angered her that he desired to draw Christian, who had been created for repose and play, delight and beauty, into his own turbid whirl. She answered with a touch of impatience: "You have always let him choose his own path, and you cannot change him now. All do not need to toil. Business is terribly unappetizing. I have borne two sons—one for you, one for myself. Demand of yours what you will and let him fulfil what he can. I like to think of mine and be happy in the thought that he is alive. If anything has worried me it is the fact that, since his trip to England, Christian has withdrawn himself more and more from us, and also, I am told, from his friends. I hope it means nothing. Perhaps there is a woman behind it. In that case it will pass; he does not indulge in tragic passions. But talking exhausts me, Albrecht. If you have other arguments, I beg you to postpone them."

She turned her head aside, and closed her eyes in exhaustion. Albrecht Wahnschaffe arose, kissed her hand with the same gallant gesture, and went out.

But her saying that she had borne one son for him and one for herself embittered him a little against his wife, whom he commonly regarded as an inviolable being of finer stuff. Why did I build all this? he asked himself, as he slowly passed through the magnificent halls.

It was more difficult for him to approach Christian than a member of the ministry or a distinguished foreigner. He vacillated between issuing a request and a command. He was not sure of his authority, and even less of any friendly understanding. But while he was spending a few days of rest and recreation in the family's ancestral house at Würzburg, he sent a message to Christian, and begged him for an interview.

XIII

Crammon wrote to Christian. It was his humour to affect an archaic manner of speech:

" Most Honoured and Worthy Friend: With deep satisfaction I learn that your Worship has ruefully returned to the god Dionysos, and as a sign thereof laid down upon his altar a jewel, whose price has caused the teeth of the Philistines in the land to rattle, and their lame digestions to work with unwelcome swiftness. Your servant, the undersigned, did, on the contrary, when the news of happy augury came to him, perform a dance in his lonely closet, which so shocked the ladies of his palace that they at once called up psychiatrists on the telephone. Thus the world, barren of understanding, is incapable of great reflections.

" Unlovely are my days. I am ensnared in amorous adventures which do not content me, and, in addition, disappoint those who are involved. At times I sit by the charming glow of

my chimney fire, and, closing my eyes, peruse the book of
memory. A bottle of golden-hued cognac is my sole companion, and while I nourish my heart upon its artificial warmth,
the higher regions are wont to sink into the cbld mystery' of
mere idiocy. My mental powers are moving, like the crab,
backward; my virile powers decline. Years ago in Paris I knew
a chess player, a purblind old German, who lost every game he
played, and exclaimed each time: 'Where are the days in
which I vanquished the great Zuckertort?' The latter, I must
explain, was a great master of the royal game. The necessary application to myself embarrasses me. There was once a
Roman emperor famous above all others for his power over
women; Maxentius was, I believe, the man's name. But were
I to exclaim: 'Where are the days in which I rivalled the great
Maxentius?' it were but damnable boasting!

"It is a pity that you cannot be a beholder when I arise from
my couch in the morning. Were this spectacle to be tested by
connoisseurs and to be enjoyed by the laity, throngs would
attend it, as whilom they did the rising of the kings of France.
The gentry of the land would come to do me reverence, and
lovely ladies would tickle me to elicit a beam of cheer upon
my face. O blessed youth, friend and playmate of my dreams,
I would have you know that the moments in which one leaves
the linen well warmed by one's own body, and goes forth to
twelve hours of the world's mischief, are to me moments of
incomparable pitifulness. I sit' on' the bed's edge, and regard
my underwear with a loud though inward rage. Sadly, I gather
the remnants of my ego, and reknot the thread of consciousness
where Morpheus cut it yestereve. My soul is strewn about,
and rolls in little globules, like mercury spilt from a broken
thermometer. Only the sacrificial fumes of the tea kettle,
the fragrance of ham and of an omelet like cowslips, and, above
all, gentle words uttered by the soft lips of my considerate
housekeepers, reconcile me to my fate.

"Dear old Regamey is dead. The Count Sinsheim has had a

paralytic stroke. My friend, Lady Constance Cuningham, a member of the highest aristocracy, has married a wealthy American bounder. The best are going, and the tree of life is growing bare. On my trip here I stopped over in Munich for three days as the guest of the young Imhofs. Your sister Judith is cutting a great figure. The painters paint her, the sculptors hew her in marble, the poets celebrate her. Yet her ambition is still vaulting. She desires passionately a little nine-pointed coronet upon her linen, her liveries, and her four motors, and flirts with everything that comes from the court or goes to it. Felix, on the contrary, being a democrat, surrounds himself with business men, speculators, explorers, and clever people of both sexes. Hence their house is a mixture of Guildhall, a grain exchange, a meeting of pettifoggers, and a jockey club. After watching the goings on for an evening, I retired to a corner with a pretty girl, and asked her to feel my pulse. She obeyed, and my suffering soul was soothed.

" Our sweet Ariel, I am told, intoxicates the Poles in Warsaw and the Muscovites in Moscow. In the latter city the students are said to have expressed their homage by a torchlight procession, and the officers to have covered the snowy streets from her dwelling to the theatre with roses. I am also told that the Grand Duke Cyril, commonly known as the human butcher, is half-mad with love of her, and is turning the world topsy-turvy to get her. It fills me with a piercing, depthless melancholy to think, O Ariel, that once I, too, felt thy breath. No more than that; but it suffices. *Le moulin n'y est plus, mais le vent y est encore.*

" With this final remark, dear brother of my heart and sorely missed friend, I commend you to God, and beseech you to give some sign to your affectionately longing Bernard Gervasius C. v. W."

When Christian had read the letter, he smiled, and laid it quietly aside.

XIV

On the slope of the hill behind the village Christian and Amadeus Voss met quite by chance.

"I have been waiting for you all week," said Voss.

"I was going to come to you to-day," said Christian. "Won't you walk a little with me?"

Amadeus Voss turned and accompanied Christian. They climbed the hill-top, and then turned toward the forest. Silently they walked side by side. The sun shone through the boughs and everything was watery. Remnants of snow rested on the dry foliage; the ground was slippery; on the road the water flowed in the deep ruts. When they left the forest the sun was just setting, the sky was greenish and pink, and when they reached the first houses of Heptrich, twilight had fallen. On the whole way they had not exchanged a syllable. At first Voss had deliberately not kept step with Christian. Later they walked in a rhythmic harmony that was like the prelude to their conversations.

"I'm hungry," said Amadeus Voss; "there is an inn yonder. Let us go."

They entered the guest room, which they found empty. They sat down at a table near the oven, for the cold air had chilled them. A bar-maid lit a lamp, and brought what they ordered. Christian, in an access of fear, which was less only than his curiosity, thought: What will happen now? and watched Voss attentively.

"The other day I read a moral tale in an old book," said Amadeus, and he used a sharpened match as a tooth-pick in a way that made Christian tremble with nervousness. "It tells about a king, who realized that men and things in his country were growing worse every day, and he asked four philosophers to find out the reason. The four wise men consulted, and then each went to one of the four gates of the city and inscribed thereon one of the chief reasons. The first wrote: 'Here might is right, and therefore this land has no law; day is night,-and therefore this land has no road; conflict is flight, and therefore this land has no honour.' The second wrote: ' One is two here, and therefore this land has no truth; friend is enemy here, therefore this land has no troth; evil is good, therefore we see no piety.' The third wrote: ' The snail pretends to be an eagle, and thieves hold all power.' The fourth wrote: ' The will is our counsellor, and its counsel is evil; the penny pronounces judgment, therefore our rule is vile; God is dead, and therefore the land is filled with sins.' "

· He threw the match away, and leaned his head upon his hand. " In the same book," he went on, " there is yet another story, and perhaps you will feel the connection between the two. Once upon a time the earth opened in the midst of Rome, and a yawning abyss was seen. The gods were questioned, and they made answer: ' This abyss will not close until some one has leaped into it of his own free will.' None could be persuaded to do that. At last a youth came and said: ' If you will let me live for one year according to my pleasure, then at the year's end I shall gladly and voluntarily plunge into the abyss.' It was decided that nothing should be forbidden him, and he used the women and possessions of the Romans freely and at his pleasure. All yearned for the moment to come when they could be rid of him. And when the year was gone, he rode up on a noble charger, and with it leaped into the abyss, which immediately closed behind him."

Christian shrugged his shoulders. " It is all dark to me," he said moodily. " Did you really want to tell me these old tales? They have no meaning."

Voss laughed hoarsely to himself. " You are not nimble," he said, " you have not a nimble mind. Have you never felt the need of seeking refuge in some metaphor? It is like a drug that stills pain."

" I don't know what you mean by that," Christian said, and again he heard the other's soft laughter.

"Let us go," said Christian and arose.

"Very well. Let us go." Voss spoke with a morose air. And they went.

XV

The night air was very still and the sky sown with stars that gleamed coldly. When the village lay behind them, they heard no sound.

"How long were you in Ribbeck's house?" Christian asked suddenly.

"Ten months," Amadeus Voss replied. "When I got to Halbertsroda, the land lay under ice and snow. When I left, the land lay under ice and snow. Between my coming and going, there was a spring, a summer, and an autumn."

He stopped for a moment, and gazed after an animal that in the darkness leaped across the road and disappeared in the furrows of a field. Then he began to talk, at first in a staccato manner and drily, then vividly and tempestuously, and at last gasping for breath. They wandered away from the road, but were not aware of it; the hour grew late, but they did not know it.

Voss told his story:

"I had never seen a house like that. The carpets, pictures, tapestries, the silver, the many servants—it was all new to me. I had never eaten of such dishes nor slept in such beds. I came from amid four bare walls, from a cot, an iron stove, a wash stand, a book shelf, and a crucifix.

"My two pupils were eleven and thirteen. The older was blond and spare, the younger brunette and stocky. Their hair hung down their shoulders like manes. From the very first hour they treated me with a jeering resistance. At first I did not see Frau Ribbeck at all. Not till a week had passed did she summon me. She made the impression of a young girl; she had rust-red hair and a pale, intimidated, undeveloped face. She treated me with a contempt that I had not expected, and

that drove the blood into my temples. My meals were served
to me,alone. I was not permitted to eat at the master's table,
and the servants treated me as their equal. That gnawed at
me,cruelly. When Frau Ribbeck appeared in the garden and I
lifted my hat, she barely nodded, blind and shameless in her
contempt for one whom she paid. I was no more to her than
thin air!

"It is as old as the world, this sin that was sinned against my
soul. Ye sinners against my soul, why did you let me famish?
Why did I taste of renunciation while ye revelled? How
shall a hungry man withstand the temptations which the living
Tempter places before him? Do you think we are not aware
of your gluttony? All action, whether good or evil, runs
through all nature. When the grape blossoms in Madeira, the
wine that has been pressed from it stirs in a thousand casks
far over sea and land, and a new fermentation sets in.

"One morning the boys locked the door of their room and
refused to come to their instruction. While I shook the knob
they mocked me from within. In the halls the servants stood
and laughed at my powerlessness. I went to the gardener, borrowed an axe, and crashed through the door with three blows.
A minute later I was in the room. The boys looked at me in
consternation, and realized at last that I would not endure
their insolence. The noise had brought Frau Ribbeck to the
scene. She looked at the broken door and then at me. I
shall never forget that look. She did not turn her eyes from
me even while she was speaking to the children, and that was
at least ten minutes. Her eyes asked: How dare you? Who
are you? When she went out, she saw the axe near the door
and stopped a moment, and I saw her shiver. But I knew that
the direction of the wind had changed. Also it came into my
consciousness that a human woman had stood before me.

"The teasing of my pupils was by no means at an end. On
the contrary, they annoyed me as much as possible. But they
did it secretively now, and the blame was hard to fix. I found

pebbles and needles in my bed, ink spilled over my books, a horrible rent in the best suit of clothes I had. They jeered at me before others, lied about me to their mother, and exchanged glances of shameless insolence when I held them responsible. What they did was not like the ordinary mischief of silly boys. They had been sophisticated by luxury. They were afraid of a draught, had the rooms so overheated that one grew faint, and thought of nothing but physical comforts. Once they fought, and the younger bit the older's finger. The boy went to bed for three days, and insisted that a physician be called. Nor was this merely a case of lazy malingering; bottomless malevolence and vengefulness entered into it. They considered me as far beneath them, and lost no chance to make me feel my dependent position. My mood was often bitter, but I determined to practise patience.

"One evening I entered the drawing-room. The hour which I had set as the boys' bed-time was past. Frau Ribbeck sat on the carpet, the boys snuggled on either side of her. She was showing them the pictures in a book. Her hair hung loose,— an unfitting thing, I thought—and its reddish splendour covered her as well as the boys like a mantle of brocade. The boys fixed green and evil eyes upon me. I ordered them to bed at once. There must have been something in my tone that frightened them and forced them to obey. Without contradiction they got up and retired.

"Adeline remained on the carpet. I shall simply call her Adeline, as, indeed, I did later during our intercourse. She looked at me exactly as she had done that day I had used the axe. One cannot well be paler than she was by nature, but her skin now became positively transparent. She arose, went to the table, lifted some indifferent object, and put it down again. At the same time a mocking smile hovered upon her lips. That smile went through and through me. And indeed the woman herself pierced me, body and soul. You'll misunderstand me. It doesn't matter. If you don't understand, no explanations

will do any good. The sheet of ice above me cracked, and
I had a glimpse of the upper world."

"I believe I do understand you," said Christian.

"To my question whether she desired me to leave the house,
she replied that, since her husband had engaged me, it was for
her to respect the arrangement. Her tone was frosty. I replied that the pressure of her dislike made it impossible for my
activities to be fruitful. With an indirect glance at me, she
answered that some method of decent co-operation could probably be found, and that she would think it over. Beginning
with that evening, I was invited to table with her, and the
boys and she treated me with respect, if not with kindness.
Late one evening she sent for me and asked me to read to
her. She gave me the book from which I was to read. It was
a current fashionable novel, and, after I had read a few pages,
I threw the volume on the table, and said that the stuff nause-
ated me. She nodded, and answered that that was quite her
feeling, too, which she had not wanted to admit even to herself, and that she was grateful to me for my frankness. I went
for my Bible, and read her the story of Samson from the Book
of Judges. It must have seemed naïve to her, for when I had
finished that mocking smile played again about her lips. Then
she asked: 'It's hardly necessary, is it, to be a hero in Judah
to share Samson's fate? And do you think that what Delilah
accomplished was so remarkable?' I replied that I had no
experience of such matters, and she laughed.

"One word led to another, and I gathered the courage to
reproach her with the morally neglected condition of her children, and with the wounding and vulgar quality of all I had so
far seen and experienced in her house. I intentionally used the
sharpest words, in order that she might flare up in wrath and
show me the door. But she remained quite calm, and begged
me to explain my ideas more fully. I did so, not without passion, and she heard me with pleasure. Several times I saw her
breathe deeply and stretch herself and close her eyes. She

contradicted me, then agreed, defended her position, and in the
end admitted it to be indefensible.   I told her that the love
which she thought she felt for her sons was really a sort of
hatred, based on a poisoning of her own soul, in which there
was yet another life and another love, which it was wicked to
condemn to withering and death.   She must have misunderstood me at this point, for she looked at me with her large eyes
suddenly, and bade me go.   When I had closed her door behind me, I heard sobs. · I opened the door again, and saw her
sitting there with her face hidden in her hands.   I had the
impulse to return to her.   But her gesture dismissed me.

"I had never before seen any woman cry except my mother.
I cannot tell you of my feelings.   If I had had a sister and
grown up in her companionship, I might have acted and felt
differently.   But Adeline was the first woman whom, in any
deeper sense, I truly saw.

"Several days later she asked me whether I had any hope of
forming her boys into human beings in my sense.   She said that
she had reflected on all I had urged, and had come to the
conclusion that things could not go on as they were.   I
answered that it was not yet too late.   She begged me to save
what was possible, and announced that, in order to leave me a
free hand, she had determined to travel for a few months.
Three days later she departed.   She took no personal farewell
of her sons, but wrote them a letter from Dresden.

"I took the boys with me to a hunting lodge, that lay isolated
in the woods, at a distance of two hours from Halbertsroda.
It belonged to the Ribbeck estate, and Adeline had assigned
it to me as a refuge.   There I settled down with the boys and
took them sternly in hand.   Sometimes dread overcame me,
when I thought of the words of Scripture: Why do you seek
constantly to change your way?   Beware lest you be deceived
by Egypt, as you were deceived by Assyria.

"A deaf, old man-servant cooked for us, and luxurious meals
were a thing of the past.   The boys had to pray, to fast once

a week, to sleep on hard mattresses, and to rise at five in the morning. In every way I broke down their stubbornness, their dull sloth, their furtive sensuality, their plots and tricks. There was no play now, and the days were divided with iron regularity. I shrank from no severity. I chastised them; at the slightest disobedience I used a whip. I taught them the meaning of pain. When they cowered naked before me, with the bloody stripes on their bodies, I spoke to them of the martyrdom of the saints. I kept a diary, in order that Adeline might know exactly what had happened. The boys started when they heard me from afar; they trembled if I but raised my head. Once I came upon them whispering to each other in bed at night. I drove them out. They screamed and fled óut of the house from me. In their night shifts they ran into the forest, and I, with two dogs following me, pursued them. Rain began to pour, and at last they broke down and threw themselves on the ground and begged for mercy. Most difficult of all it was to lead them to Confession. But I was stronger than the Evil One within them, and forced them to cleanse their souls. Bitter hours were the hours I endured. But I had made a vow to Adeline in my heart.

"The boys became thoughtful, subdued, and silent. They went into corners and wept. When Adeline returned I took them to Halbertsroda, and she marvelled at the change in them. They flung themselves into her arms, but they uttered no complaint against me, either then or when they were left alone with her. I had told them that if they were disobedient or stubborn, we would return to the hunting lodge. One or two days a week were spent there under any circumstances. Gradually they came to avoid their mother, and Adeline herself was more indifferent to them. The softish, hectic, over-tender element in their relations had disappeared.

"Adeline sought my companionship and conversation. She watched me, and was condescending, weary, distracted in mind, and restless. She adorned herself as though guests were

coming, and combed her hair thrice daily. In all respects she
submitted to my regulations. There are dulled, worm-eaten,
smouldering souls that kneel before the raised axe in another's
hand, and give only mockery to those who bend before them.
Often her loftiness and reserve overwhelmed me, and I thought
that she had no space for me in her mind. Then a look came
into her eyes that made me forget whence I came and what I
was in her house. Everything seemed possible with her. She
was capable of setting fire to the house by night, because she was
bored, and because the cancer that ate at her soul would cease
its gnawing for no nobler ecstasy: she was capable of standing
from noon to night before her mirror to watch a deepening
furrow on her brow. Everything seemed possible. For is it
not written: What man knoweth what is in man except only the
spirit of man that is in him?

" My deep temptations began on an evening when, in the
course of conversation, she carelessly laid her hand over mine,
and withdrew it hastily. That gesture snatched from my
sight the things about us. In the space between one thought
and the next I had become the slave of visions and desires.

" She asked me to tell her about my life. I fell into that
snare too, and told her.

" Once in the twilight I met her in the hall. She stood still,
and looked at me piercingly. Then she laughed softly and
moved away. I reeled, and the sweat stood in beads on my
forehead.

" My heart was heavy when I was alone. Visions appeared
that set my room in flames. My rosary and my missal were
hidden from me, and I could find neither. Always there rose
the cry in me: Once only! Let me taste that ecstasy but once!
Then demons came and tormented me. All the muscles and
nerves and sinews of my body seemed lacerated. Do with me
as God wills, I whispered to the demons, for my heart is prepared. During sleep a strange force hurled me from my bed,
and unconsciously I battered the walls with my head. One

whole week I fasted upon bread and water, but it did not avail.
Once when I had sat down to read, a huge ape stood before
me and turned the leaves of my book. Every night a seductive vision of Adeline came to my bed-side. She stood there
and spoke: 'It is I, my beloved.' Then I would rise and run
senselessly about. But she would follow me and whisper:
'You shall be my master and have all the good things of this
world.' But when I sought to grasp that vision of her, it
showed a sudden aversion, and she called fluttering shadows to
her aid. One was a notary with a pen and an ink-well,
another a locksmith with a red-hot hammer, there was a mason
with his trowel, an officer with naked sword, a woman with a
painted face.

" So terrible was my state, that I understood but slowly and
gradually the dreadful realities that took place about me. One
morning Adeline came into the room where I was teaching the
boys, sat down, and listened. She drew from her finger a ring
that had in it a great, lovely pearl, played with it thoughtfully, arose, went to the window to watch the falling of the
snow, and then left the room to go into the garden. I could
not breathe or see any longer. There was an intolerable pressure on my chest, and I had to leave the room for a little to
catch my breath. When I returned I saw in the eyes of my
pupils a look of unwonted malevolence. I paid no attention
to it. From time to time the old rebelliousness flared up in
them, but I let them be. They sat before me half-crouching,
and recited their catechism softly and with glances full of fear.

" About ten minutes passed when Adeline returned. She said
she had left her ring on the table, and asked me whether I
had seen it. She began to search for it, and so did I. She
called her maid and a footman, who examined everything in
the room; but the ring was gone. Adeline and her servants
looked at me strangely, for I stood there and could not move.
I felt at once and in every fibre that I was exposed to their
suspicion. They searched on the stairs and in the hall, in the

new fallen snow of the garden, and again in the room, since Adeline insisted that she had taken the ring off there and forgotten it on the table. And I confirmed this statement, although I had not actually seen the ring on the table, since I had seen her and her gestures but as things in a dream. All the words that were exchanged between her and the servants seemed directed against me. I read suspicion in their looks and changed colour, and called the boys, who had stolen away as soon as they could, and questioned them. They suggested that their rooms be searched, and looked at me with malignity. I begged Adeline to have my room searched as well. She made a deprecating gesture, but said, as though in self-justification, that she attached a peculiar value to this ring and should hate to lose it.

" Meantime the manager of the estate, who happened to have spent that night at Halbertsroda, entered. He passed me by without greeting, but with a dark and hostile glance. Then it all came over me. I saw myself delivered over to their suspicions without defence, and I said to myself: Perhaps you have really stolen the ring. The fall from my previous spiritual condition to this vulgar and ugly one was so sudden, that I broke out into wild laughter, and insisted more urgently than ever that my room and effects and even my person be searched. The manager spoke softly to Adeline. She looked at me wanly and went out. I emptied my pockets in the man's presence. He followed me to my room. I sat down by the window while he opened drawer after drawer in my chest and opened my wardrobe. The footman, the maid, and the two boys stood by the door. Suddenly the manager uttered a hollow cry and held up the ring. I had known with the utmost certainty a moment before that he would find the ring. I had read it in the faces of the boys. Therefore I remained quietly seated while the others looked at one another and followed the manager out. I locked my door and walked up and down, up and down, for many, many hours.

"When the night was over, there was a solemn calm in my soul. I sent a servant to ask Adeline whether she would receive me. She refused. To justify myself in writing was a thing I scorned to do. I would but degrade myself by asserting my innocence thus. My soul felt pure and cold. I learned next day that the manager had long heard rumours of the frightful cruelties I was said to inflict on the boys, who had, moreover, accused their mother and myself of an adulterous intimacy. Hence he had visited Halbertsroda secretly on several occasions, had questioned the servants, and had, that very morning, caused the boys to strip in his presence and had seen on· their bodies· the marks of the stripes that they had received. Since, in addition, their entire state of mind made him anxious, he sent a telegram to the Councillor, who arrived during the night with an official of the police.

"I suspect that Adeline at once saw through the plot concerning the ring, for it was not mentioned. The commissary turned to me and spoke vaguely of serious consequences, but I made no attempt to explain or excuse anything I had done. I left Halbertsroda that same night. I did not see Adeline again. She was, I have been told, sent off to a sanatorium. Three weeks later a little package came to me by post. I opened it and found in it the ring with the pearl. In our yard is a very ancient well. I went to that well and cast the ring into its depths.

"And now you know what happened to me in that world of the higher classes, in the house of the Councillor Ribbeck."

XVI

They had to walk a while longer before they reached the gate of the park of Christian's Rest. As Voss was about to take his leave, Christian said: "You're probably tired. Why trouble to walk to the village? Be my guest over night."

"If it does not inconvenience you, I accept," Voss answered.

They entered the house and passed into the brightly lit hall.

Amadeus Voss gazed about him in astonishment. They went up the stairs and into the dining hall, which was furnished in the purest style of Louis XV. Christian led his guest through other rooms into the one that was to be his. And Amadeus Voss wondered more and more. " This is quite another thing from Halbertsroda," he murmured; " it is as a feast day compared to every day."

Silently they sat opposite each other at table. Then they went into the library. A footman served the coffee on a silver platter. Voss leaned against a column and looked upward. When the servant had gone, he said: " Have you ever heard of the Telchinian pestilence? It is a disease created by the envy of the Telchines, the hounds of Actæon who were changed into men, and it destroys everything within its reach. A youth named Euthilides saw with that eye of envy the reflection of his own beauty in a spring, and his beauty faded."

Christian looked silently at the floor.

" There is another legend of a Polish nobleman," Amadeus continued. " This nobleman lived alone in a white house by the Vistula river. All his neighbours avoided him, for his envious glance brought them nothing but misfortune. It killed their herds, set fire to their barns, and made their children leprous. Once a beautiful maiden was pursued by wolves and took refuge in the white house. He fell in love with her and married her. But because the evil that was in him passed into her also, he tore out the gleaming crystals of his eyes, and buried them near the garden wall. He had now recovered. But the buried eyes gained new power under the earth, and an old servitor who dug them up was slain by them."

Sitting on a low stool, Christian had folded his arms over his knee, and looked up at Voss.

" From time to time," said Amadeus Voss, " one must expiate the lust of the eye. Over in the village of Nettersheim a maid servant lies dying. The poor thing is deserted by all the world. She lies in a shed by the stables, and the peasants who think her merely lazy will not believe that she is about to die. I have visited her more than once, in order to expiate the lust of the eye."

A long silence fell upon them. When the clock in the tall Gothic case struck twelve, they went to their rooms.

XVII

In obedience to his father's summons, Christian travelled to Würzburg.

Their greeting was most courteous. "I hope I have not interfered with any plans of yours," said Albrecht Wahnschaffe.

"I am at your disposal," Christian said coolly.

They took a walk on the old ramparts but said little. The beautiful dog Freia, who was the constant companion of Albrecht Wahnschaffe, trotted along between them. It surprised the elder Wahnschaffe to observe on Christian's face the signs of inner change.

That evening, over their tea, he said with an admirably generous gesture. "You're to be congratulated, I understand, on a very unusual acquisition. A wreath of legends surrounds this diamond. The incident has caused quite a whirl of dust to fly and not a little amazement. Not unjustly so, it seems to me, since you are neither a British Duke nor an Indian Maharajah. Is the stone so very desirable?"

"It is marvellous," Christian said. And suddenly the words of Voss slipped into his mind: One must expiate the lust of the eye.

Albrecht Wahnschaffe nodded. "I don't doubt it, and I understand such passions, though, as a man of business, I must regret the tying up of so much capital. It is an eccentricity; and the world is endangered whenever the commoners grow eccentric. And so I should like to ask you to reflect on this aspect of things: all the privileges which you enjoy, all the easements of life, the possibility of satisfying

your whims and passions, the supremacy of your social station
—all these things rest on work. Need I add—on the work of
your father?'"

The dog Freia had strolled out from a corner of the room,
and laid her head caressingly on Christian's knee. Albrecht
Wahnschaffe, slightly annoyed and jealous, gave her a smart
slap on one flank.

He continued. "An exploitation of one's capacity for work
which reaches the extent of mine involves, of course, the
broadest self-denial in all other matters. One becomes a
ploughshare that tears up the earth and rusts. Or one is like
a burning substance, luminiferous but self-consumed. Marriage, family, friendship, art, nature—these things scarcely
exist for me. I have lived like a miner in his shaft. And what
thanks do I get? Demagogues tell those whom they delude
that I am a vampire, who sucks the blood of the oppressed.
These poisoners of our public life either do not know or do
not wish to know the shocks and sufferings and renunciations
that have been mine, and of which their peaceful 'wage-slave'
has no conception."

Freia snuggled closer up to Christian, licked his hand, and
her eyes begged humbly for a look. The beast's dumb tenderness soothed him. He frowned, and said laconically: ". If it is
so, and you feel it so keenly, why do you go on working?"

"There is such a thing as duty, my dear spoiled boy, such
a thing as loyalty to a cause," Albrecht Wahnschaffe answered,
and a gleam of anger showed in his pale-blue eyes. "Every
peasant clings to the bit of earth into which he has put his
toil. When I began to work, our country was still a poor
country; to-day it is rich. I shall not say that what I have
accomplished is considerable, when compared to the sum of
our national accomplishment, but it has counted. It is a symptom of our rise, of our young might, of our economic welfare.
We are one of the very great nations now, and have a body as
well as a countenance."

"What you say is doubtless most true," Christian answered. "Unhappily I have no instinct for such matters; my personality is defective in things of that kind."

"A quarter of a century ago your fate would have been that of a bread earner," Albrecht Wahnschaffe continued, without reacting to Christian's words. "To-day you are a descendant and an heir. Your generation looks upon a changed world and age. We older men have fastened wings upon your shoulders, and you have forgotten how painful it is to creep."

Christian, in a sombre longing for the warmth of some body, took the dog's head between his hands, and with a grunt of gratitude she raised herself up and laid her paws on his shoulders. With a smile, that included his petting of the dog, he said: "No one refuses the good things that fall into his lap. It is true I have never asked whence everything comes and whither it tends. To be sure, there are other ways of living; and I may yet embrace one of them some day. Then it will be apparent whether one becomes another man, and what kind, when the supports or the wings, as you put it, are gone." His face had grown serious.

Albrecht Wahnschaffe suddenly felt himself rather helpless before this handsome, proud stranger who was his son. To hide his embarrassment, he answered hastily: "A different way of living—that is just what I mean. It was the conviction that a life which is nothing but a chain of trifles must in the end become a burden, that made me suggest a career to you that is worthier of your powers and gifts. How would you like the profession of diplomacy? Wolfgang seems thoroughly satisfied with the possibilities that he sees opening up before him. It is not too late for you either. It will not be difficult to make up the time lost. Your name outweighs any title of nobility. You would stay in a suitable atmosphere; you have large means, the necessary personal qualities and relations. Everything will adjust itself automatically."

Christian shook his head. "You are mistaken, father," he

said, softly but firmly. " I have no capacity for anything like that, and no taste for it at all."

" I suspected as much," Albert Wahnschaffe said, in his liveliest manner. " Let us not speak of it any more. My second proposal is far more congenial to myself. I would encourage you to co-operate in the activities of our firm. My plan is to create a representative position for you in either our home or our foreign service. If you choose the latter you may select your own field of activity—Japan, let us say, or the United States. We would furnish you with credentials that would make your position very independent. You would assume responsibilities that are in no wise burdensome, and enjoy all the privileges of an ambassador. All that is needed is your consent. I shall arrange all details."

Christian arose from his chair. " I beg you very earnestly, father, to drop that subject," he said. His expression was cold and his eyes cast down.

Albrecht Wahnschaffe arose too. " Do not be rash, Christian," he admonished his son. " I shall not conceal the fact that a definitive refusal on your part would wound me deeply. I have counted on you." He looked at Christian with a firm glance. But Christian was silent.

After a while he asked: " How long ago is it since you were at the works? "

" It must be three or four years ago," Christian answered.

" It was three years ago on Whitsuntide, if I remember rightly," Albrecht Wahnschaffe said, with his habitual touch of pride in his memory, which was rarely at fault. " You had agreed on a pleasure trip in the Harz mountains with your cousin, Theo Friesen, and Theo was anxious to pay a flying visit to the factories. He had heard of our new welfare movement for workingmen, and was interested in it. But you scarcely stopped after all."

" No, I persuaded Theo to go on. We had a long way ahead of us, and I was anxious to get to our quarters."

Christian remembered the whole incident now. Evening
had come before the car drove through the streets of the factory village. He had yielded to his cousin's wish, but suddenly his aversion for this world of smoke and dust and sweat
and iron had awakened. He had not wanted to leave the car,
and had ordered the driver to speed up.

Nevertheless he recalled the hellish music made up of beaten
steel and whirring wheels. He could still hear the thundering,
whistling, wheezing, screeching, hissing; he could still see the
swift procession of forges, cylinders, pumps, steam-hammers,
furnaces, of all kinds; the thousands of blackened faces, a race
that seemed made of coal in the breath of the fierce glow of
white and crimson fires; misty electric moons that quivered in
space; vehicles like death barrows swallowed up in the violet
darkness; the workingmen's homes, with their appearance of
comfort, and their reality of a bottomless dreariness; the baths,
libraries, club-houses, crèches, hospitals, infants' homes, ware-
houses, churches, and cinemas. The stamp of force and servi-
tude, of all that is ugliest on earth, was bedizened and tinted in
fair colours here, and all menaces were throttled and fettered.

Young Friesen had exhausted himself with admiration, but
Christian had not breathed freely again until their car was
out on the open road and had left the flaring horror in its
panic flight.

"And you have not been there since?" Albrecht Wahnschaffe asked.

"No, not since that day."

For a while they stood opposite each other in silence.
Albrecht Wahnschaffe took Freia by her collar, and said with
notable self-control: "Take counsel with yourself. There is
time. I shall not urge you unduly, but rather wait. When you
come to weigh the circumstances, and test your own mind,
you will realize that I have your welfare at heart. Do not
answer me now. When you have made a clear decision—
let me know what it is."

"Have I your permission to retire?" Christian asked. His father nodded, and he bowed and left the room.

Next morning he returned to Christian's Rest.

XVIII

In a side street of the busiest quarter of Buenos Ayres, there stood a house that belonged to the Gunderam family. The parents of Gottlieb Gunderam had bought it when they came to the Argentine in the middle of the nineteenth century. In those days its value had been small, but the development of the city had made it a considerable property. Gottfried Gunderam received tempting offers for it, not only from private dealers, but from the municipality. The rickety house was to be torn down, and to be replaced by a modern apartment house.

But Gottfried Gunderam turned a deaf ear to all offers. "The house in which my mother died," he declared, "shall not be sold to strangers so long as the breath is in my body."

This determination did not arise so much from filial piety, as from a superstition that was powerful enough to silence even his greed. He feared that his mother would arise from her grave and avenge herself on him, if he permitted the family's ancestral home to be sold and destroyed. Wealth, good harvests, a great age, and general well-being were, in his opinion, dependent on his action in this matter. He would not even allow strangers to enter the house.

His sons and kinsmen mockingly called it the Escurial. Gottfried Gunderam took no notice of their jeers, but he himself had, gradually and quite seriously, slipped into the habit of calling the house the Escurial.

One day, long before his voyage to Germany, Stephen had cleverly taken advantage of his father in an hour when the old man was tipsy and merry, and had extorted a promise that the Escurial was to be his upon his marriage. When he came home with Letitia he counted upon the fulfilment of this promise. He intended to establish himself as a lawyer in Buenos Ayres, and restore the neglected house.

He reminded his father of the compact. The old man denied it bluntly. He winked gravely. "Can you show me any record—black on white? Well, then, what do you want? A fine lawyer you are to think that you can enforce an agreement of which there is no record!".

Stephen did not reply. But from time to time—coldly, methodically, calmly—he reminded the old man of his promise.

The old man said: "The woman you have married is not to my taste. She doesn't fit into our life. She reads and reads. It's sickening. She's a milk-faced doll without sap. Let her be content with what she has. I shan't be such a fool as to plunge into expenditures on your account. It would cost a pretty penny to make the Escurial habitable. And I have no cash. Absolutely none."

Stephen estimated the available capital of his father as amounting to between four and five millions. "You owe me my patrimony," he answered.

"I owe you a damned good thrashing!" the old man replied grimly.

"Is that your last word?"

The old man answered: "Far from it. I won't speak my last word for a dozen years. But I like peace at home, and so I'll make a bargain with you. Whenever your wife gives birth to a man-child, you shall have the Escurial, and fifty thousand pesos to boot."

"Give me the promise in writing! Black on white counts —as you yourself said."

The old man laughed a dry laugh. "Good!" he cried, and winked with both eyes. "You're improving. Glad to see that the money spent on your legal studies wasn't quite wasted." With a sort of glee he sat down at his desk, and made out the required document.

A few weeks later Stephen said to Letitia: "Let us drive to the city. I want to show you the Escurial."

The only living creature in that house was a mulatto woman ninety years old. To rouse her one had to throw stones against the wooden shutters. Then she appeared, bent almost double, half-blind, clothed in rags, a yellow growth on her forehead.

The street, which had been laid out a century before, was a yard deeper than the more recent ones; and Stephen and Letitia had to use a short ladder to reach the door of the house. Within everything was mildewed and rotten, the furniture and the floors. In the corners the spiders' webs were like clouds, and fat hairy spiders sat in them peacefully. The wall-paper, was in rags, the window-panes were broken, and the fire-places had caved in.

But in the room in which the mother of Gunderam had died, there stood a beautiful inlaid table, an antique piece from a convent of Siena. The mosaic showed two angels inclining palm-branches toward each other, and between the two sat an eagle. Upon the table lay the dead woman's jewels. Brooches and chains, rings and ear-rings and bracelets, had lain here dust-covered for many, many years. The reputation of the old house as being haunted had protected them more effectually than barred windows.

Letitia was frightened, and thought: "Am I to live here where ghosts may appear at night to don their old splendour? "

But when Stephen explained his plans for rebuilding and redecorating, she recovered her gaiety, and her imagination transformed these decayed rooms into inviting chambers and dainty boudoirs, cool halls with tall windows and airy, carpeted stairs.

"It depends quite simply on you whether we can have a happy and beautiful home very soon," Stephen declared. "I'm doing my share. I wish I could say the same of you."

Letitia looked away. She knew the condition which old Gunderam had made.

Again and again she had to disappoint Stephen. The Escurial lay in its deathlike sleep, and her husband's face grew more and more sombre. He sent her to church to pray; he strewed her bed with ground wall-nuts; he made her drink a powder of bones dissolved in wine. He sent for an old crone who was gifted in magic, and Letitia had to stand naked, surrounded by seven tapers, and let the woman murmur over her body. And she went to church and prayed, although she had no faith in her praying and felt no devotion and knew nothing of God. Yet she shuddered at the murmurs of the Italian witch, although when it was all over, she laughed and made light of the whole thing.

In spirit she conceived the image of the child which her body denied her. The image was of uncertain sex, but of flawless loveliness. It had the soft eyes of a deer, the features of one of Raphael's angels, and the exquisite soul of an ode by Hölderlin. It was destined to great things, and the dizzying curve of its fortune knew no decline. The thought of this dream child filled her with vaguely beautiful emotions, and she was amazed at Stephen's anger and growing impatience. She was amazed and was conscious of no guilt.

Stephen's mother, who was known as Doña Barbara to every one, said to her son: " I bore your father eight living creatures. Three are dead. Four are strong men. We need not even count your sister Esmeralda. Why is this woman barren? Chastise her, my son, beat her! "

Stephen gritted his teeth, and took up his ox-hide whip.

XIX

It was evening, and Christian went to the forester's house. The way was very familiar to him now. He did not analyze the inner compulsion that drew him thither.

Amadeus Voss sat by his lamp and read in an old book. Through the second door of the room the shadow of his mother slipped away.

After a while he asked: "Will you go with me to-morrow to Nettersheim? "

"What am I to do there? " Christian questioned in his turn.

Amadeus raised his face, and his spectacles glimmered. He murmured: "She may be dead by this time."

He drummed on his knees with his fingers. Since Christian said nothing, he began to tell him the story of the woman Walpurga, who was in the service of his uncle, the wealthy farmer Borsche.

"She was born in the village, a cottager's daughter. At fifteen she went to the city. She had heard of the fine life one leads there and had great ambitions. She was in service here and there. Last she was in the house of a merchant whose son seduced her; and of course, when it was discovered, she was driven out. So it comes to pass that those who are by nature the victims must bear a punishment in addition.

"She bore a child, but the child died. She fell deeper and deeper, until she became a street-walker. She practised this calling in Bochum and in Elberfeld. But the life wore on her, and she fell ill. One day a great home-sickness came upon her. She mustered her last strength, and returned to her native village. She was penniless and weak, but she was anxious to earn her bread, no matter at what wage or through what labour.

"But no one would hire her. Her parents were dead and she had no relatives, so she became a pubic charge. She was made to feel it grievously. One Sunday the minister inveighed against her from the pulpit. He did not mention her name, but he spoke of vile lives and sinks of iniquity, of visitations and punishments, and of how the anger of the Lord was visible in an example that was before the eyes of all. Thus she was branded and publicly delivered over to the scorn of all people, and she determined to put an end to her life. One evening, as Borsche was returning from his inn, he saw a woman lying in the road in dreadful convulsions. It was Walpurga. No man was near. Borsche lifted her on his broad back, and

carried her to his farm. She confessed that she had scraped
the phosphorus from many matches and eaten it. The farmer
gave her milk as an antidote. She recovered, and was permitted to stay on the farm.

"On some days she could work, and then she dragged herself
to the fields. On others she could not, and lay in a remote
corner. The men servants, of whom there were many, regarded her body as common property. Resistance was useless.
Not until Borsche learned this, and blazed out in anger, did
things get better. She was only twenty-three, and despite her
illness and the wretchedness of her life, she had preserved much
of her youthful good looks. Her cheeks had a natural glow
and her eyes were clear. So whenever she could not work,
the other maids fell upon her, and called her a malingering
bawd.

"Two weeks ago I happened to be wandering in the neighbourhood of Nettersheim, and stopped at Borsche's house. I
was well received there, for the family think highly of me as a
future priest. They talked about Walpurga. The farmer told
me her story, and asked me to have a look at her and give my
opinion as to whether she was really ill. I objected, and asked
why a physician had not seen her. He said that the doctor
from Heftrich had examined her and could find nothing
wrong. So I went to her. She lay in a shed, separated from
the cows only by a wooden partition. She was wrapped in an
old horse-blanket, and a little straw kept the chill of the
earth from her body. Her healthy colour and her normal
form did not deceive me. I said to the farmer: 'She's like
a guttering candle.' He and his wife seemed to believe me.
But when I demanded of them that they give the sick woman
decent lodging and care, they shrugged their shoulders, and
said that it was as warm in the stable as anywhere, and that
there was no sense in taking trouble or undergoing discomfort
on account of a creature who had fallen so low.

"On the third day I saw her again, and I have seen her on

every other day since then. My thoughts could not get rid
of her any more. In all my life no human creature has so
tugged at my heart. She could no longer get up; the most
malevolent had to admit that. I sat with her in the evil
smelling shed on a wooden bench near where she lay. Each
time I came she was happier to see me. I picked wild flowers
on the way, and she took them in her hands and held them
against her breast. They told her who I was, and gradually
she put many questions to me. She wanted to know whether
there really was an eternal life and eternal bliss. She wanted
to know whether Christ had died on the cross for her too.
She was afraid of the torments of purgatory, and said if they
were as bad as the torments men could inflict she was sorry
for the immortal part of her. She meant neither to re-
vile men nor to complain of them. She merely wanted to
know.

"And what answer could I give her? I assured her that
Christ had taken her cross upon Him too. Her other questions
left me silent. One is so dumb and desperate when a living
heart thirsts after truth, and the frozen Christ within would
melt into a new day and a new sun. They are even now in
purgatory and ask when it will begin. Hidden in blackness,
they do not see the dark; consumed by flames, they are un-
aware of the fire. Where is Satan's true kingdom—here or
elsewhere? And can that elsewhere be upon any star more
accursed than this? The poor man is thrust from the wayside,
the oppressed of the land creep into hiding; from the cities
come the moans of the dying, and the souls of those who are
wounded to death cry out. Yet God does not put an end to the
iniquity. And is it not written that the Lord said to Satan:
'From whence comest thou? And Satan answered the Lord,
and said, From going to and fro in the earth and from walking
up and down in it.'

"She confessed her sins to me, and begged me to grant her
absolution. But nothing that seemed sinful to her seemed so

to me. I saw the desolateness and loneliness of the world. I
saw the bleak rooms and the barren walls, the streets by night
with their flickering lamps, and the men with no compassion
in their eyes. That is what I saw and what I thought of, and
I took it upon my conscience to absolve her from all guilt. I
set her free and promised her Paradise. She smiled at me
and grasped my hand, and before I could prevent her she had
kissed it. That was yesterday."

Amadeus was silent. "That was yesterday," he repeated,
after a long and meditative pause. "I did not go to-day, out
of fear of her dying. Perhaps she is dead even now."

"If you still want to go, I am ready," said Christian timidly.
"I'll go with you. It's only an hour's walk.

"Then let us go," said Amadeus, with a sigh of relief, and
arose.

XX

An hour later they were in Borsche's farm yard. The stable
door was open. The men servants and the maid servants stood
in front of it. An old man held a lantern high up, and they
all stared into the shed. In the dim and wavering light, their
faces showed a mixture of reverence and amazement. Within,
on a pallet of straw, lay the body of Walpurga. Its cheeks
were rosy. Nothing in that countenance recalled death, but
only a peaceful sleep.

On the wooden bench a single candle was burning; but it
was near extinction.

Amadeus Voss passed through that group of men and women,
and kneeled at the dead woman's feet. The old man who held
the lantern whispered something, and all the men and women
kneeled down and folded their hands.

A cow lowed. After that there was no sound save from the
bells of the unquiet cattle. The darkness of the stable, the
face of the dead woman, which was like a face in a painting, the
faces of the kneeling people, with their blunted foreheads and

hard lips, in the yellow glimmer of the light—all these things Christian beheld, and something melted in his breast.

He himself watched it all from the darkness of the yard behind.

When Amadeus Voss joined Christian, the village carpenter came to measure the dead woman for her coffin. They started on their homeward way in silence.

Suddenly Christian stopped. It was near a tall mile-post. He grasped the post with both hands, and bent his head far back, and gazed with the utmost intensity into the drifting clouds of the night. Then he heard Amadeus Voss say: " Is it possible? Can such things be? "

Christian turned to him.

" I have a strange feeling in your presence, Christian Wahnschaffe," Voss said in a repressed and toneless voice. And then he murmured to himself: " Is it possible? Can the monstrous and incredible come to pass? "

Christian did not answer, and they wandered on.

XXI

Crammon gave a dinner. Not in his own house; meetings of a certain character were impossible there, on account of the innocent presence of the two old maiden ladies, Miss Aglaia and Miss Constantine. The disillusion would have been too saddening and final to the good ladies, who were as convinced of the virtue of their lord and protector as they were of the emperor's majesty.

In former years it had indeed sometimes seemed to them that their adored one did not always tread the paths of entire purity. They had closed an eye. Now, however, the dignity and intellectual resonance of his personality forbade any doubt.

Crammon had invited his guests to the private dining-room of a well-known hotel, in which he was familiar and esteemed. The company consisted of several young members of the nobility, to whom he was under social obligations, and, as for

ladies, there were three beauties, entertaining, elegant, and yielding, in the precise degree which the occasion required. Crammon called them his friends, but in his treatment of them there
was something languid and even vexed. He gave them clearly
to understand that he was only the business manager of the
feast, and that his heart was very far away.

No one, in fact, was present to whom he was not completely
indifferent. Best of all he liked the old pianist with long, grey
locks, who closed his eyes and smiled dreamily whenever he
played a melancholy or languishing piece, just as he had done
twenty years ago, when Crammon was still fired by the dreams
and ambitions of youth. He gave the old man sweets and
cigarettes, and sometimes patted his shoulder affectionately.

The table groaned under its burden of food and wine. Pepper
was added to the champagne to heighten every one's thirst.
There were cherries in the fruit bowls, and the gentlemen found
it amusing to drop the pits down the semi-exposed bosoms of
the ladies. The latter found it easier and easier, as the
evening advanced, to resist the law of gravitation, and to display their charming shoes and the smooth silks and rustling
laces of their legs in astonishingly horizontal attitudes. The
most agile among them, a popular soubrette, climbed on the
grand piano, and, accompanied by the grey-haired musician,
sang the latest hit of the music halls.

The young men joined in the chorus.

Crammon applauded with just two fingers. "There is a
sting in my soul," he whispered into the din. He got up and
left the room.

In the corridor the head-waiter Ferdinand was leaning alone
and somewhat wearily against the frame of a mirror. A tender
intimacy of two decades bound Crammon to this man, who had
never in his life been indiscreet, in spite of the innumerable
secrets he had overheard.

"Bad times, Ferdinand," Crammon said. "The world is
going to the deuce."

"One must take things as they are, Herr von Crammon," that dignified individual consoled him, and handed him the bill.

Crammon sighed. He gave directions that if his guests inquired after him, they were to be told that he was indisposed and had gone home.

"There is a sting in my soul," he said, when he found himself on the street. He determined to travel again.

He yearned for his friend. It seemed to him that he had had no friend but that one who had cast him off.

He yearned for Ariel. It seemed to him that he had possessed no woman, because she had not yielded to him who was his very conception of genius and beauty.

At the door of his house stood Miss Aglaia. She had heard him coming and had hastened to meet him. It frightened Crammon, for the hour was late.

"There is a lady in the drawing-room," Miss Aglaia whispered. "She arrived at eight, and has been waiting since then. She besought us so movingly to let her stay that we had not the heart to refuse. She is a distinguished lady, and she has a dear face——"

"Did she tell you her name?" Crammon asked, and the thunder-clouds gathered on his brow.

"No, not exactly——"

"People who enter my dwelling are required to give their names," Crammon roared. "Is this a railway station or a public shelter? Go in and ask her who she is. I shall wait here."

In a few minutes Miss Aglaia returned and said in a compassionate tone: "She's fallen asleep in an armchair. But you can take a peep at her. I've left the door ajar."

On tip-toes Crammon passed through the hall, and peered into the well-lit drawing-room. He recognized the sleeper at once. It was Elise von Einsiedel. She slept with her head leaned back and inclining a little to one side. Her face was pale, with blue circles under her eyes, and her left arm hung down limply.

Crammon stood there in his hat and overcoat, and gazed at her with sombre eyes. "Unhappy child!" he murmured.

He closed the door with all possible precaution. Then he drew Miss Aglaia toward the door and said: "The presence of a strange lady makes it unseemly, of course, for me to pass the night here. I shall find a bed elsewhere. I hope you appreciate my attitude."

Miss Aglaia was speechless over such purity and sternness. Crammon continued: "As early as possible in the morning, pack my bags and bring them to meet me in time to catch the express to Ostende. And let Constantine come with you, so that I may say good-bye to her as well. Let the strange lady stay here as long as she desires. Entertain her courteously and fulfil all her wishes. She has a sorrow, and deserves kindness. If she asks after me, tell her that urgent affairs require my presence elsewhere."

He went out. Sadly, and quite astonished, Miss Aglaia looked after him. "Good-night, Aglaia," he called out once more. Then the door closed behind him.

XXII

During the last days of April Christian received a telegram from Eva Sorel. The message read: "From the third to the twentieth of May, Eva Sorel will be at the Hotel Adlon, Berlin, and feels quite sure that Christian Wahnschaffe will meet her there."

Christian read the message over and over. In his inner and in his outer life all circumstances pointed to an approaching crisis. He knew that this summons would be decisive in its influence upon his fate. Its exact character and the extent of its power he could not predict.

For weeks there had been a restlessness in him that robbed him of sleep during many long hours of the night. On certain days he had called for his motor in order to drive to some near-by city. When the car had covered half the distance, he ordered his chauffeur to turn back.

He had gone to Waldleiningen, and had patted his horses and played with his dogs. But he had suddenly felt like a schoolboy who lies and plays truant, and his pleasure in the animals had gone. At parting he had put his arms about his favourite dog, a magnificent Great Dane, and as he looked into the animal's eyes it had seemed to Christian, still in his character of a truant, that he wanted to say: "I must first go and pass my examination." And the dog seemed to answer: "I understand that. You must go."

Also the slender horse of Denis Lay had said, with a turn of its excessively graceful neck: "I understand that. You must go."

It was settled that the horse was to run in the races at Baden-Baden, and the Irish jockey was full of confidence. But on the day of his departure Christian was told that the animal had sickened again. He thought: "I have loved it too insistently. Now it wants the caressing hand, and is lonely without it."

With the coming of spring guests from the cities had appeared almost daily at Christian's Rest. But he had rarely received any one. A single guest he could not bear at all. If there were two they could address each other and make his silence easier.

One day came Conrad von Westernach and Count Prosper Madruzzi, bringing messages from Crammon. They were on their way to Holland. Christian asked them to dine with him, but he was very laconic. Conrad von Westernach remarked later, in his forthright fashion, to Madruzzi: "That fellow has a damned queer smile. You never know whether he's a born fool or whether he's laughing at you."

"It's true," the count agreed; "you never know where you are with him."

XXIII

Christian had given his valet orders to prepare for his journey. Then he had gone to the green-houses to interview the gardeners. In the meantime twilight had set in. It had rained all day, and the trees were still dripping. But now the fresh greenery gleamed against the afterglow, and the windows of the beautiful house were dipped in gold.

"Herr Voss is in the library," an old footman announced.

Christian had begged Amadeus Voss to use the library quite freely, whether he himself was at home or not. The servants had been instructed. Voss had offered to catalogue the library, but as yet he had made no beginning. He merely passed from book to book, and if one interested him he read it and forgot the passage of time.

The afterglow fell into the library too. Voss had taken fifty or sixty volumes from the shelves, and he was now arranging them in stacks on a large oak table.

"Why do you do that, Amadeus?" Christian asked carelessly.

"If you give me your permission, I'd like to burn these," Amadeus Voss answered.

Christian was surprised. "Why?" he asked.

"Because I lust after an *auto-da-fé*. It is worthless and corrupt stuff, the product of idle and slothful minds. Don't you scent the poison of it in the atmosphere?"

"No, I scent nothing," said Christian, more absent-mindedly than ever. "But burn them if it amuses you," he answered.

Amadeus had been in the library since three o'clock that afternoon, and he had had a remarkable experience there. In looking about among the shelves he had come upon a bundle of letters. By some accident it had probably fallen behind the books and been lost sight of. He had read a few lines of the topmost letter, and from the first words there breathed upon him the glow of an impassioned soul. Then he had yielded to the temptation of untying the package. He had taken the letters into a corner, and read them swiftly and with fevered eyes.

A few bore dates. The whole series had been written about two years before. They were signed merely by the initial F. But in every word, in every image, in every turn of speech there was such a fullness of love and devotion and adoration and self-abnegation, and so wild and at the same time so spiritual a stream of tenderness and pain, of happiness and yearning, that Amadeus Voss seemed to glide from a world of shadows and appearances into a far more real one. Yet in that, too, all was but feigned and represented to lure and madden him.

And F.—this unknown, eloquent, radiant, profoundly moved and nameless woman—where was she now? What had she done with her love? Pressed flowers lay between certain pages. Was the hand that plucked them withered as they? And what had he done with her love, he whom she had wooed so humbly and who was so riotous a spendthrift of great gifts? He had been only twenty. He had probably taken as a pastime all that was the fate of this full heart, and had used it and trampled it in a consciousness of wealth that neither counts nor reckons.

Deeper and deeper, as he read, a spear penetrated into the breast of Amadeus. The Telchines gained power over him. He turned pale and crimson. His fingers trembled, and his mouth shrivelled in dryness, and his head seemed to be full of needles. Had Christian entered then, he would have flung himself upon him in foaming hatred, to throttle or to stab him. Here was the unattainable, the eternally closed door. And a demon had hurled him down before it.

He sat long in dull brooding. Then he looked about furtively, and dropped the letters into his pocket. And then there arose in him the desire to destroy, to annihilate something. He chose books as sacrifices, and awaited Christian's coming with repressed excitement.

"It's practically all contemporary trash," he said drily, and
pointed. to the books. "Stories like tangled thread, utterly
confused, without beginning or end. If you've read one page,
you know a thousand. There are descriptions of manners
with a delight in what is common and mean. The emotions
riot like weeds, and the style is so noisy that you lose all perception. Love, love, love! That's one theme. And the other
is wretchedness! There are histories and memoirs, too. Sheer
gossip! The poems are empty rhymings by people with inflated
egos. There's popular philosophy—self-righteous twaddle. A
sincere parson's talk were more palatable. What is it for?
Reading is a good thing, if a real spirit absorbs me, and I
forget and lose myself in it. But the unspiritual has neither
honesty nor imagination; he is a thief and a swindler."

"Burn it, burn it!" Christian repeated, and sat down at
the other side of the room.

Amadeus went to the marble fire-place, which was so large
that a man could easily have lain down in it, and opened the
gates of brass. Then he carried the books there—one pile
after another, and heaped them on the flat stones. When he
had thrown them all in, he set fire to the pages of one book,
and lowered his head and watched the flames spread.

"You know that I am going to leave Christian's Rest,"
Christian said, turning to him. It had grown quite dark
now.

Voss nodded.

"I don't know for how long," Christian continued. "It
may be very long before I return."

Amadeus Voss said nothing.

"What are you going to do, Amadeus?" Christian asked
him.

Voss shrugged his shoulders. Involuntarily he pressed his
hand against the inner pocket in which lay the letters of the
unknown woman.

"It is dark and oppressive in the forester's house," said

Christian. "Won't you come and live here? I'll give the necessary orders at once."

" Don't make me a beggar with your alms, Christian Wahnschaffe," Voss answered. " If you were to give me the house, with all its forests and gardens, you would but rob me, and leave me poorer by so much."

" I don't understand that," said Christian.

Voss walked up and down. The carpet muffled his sturdy tread.

" You are far too passsionate, Amadeus," Christian said.

Amadeus stopped in front of a lectern that had been placed in a niché. Upon it lay the great Bible that Christian had bought. It was open. The flames of the burning books flared so brightly that he could read the words. For a space he read in silence. Then he took the book, and going nearer to the fire, sat down opposite Christian, and read aloud:

" Rejoice, O young man, in thy youth, and let thy heart cheer thee in the days of thy youth, and walk in the ways of thine heart and in the sight of thine eyes: but know thou that for all these things God will bring thee into judgment."

At the word, God, the almost unemphatic voice sounded like a bell.

" Remember now thy Creator in the days of thy youth, while the evil days come not, nor the years draw nigh, when thou shalt say, I have no pleasure in them; while the sun, or the light, or the moon, or the stars be not darkened, nor the clouds return after the rain: In the day when the keepers of the house shall tremble, and the strong men shall bow themselves, and the grinders cease because they are few, and those that look out of the windows be darkened, and the doors shall be shut in the streets; when the sound of the grinding is low, and he shall rise up at the voice of the bird, and all the daughters of music shall be brought low; also when they shall be afraid of that which is high, and fears shall be in the way, and the almond tree shall flourish, and the grasshopper shall be a

burden and desire shall fail: because man goeth to his long
home, and the mourners go about the street: or ever the silver
cord be loosed, or the golden bowl be broken, or the pitcher
be broken at the fountain, or the wheel broken at the
cistern." . . .

He stopped. Christian, who had seemed scarcely to listen,
had arisen and come nearer to the fire. Now he sat down on
the floor, with his legs crossed under him, and gazed with a
serene wonder into the flames.

"How beautiful is fire! " he said softly.

Speechlessly Amadeus Voss regarded him. Then he spoke
quite suddenly. "Let me go with you, Christian Wahnschaffe."

Christian did not take his eyes from the fire.

"Let me go with you," Voss said more insistently. "It is
possible that you may need me: it is certain that without you
I am lost. Darkness is in me and a demon. You alone break
the spell. I do not know why it is thus, but it is. Let me go
with you."

Christian replied: "Very well, Amadeus, you shall stay with
me. I want some one to stay with me."

Amadeus grew pale, and his lips quivered.

Christian said: "How beautiful is fire!"

And Amadeus murmured: "It devours uncleanness and
remains clean."

THE NAKED FEET

I

WITH her companion, Fräulein Stöhr, the Countess Brainitz travelled about the world.

She had been the guest of an incredibly aged Princess Neukirch at Berchtesgaden. But she grew to be immensely bored, and fled to Venice, Ravenna, and Florence. Armed with a Baedeker, and accompanied by a guide, she " did " the galleries, churches, basilicas, palaces, sarcophagi, and monuments, and her tirelessness reduced Fräulein Stöhr to despair.

She quarrelled with the gondoliers over their fare, with waiters over a tip, with shopkeepers over the price of their wares. She thought every coin a counterfeit, and in her terror of dirt and infection she touched no door-knob or chair, no newspaper and no one's hand. She washed herself repeatedly, screeched uninterruptedly, and by her appetite struck her companions at the table d'hôte with awe.

With rancour in her heart she left the land of miracles and of petty fraud. She visited her nephews, the brothers Stojenthin, in Berlin. They were charmed at her coming, and borrowed a thousand marks of her over the oysters and champagne. Then she proceeded to Stargard, to be with her sisters Hilde Stojenthin and Else von Febronius.

She was vastly amused at the middle-class ladies in Stargard, who curtsied to her as to a queen. At their teas she lorded it over them from the heights of a sofa covered with dotted calico. She entertained her devoutly attentive audience with stories of the great world. At times these anecdotes were of such a character that the judge's widow had to administer a warning pinch to the arm of her noble sister.

. Frau von Febronius had been ailing since the beginning of winter. Careless exposure on a sleigh drive had brought on an attack of pneumonia. The consequences threatened to be grave. The countess, who not only feared illness for herself but hated it in others, grew restive and talked of leaving.

"When my dear husband saw his end approaching, he sent me to Mentone," she told Fräulein Stöhr. "Stupid and devoid of understanding as he was—though not more so than most men—in this respect he showed a praiseworthy delicacy of feeling. I was simply not made to bear the sight of suffering. Charity is not among my gifts."

Fräulein Stöhr assumed a pastoral expression and cast her eyes to heaven. She knew her mistress sufficiently to realize that the anecdote of the dying count and the expedition to Mentone was a product of the imagination. She said: "Man should prepare himself in time for his latter end, Madame."

The countess was indignant. "My dear Stöhr, spare me your spiritual wisdom! It suits only times of trouble. Pastoral consolations are not to my taste. It is not your proper task to preach truths to me, but to offer me agreeable illusions."

One evening Frau von Febronius asked to see the countess. The latter went. But terror made her pale. She put on a hat, swathed her face in a veil and her hands in gloves. Sighing she sat down beside her sister's bed, and carefully measured the distance, so as to be out of reach of the patient's breath.

Frau von Febronius smiled indulgently. Her illness had smoothed the lines of petty care and sorrow from her face, and, among her white pillows, she looked strikingly like her daughter Letitia. "I'm sorry to trouble you, Marion," she began, "but I must talk to you. There's something that weighs on my mind, and I must confide in some one. The fact in question should be told to one who knows me, and should not be buried with me."

"I beseech you, Elsie, my poor darling, don't talk of graves

and such things," the countess exclaimed in a whining voice.
" My appetite will be gone for a week. If you'll only fling the
medicine bottles out of the window, and tell all quacks to go
to the devil, you'll be well by day after to-morrow. And, for
heaven's sake, don't make a confession. It reminds one of
quite dreadful things."

But Frau von Febronius went on: " It's no use, Marion.
I must tell you this. The reason I turn to you is because
you've really been so very good and kind to Letitia, and
because Hilde, sensible and faithful as she is, wouldn't quite
understand. Her notions are too conventional."

In whispers she now related the story of Letitia's birth. An
illness of his earlier years had deprived her husband of the hope
of posterity; but he had yearned for a son, a child. This
yearning had finally silenced all scruples and all contradictory
emotions to such an extent that he had chosen a congenial
stranger to continue his race. He had persuaded her, his
wife, whom he loved above all things, after a long struggle.
Finally she had yielded to his unheard-of demand. But when
the child was born, a progressive melancholy had seized upon
her husband. It had become incurable, and under its control
he had ruined his estate and in the end himself. He had felt
nothing of the happiness he had expected. He had, on the
contrary, always shown a contemptuous dislike of Letitia, and
had avoided her as far as possible.

" It doesn't surprise me a bit," the countess remarked.
" You were uncommonly naïve to be astonished. A strange
child is a strange child, no matter how it got into the nest.
But it's really like a fairy tale. I confess I underestimated
you. Such delightful sophistication! And who is the child's
father? Who is responsible for the life of that darling angel?
He deserves great credit for his achievement."

Frau von Febronius mentioned the name. The countess
screamed, and leaped up as though she had been stung.
" Crammon? Bernard von Crammon? " She clasped her

hands in agony. "Is that true? Aren't you dreaming? Consider, my dear! It must be the fever. Oh, certainly, it's sheer delirium. Take a little water, I beg of you, and then think carefully, and stop talking nonsense."

Frau von Febronius gazed at her sister in utter amazement. " Do you know him? " she asked.

The countess' voice was bitter. " Do I know him? I do. And tell me one more thing: Does this—this—creature know? Has he always known? "

" He knows. Two years ago he saw Letitia at our old home. Since that time he has known. But you act as if he were the fiend incarnate, Marion. Did you have a quarrel with him or what? You always exaggerate so! "

Excitedly the countess walked up and down. " He knows it, the wretch! He has always known it, the rogue! And such dissembling as he has practised! Such hypocrisy! The wretched rogue, I'll bring it home to him! I'll seek him out!" She turned to her sister. " Forgive me, Elsie, for letting my temperament run away with me. You are right. His name awakened an anger of some years' standing. My blood boils, I confess. He may have been a man of honour and a gentleman in his youth. He must have been, or you would never have consented to such an adventure. But I hesitate to say what he is to-day. He is still perfectly discreet; you need have no anxiety on that score. But I assert that even discretion has its limits. Where these are passed, decent people shake their heads, and virtue looks like mere baseness. *Voilà.*"

" All that you say is quite dark to me," Frau von Febronius replied wearily, " and I really haven't any desire to fathom it. I wanted to tell you this oppressive secret. Keep it to yourself. Never reveal it, except to prevent some misfortune, or to render Letitia a service. I don't quite see how either purpose will ever be served by a revelation. But it consoles me that one other human being, beside myself and that man, knows the truth."

The countess gazed thoughtfully at her sister. "Your life wasn't exactly a gay one, was it, Elsie?".

The sick woman answered: "No, hardly gay."

During the following days she rallied a little. Then came a relapse that left no room for hope. In the middle of March she died.

By this time the countess was already far away. Her goings and comings were as purposeless as ever. But she nursed a favourite vision now. Some day she would meet Crammon, confront him with her knowledge, avenge herself upon him, challenge him and annihilate him, in a word, enjoy a rich triumph. At times when she was alone, or even in the presence of Miss Stöhr, whom it astonished, she would suddenly wrinkle her childlike forehead, clench her little fists, and her shiny face would turn red as a lobster, and her violet-blue eyes blaze as for battle.

II

It was three o'clock in the morning when Felix Imhof left a party in the Leopoldstrasse, where there had been gaming for high stakes. He had won several thousand marks, and the gold coins clinked in the overcoat pocket into which he had carelessly stuffed them.

He had had a good deal to drink, too. His head was a bit heavy. At his first steps into the fresh air he reeled a little.

Nevertheless he was in no mood to go home. So he wandered into a coffee-house that was frequented by artists. He thought he might still find a few people with whom he could chat and argue. The day he had passed was not yet full enough of life for him. He wanted it brimming.

In the room, which was blue with smoke, there were only two men, the painter Weikhardt, who had recently returned from Paris, and another painter, who looked rather ragged and stared dejectedly at the table.

Felix Imhof joined the two. He ordered cognac and served

them, but, to his annoyance, the conversation would not get started. He got up and invited Weikhardt to walk with him. With contemptuous joviality he turned to the other: "Well, you old paint-slinger, your lamp seems about burned out! "

The man didn't stir. Weikhardt shrugged his shoulders, and said softly: "He has no money for bread and no place to sleep."

Felix Imhof plunged his hand into his pocket, and threw several gold coins on the table. The painter looked up. Then he gathered the gold. "Hundred and sixty marks," he said calmly. "Pay you back on the first."

Imhof laughed resoundingly.

. When they were in the street, Weikhardt said good-naturedly: "He believes every word of it. If he didn't absolutely believe it, he wouldn't have taken the money. There are still eleven days before the first—time for a world of illusions."

"It may be that he believes it," Imhof replied, with an unsteady laugh, "it may be. He even believes that he exists, and yet he's nothing but a melancholy corpse. O you painters, you painters! " he cried out into the silent night. "You have no feeling for life. Paint life! You're still sitting by a spinning-wheel, instead of at some mighty wheel of steel, propelled by a force of sixteen thousand horse-power. Paint my age for me, my huge delight in being! Smell, taste, see, and grasp that colossus! Make me feel that great rhythm, create my grandiose dreams. Give me life—my life and its great affirmation!"

Weikhardt said drily: "I have heard that talk before—between midnight and dawn. When the cock crows we all calm down again, and every man pulls the cart to which fate has hitched him."

Imhof stopped, and somewhat theatrically laid his hand on Weikhardt's shoulder. He gazed at him with his intensely black, bloodshot eyes. "I give you a commission herewith, Weikhardt," he said. "You have talent. You're the only

one with a mind above your palette./ Paint my portrait. I
don't care what it costs—twenty, fifty thousand. Doesn't
matter. Take your own time—two months or two years. But
show me—me—the innermost me. Take this vulture's nose,
this Hapsburg lip, these gorilla arms and spindle shanks, this
coat and this chapeau claque, and drag from it all the animat-
ing Idea. To hell with the accidents of my phiz, which looks
as though an unskilful potter had bungled it in the making.
Render my ambition, my restlessness, my inner tempo and
colourfulness, my great hunger and the time-spirit that is in
me. But you must hurry; for I am self-consumed. In a few
years I shall have burned out. My soul is tinder. Render this
process with the divine objectivity of art, and I'll reward you
like a Medici. But I must be able to see the flame, the flaring
up, the dying down, the quiver of it! I want to see it, even
if to make me see it you have to lash the whole tradition since
Raphael and Rubens into rags! "

"You are an audacious person," Weikhardt said, in his dry
way. "But have patience with us, and restrain your admiration for your particular century. I do not let the age over-
whelm me to the point of folly. I do not share the reverential
awe of speed and machinery that has seized upon many young
men like a new form of epilepsy. I haven't any attitude
of adoration toward seven-league boots, express trains, dread-
noughts, and inflated impressionism. I seek my gods elsewhere. I don't believe I'm the painter you're looking for.
Where were you? You've been travelling again? "

"I'm always on some road," Felix Imhof replied. "It's a
crazy sort of life. Let me tell you how I spent the last five
days. Monday night I went to Leipzig. Tuesday morning
at nine I had a conference with some literary people in regard
to the founding of a new review. Splendid fellows—keen critics and intellectual Jacobins, every one of them. Then I went
to an exhibition of majolicas. Bought some charming things.
At noon I left for Hamburg. On the train I read two manu-

scripts and a drama, all by a young genius who'll startle the world. That evening attended a meeting of the directorate of the East African Development Corporation. Festivities till late that night. Slept two hours, then proceeded to Olden-burg to a reunion of the retired officers of my old regiment. Talked, drank, and even danced, though the party was stag. Six o'clock in the morning rushed to Quackenbrück, a shabby little country town on the moors, where the officers had arranged for a little horse race. My beast was beaten by a head. Drove to the station and took a train for Berlin. Attended to business next morning in the Ministry of Foreign Affairs, interviewed agents, witnessed a curious operation in the clinic, made a flying-trip to Johannisthal, where a new aeroplane was tried out; went to the Deutsches Theater that evening, and saw a marvellous performance of 'Peer Gynt.' Drank the night away with the actors. Next morning Dresden. Confer-ence with two American friends. Home to-day. Next week won't be very different, nor the one after that. I ought to sleep more; that's the only thing." He waved his thick bam-boo cane in air.

"It is enough to frighten any one," said Weikhardt, who took more comfort in the contrast between his own phlegm and his companion's excitement. "How about your wife? What does she say to your life? She was pointed out to me recently. She doesn't look as if she would let herself be pushed aside."

Imhof stopped again. He stood there, with his legs far apart and his trunk bent forward, and rested on his cane. "My wife!" he said. "What a sound that has! I have a wife. Ah, yes. I give you my word, my dear man, I should have clean forgotten it to-night, if you hadn't reminded me. It's not her fault, to be sure. She's a born Wahnschaffe; that means something! But somehow . . . God knows what it is—the damned rush and hurry, I suppose. You're quite right. She's not the sort to be neglected or pushed to the wall. She

creates her own spaces, and within these "—he described
great circles in the air with his cane—" she dwells, cool to her
fingertips, tense as a wire of steel. A magnificent character—
energetic, but with a strong sense for decorative effects. She's
to be respected, my dear man."

Weikhardt had no answer ready for this outburst. ·Its
mixture of boasting and irony, cynicism and ecstatic excitement disarmed and wearied him at once. They had reached
a side street, which led to the Englischer Garten, and in which
stood the painter's little house. He wanted to say good-night.
But Imhof, who seemed still unwilling to be alone, asked:
" Are you working at anything? "

Weikhardt hesitated before answering. That was enough
to make Imhof accompany him. The sky grew grey with dawn.
Felix Imhof recited softly to himself:

> " Where the knights repose, and streaming
> Banners fold at last their gleaming,
> Towers rise to the way-farers,
> And the wanderers seek a spring;
> And the lovely water-bearers
> Lift a goblet to the dreaming
> Shadow of the fleeing king."

Weikhardt, who would not yield to Imhof in a knowledge or
love of the poet Stefan George, continued the quotation in a
caressing voice:

> " With a smile serene he watches,
> Yet flits on with shyer seeming,
> For beneath him fades the height,
> And he fears all mortal touches,
> And he almost dreads the light."

They entered the studio. Weikhardt lit the lamp, and let
its glow fall upon a picture that was not quite completed. It
was a Descent from the Cross.

"Rather old-fashioned, isn't it?" Weikhardt asked, with a sly smile. He had grown pale.

Imhof looked. He was a connoisseur through and through. No other had his eye. The painters knew it.

The picture, which reminded one of the visionary power as well as of the brushwork of El Greco, was bizarre in composition, intense in movement, and filled with an ecstatic passion. The forms of an old master, through which the painter had expressed himself, were but an appearance. The vision had been flung upon the canvas with a burning splendour. The figures had nothing old-fashioned about them; there was no cliché; they were like clouds, and the clouds like architecture. There were no concrete things. There was a chaos, which drew meaning and order only from the concentrated perceptions of the beholder.

Felix Imhof folded his hands. "To have such power," he murmured. "Great God, to have the power to project such things!"

Weikhardt lowered his head. He attributed little significance to these words. A few days before he had stood in front of his canvas, and he had imagined that a peasant was standing beside him—an old peasant or any other simple man of the people. And it had seemed to him that this peasant, this humble man, who knew nothing of art, had kneeled down to pray. Not from piety, but because what he saw had in its own character overwhelmed him.

Almost rudely Imhof turned to the painter and said: "The picture is mine. Under all circumstances. Mine. I must have it. Good-night." With his top hat set at a crazy angle, and his sleepless, dissipated face, he was a vision to frighten one.

At last he went home.

Next day Crammon informed him of his arrival in Munich. He had come because Edgar Lorm was about to give a series of performances there.

III

Christian considered how he could convey money to Amadeus Voss without humiliating him. Since it was agreed that they travel together, it was necessary for Voss to have the proper outfit; and he possessed nothing but what he had on.

Amadeus Voss understood the situation. The social abyss yawned between them. Both men gazed helplessly into it, one on each shore.

In his own heart Voss mocked at the other's weakness, and at the same time loved him for his noble shame—loved him with that emotional self that had been humiliated, estranged from the world, stamped on and affronted from his youth on. He shuddered at the prospect of sitting in the forester's house again with perished hopes and empty hands, and letting his soul bleed to death from the wounds of unattainable lures. He brooded, regarding Christian almost with hatred. What will he do? How will he conquer the difficulty?

Time passed. The matter was urgent.

On the last afternoon Christian said: "The hours crawl. Let us play cards." He took a pack of French cards from a drawer.

"I haven't touched a card in my life," Voss said.

"That doesn't matter," Christian replied. "All you need do is to tell red from black. I'll keep the bank. Bet on a colour. If you've bet on red and I turn up red, you've won. How much will you risk? Let us start with one taler."

"Very well, here it is," said Voss, and put the silver coin on the table. Christian shuffled the cards and drew one. It was red.

"Risk your two talers now," Christian advised. "Novices have luck."

Voss won the two talers. The betting continued. Once or twice he lost. But finally he had won thirty talers.

"Now you take the bank," Christian proposed. He was secretly pleased that his ruse was working so well.

He bet ten talers and lost. Then fifteen, then twenty, then thirty, and lost again. He risked a hundred marks, two hundred, five hundred, more and more, and still lost. Voss's cheeks turned hectic red, then white as chalk: his hands trembled; his teeth rattled. He was seized by a terror that his luck would change, but he was incapable of speech or of asking for an end of the game. The bank notes were piled up in front of him. In half an hour he had won over four thousand marks.

Christian had previously marked the cards in a manner that no inexperienced eye could detect. He knew exactly which colour Voss would find. But the curious thing was that, though he forgot occasionally to watch the markings, Voss still won.

Christian got up. "We're in a hurry," he said. "You must get ready for our journey, Amadeus."

Voss was overwhelmed by the change which had come over his life within a few minutes. If a spark of suspicion glowed in his soul, he turned away from it, and plunged into rich dreams.

The motor took them to Wiesbaden, and there, with Christian's help, Amadeus bought garments and linen, boots, hats, gloves, cravats, a razor, a manicure set, and a trunk.

At ten o'clock that evening they sat in the sleeper. "Who am I now?" asked Amadeus Voss. He looked about him with a curious and violent glance, and pushed the blond hair from his forehead. "What do I represent now? Give me an office and a title, Christian Wahnschaffe, in order that I may know who I am."

Christian watched the other's excitement with quiet eyes. "Why should you think yourself another to-night or changed from yesterday?" he asked in surprise.

IV

Eva Sorel passed through the countries of Europe—a comet leaving radiance in its wake.

Her day was thickly peopled. It needed the flexibility of an experienced practitioner to test and grant the many-sided demands upon her. Monsieur Chinard, her impresario, served admirably in this capacity. Only Susan Rappard treated the man morosely. She called him a Figaro *pris à la retraite*.

In addition, the dancer employed a courier and a secretary.

Several of her adorers had been following her from city to city for months. They were Prince Wiguniewski, a middle-aged American, named Bradshaw, the Marquis Vicente Tavera, of the Spanish legation at Petrograd, Herr Distelberg, a Jewish manufacturer of Vienna, and Botho von Thüngen, a very young Hanoverian, a student in his second year.

These, as well as others who drifted with the group from time to time, neglected their callings, friends, and families. They needed the air that Eva breathed in order to breathe themselves. They had the patience of petitioners and the optimism of children. They were envious of one another's advantage, knowledge, and witticisms. Each noted with malicious delight if another blundered. They vied zealously for the friendship of Susan, and made her costly presents, in order that she might tell them what her mistress had said and done, how she had slept, in what mood she had awakened, and when she would receive.

Since Count Maidanoff had joined Eva's circle they had all been profoundly depressed. They knew, everybody knew, who was concealed behind this pseudonym. Against him—mighty and greatly feared—no one hoped to prevail.

Eva consoled them with a smile. They counted for nothing in her eyes. "How are my chamberlains?" she asked Susan, "how do my time-killers kill their time?"

But she was not quite as light and serene of soul as she had once been.

V

' She had made the acquaintance of Count Maidanoff in Trouville. . She had been presented to him on the promenade, and a far-flung circle of fashionables had looked on. Careful murmurs had blended with the thunder of the sea.

She came home and grasped Susan by the shoulders. " Don't let me go out again," she said, pale and breathing heavily. " I don't want to look into those eyes again. I must not meet that man any more."

Susan exhausted herself promising this. She did not know who had awakened such horror in her mistress. " Elle est un peu folle," she said to M. Labourdemont, the secretary, " mais ce grain de folie est le meilleur de l'art."

The next day Count Maidanoff announced his formal call, and had to be received.

The conventional act of homage, to which he was entitled by his birth, he repaid with a personal and sincere one.

His speech was heavy and slow. He seemed to despise the words, the use of which caused him such exertion. Sometimes he stopped in the middle of a sentence and frowned in annoyance. Between his eyebrows there were two straight, deep lines that made his face permanently sombre. His smile began with an upward curl of the lips, and quivered down into his thin, colourless beard, like the effect of a muscular paralysis.

He went straight and without circumlocution toward his purpose. It was commonly the office of his creatures to clear the road toward his amatory adventures. By doing the wooing himself in this instance he desired to single out its object by an act of especial graciousness.

The cool timidity of the dancer had pleased him at first. Fear was to him the most appealing quality in men. But Eva's repressed chill in the face of his courteous proposals confused him. His eyes became empty, he looked bored, and asked for permission to light a cigarette.

He talked of Paris, of a singer at the Grand Opera there. Then he became silent, and sat there like some one who has all eternity ahead of him. When he arose and took his leave, he looked as though he were really asleep.

With arms crossed Eva walked about the room till evening. During the night she picked up books which she did not read, thought of things that were indifferent to her, called Susan only to torment her, wrote a letter to Ivan Becker and tore it up again. Finally, in spite·of the driving rain, she wrapped herself in a cloak and went out on the terrace.

Maidanoff repeated his visit. At the inevitable point Eva conveyed to him with great delicacy that his expectations were doomed to disappointment. He looked at her with slothful, oblique glances, and condescended to smile. What nonsense, his morose frown seemed thereupon to say.

Suddenly he opened his eyes very wide. The effect was uncanny. Eva bent her head forward in expectation, and spread out her fingers.

He said: " You have the most beautiful hands I have ever seen, To have seen them is to desire to know their touch."

Three hours later she left Trouville, accompanied by Susan and by M. Labourdemont, and travelled to Brussels, where Ivan Becker was staying.

VI

Becker lived in the suburbs, in a lonely house that stood in a neglected garden. He received her in a tumbled room that was as big as a public hall. Two candles burned on the table.

He looked emaciated, and moved about restlessly, even after he had bidden Eva welcome.

She told him with some haste of her engagement in Russia, which she was about to fulfil, and asked whether he had any commissions to give her. He said that he had not.

" The Grand Duke was attentive to me," she said, and looked at him expectantly.

He nodded. After a little he sat down and said: " I must tell you a dream I had; or, rather, a hallucination, for I lay with my eyes wide open. Listen!

" About a richly laid board there sat five or six young women. They were in evening dress, with very deep décolletage, and laughed wildly and drank champagne. With frivolous plays on words and seductive gestures, they turned to one who sat at the head of the table. But that one had no form: he was like a lump of dough or clay. The footmen trembled when they approached him, and the women grew pale under their rouge when he addressed them. In the middle of the gleaming cloth there lay, unnoticed by any one, a corpse. It was covered with fruits, and from its breast, between the peaches and the grapes, projected the handle of a dagger. Blood trickled through the joints of the table and tapped in dull drops on the carpet.

" The meal came to an end. All were in a wildly exuberant mood. Then that formless one arose, grasped one of the women, drew her close to him, and demanded music. And while the thunderous music resounded, that lump expanded and grew, and a skull appeared on it, and eyes within that skull, and these eyes blazed in a measureless avidity. The woman that he held became paler and paler, and sought to free herself from his embrace. But long, thin arms grew out of his trunk. And with these he pressed her so silently and so cruelly that she began to moan and turn blue. And her body snapped in two in the middle. Lifeless she lay in his arms, and nothing seemed left of her but her dress. Then the corpse, that lay with pierced breast amid the fruit and sweets, raised its head, and said with closed eyes: ' Give her back to me.'

" Suddenly many people streamed into that room—peasants and factory workers, soldiers and ragged women, Jews and Jewesses. An old man with a white beard said to the formless

one: ' Give me back my daughter.' Others who stood behind
screamed frantically: ' Give us our daughters, our brides, our
sisters.' Then peasants pressed forward, and bent to the earth
their melancholy faces, and said: ' Give us our lands and our
forests.' Over all rose the piercing voices of mothers: ' Give
us our sons, our sons.' The formless one receded step by step
into empty space. But even as he receded he assumed a more
clearly defined shape. The face, the hands, and the garments
were brown as though encrusted with rust or dried- slime.
The features of the face gave not the least notion of that
being's character, and precisely this circumstance heightened
the despair of all beyond endurance. They cried without ceas-
ing: ' Our brothers! Our sons! Our sisters! Our lands!
Our forests, O thou accursed unto all eternity! ' "

Eva said no word.

Ivan Becker rested his head upon his hand. " One thing is
certain. He has caused so many tears to be shed, that were
they gathered into one lake, that lake were deeper than the
Kremlin is tall; the blood that he has caused to flow would
be a sea in which all Moscow could be drowned."

He walked to and fro a few times. Then he sat down again
and continued: " He is the creator and instigator of an incomparable reign of terror. Our living souls are his victims. Wherever there is a living soul among us, it becomes his prey. Six
thousand intellectuals were deported during the past year.
Where he sets his foot, there is death. Ruins and fields full of
murdered men mark his path. These expressions are not to be
taken metaphorically but quite, quite literally. It was he who
created the organization of the united nobility, which holds
the country in subjection, and is a modern instrument of torture on the hugest scale. The pogroms, the murderous Finnish
expedition, the torturing of the imprisoned, the atrocities of the
Black Hundreds—all these are his work. He wastes untold
millions from the public treasury; he pardons the guilty and
condemns the innocent. He throttles the spirit of man and

extinguishes all light. He is all-powerful. He is God's living adversary. I bow before him."

Eva looked up in astonishment. But Becker did not observe her.

"There is no one who knows him. No one is able to see through him. I believe he is satiated. Nothing affects him any longer except some stimulus of the epidermis. The story is told that sometimes he has two beautiful naked women fight in his presence. They have daggers and must lacerate each other. One must bow down before that."

"I do not understand," Eva whispered wide-eyed. "Why bow?"

Becker shook his head warningly, and his monotonous voice filled the room once more. "He has found everything between heaven and earth to be for sale—friendship, love, the patience of a people, justice, the Church, peace and war. First he commands or uses force; that goes without saying. What these cannot conquer he buys. It seems, to be sure, that pressure and force can accomplish things that would defy and wreck ordinary mortals. While hunting bears in the Caucasus his greatest favourite, Prince Szilaghin, fell ill. His fever was high and he was carried into the hut of some Circassians. Szilaghin, by the way, is a creature of incredible corruption—only twenty years old and of astonishing though effeminate beauty. To win a bet he once disguised himself as a cocotte, and spent a night in the streets and amusement resorts of Petrograd. In the morning he brought back a handful of jewels, including a magnificent bracelet of emeralds, that had been given him as tributes to his mere beauty. It was he who fell ill in the mountains. A mounted messenger was sent to the nearest village, and dragged back with him an old, ignorant country doctor. The Grand Duke pointed to his favourite writhing in delirium, and said to the old man: 'If he dies, you die too.' Every hour the physician administered a draught to the sick man. In the intervals he kneeled trembling by the bed and prayed. As fate would have it, Szilaghin recovered consciousness toward morning, and gradually became well. The Grand Duke was convinced that the inexorable alternative which he had offered the old physician had released mysterious forces in him and worked something like a miracle. Thus he does not feel nature as a barrier to his power."

A swift vividness came into Eva's features. She got up and walked to the window and opened it. A storm was shaking the trees. The ragged clouds in the sky, feebly illuminated by moonlight and arching the darkness, were like a picture of Ruysdael. Without turning she said: "You say no one can penetrate him. There is nothing to penetrate. There is an abyss, dark and open."

"It may be that you are right and that he is like an abyss," Ivan Becker answered softly, "but who will have the courage to descend into it?"

Another silence fell upon them. "Speak, Ivan, speak out at last the thought in your mind!" Eva cried out into the night. And every fibre of her, from the tips of her hair to the hem of her gown, was tense with listening.

But Becker did not answer. Only a terrible pallor came over his face.

Eva turned around. "Shall I throw myself into his arms in order to create a new condition in the world?" she asked proudly and calmly. "Shall I increase his opinion of the things that can be bought among men by the measure of my worth? Or do you think that I could persuade him to exchange the scaffold for the confessional and the hangman's axe for a flute?"

"I have not spoken of such a thing; I shall not speak of it," said Ivan Michailovitch with solemnly raised hand.

"A woman can do many things," Eva continued. "She can give herself away, she can throw herself away, she can sell herself, she can conceal indifference and deny her hatred. But against horror she is powerless; that tears the heart in two.

Show me a way; make me insensitive to the horror of it; and I shall chain your tiger."

"I know of no way," answered Ivan Michailovitch. "I know none, for horror is upon me too. May God, the Eternal, enlighten you."

The loneliness of the room, of the house, of the storm-ploughed garden, became as the thunder of falling boulders.

VII

Her friends awaited developments in suspense. None expected her to offer Maidanoff any serious resistance. When she seemed to hold out, her subtlety was admired. Paris predicted a radiant future for her. Much public curiosity centred upon her, and many newspaper columns were devoted to her.

When she arrived in Russia it was clear that the authorities and officials had received special instructions. No queen could have been treated with more subtle courtesy. Palatial rooms in a hotel were in readiness and adorned. A slavish humility surrounded her.

When the Grand Duke called, she begged him to rescind the orders that made her his debtor. He devoured her words with a frosty and lurking expression, but remained inactive. She was indignant at this slothfulness of a rigid will, this deaf ear that listened so greedily.

His contempt of mankind had something devastating in it. His slow eyes seemed to say: Man, thou slimy worm, grovel and die!

In his presence Eva felt her thoughts to be so loud at times that she feared he would perceive them.

She ventured to oppose and judge him. A young girl, Vera Cheskov, had shot the governor of Petrograd. Eva had the courage to praise that deed. The Grand Duke's answer was smooth, and he left quite unruffled. She challenged him more vigorously. Her infinitely expressive body vibrated in rhythms of bitterness and outrage. She melted in grief, rage, and sympathy.

He watched her as one would watch a noble beast at its graceful antics and said: "You are extraordinary, Madame. I cannot tell what wish of yours I would leave ungranted for the reward of winning your love." He said that in a deep voice, which was hoarse. He had also a higher voice, which had a grinding sound like that of rusty hinges.

Eva's shoulders quivered. His iron self-sufficiency reflected no image of her or her influence. Against it all forces were shattered.

Twice she saw him change countenance and give a start. The first time was when she told him of her German descent. An inbred hatred against all Germans and everything German filled him. An evil mockery glared in his face. He determined not to believe her and dropped the subject.

And the second time was when she spoke of Ivan Michailovitch Becker. She could not help it; she had to bring that name to the light. It was her symbol and talisman.

A glance like a whip's lash leaped out of those slothful eyes. The two deep grooves between the eyebrows stretched like the antennæ of an insect. A diagonal groove appeared and formed with the others a menacing cross. The face became ashen.

Susan was impatient. She urged her on and lured her on. "Why do you hesitate?" she said to her mistress one evening. "So near the peak one cannot go back. Remember our dreams in Toledo! We thought they were insolent then. Reality puts us to shame. Take what is given you. Never will your sweet, little dancing feet win a greater prize."

Eva walked in a circle about the rug. "Be quiet," she said thoughtfully and threateningly, "You don't know what you are advising me to do."

Crouching near the fire-place, Susan's lightless, plum-like eyes followed her mistress. "Are you afraid?" she asked with a frown.

" I believe I am afraid," Eva replied.

" Do you remember the sculptor whom we visited in Meudon last winter? He showed us his work, and you two talked art. He said: ' I mustn't be afraid of the marble; the marble must be afraid of me.' You almost kissed him in gratitude for those words. Don't be afraid now. You are the stronger."

Eva stood still, and sighed: " Cette maladie, qu'on appelle la sagesse! "

Then Susan went to the piano-forte, and with her fluttering angularity of movement began to play a Polonaise of Chopin. Eva listened for a while. Then she went up to Susan from behind, tapped her shoulder, and said, as the playing ceased, with a dark, strange cooing in her voice:

" If it must be, I shall first live one summer of love, the like of which has not been seen on earth. Do not speak, Susan. Play on, and do not speak."

Susan looked up, and shook her puzzled head.

VIII

On the day of Eva's last appearance in Petrograd, a well laid high explosive mine blew up the central building of the Agricultural Exposition.

The plot had been aimed at the person of the Grand Duke. His visit had been expected, the order in which he would inspect the buildings had been carefully mapped out. A slight mal-adjustment in the machinery of his car delayed him and his train a few minutes beyond the precisely fixed hour.

At the very moment when he put his foot on the first step of the building, a terrific crash resounded. The sky disappeared behind fume and fragments. Several manufacturers and bureaucrats, who had officiously hurried ahead, as well as ten or twelve workingmen, were killed. The air pressure smashed the window panes in all the houses within a mile of the spot.

For a while the Grand Duke stood quite still. Without

curiosity or fear, but with an indescribably sombre look, he surveyed the devastation. When he turned to go, the great crowds who had streamed thither melted back silently at his approach. They left him a broad path through which his abnormally long legs, accompanied by the clinking of his sword, strode with the steps of a sower.

For her final performance Eva had selected the rôle of the fettered and then liberated Echo, in the pantomime called The Awakening of Pan. It had always created enthusiasm; but this time she celebrated an unparalleled triumph.

She danced a dance of freedom and redemption, that affected with complete immediacy the nerves of the thronging audiences, and released the tensions of the day of their lives. There was a present and significant eloquence in the barbaric defiance, the fiery terror of the pursued. Then came her sudden rallying, her heroic determination, her grief over a first defeat, her toying with the torch of vengeance, her jubilant welcome of a rising dawn.

The curtain dropped, and the twenty-five hundred people sat as though turned to stone. Innumerable glances sought the box of the Grand Duke and found those slothful, unseeing eyes of his. They saw the slightness and disproportionate length of his body, the sinewy, bird-like neck above the round collar of his uniform, the thin beard, the bumpy forehead, and felt the atmosphere that rolled silently out from him and dwelled in his track—the atmosphere of a million-atomed death. And in the midst of these were those slothful eyes.

Then the applause broke out. Distinguished ladies contorted their bodies, toothless old men yelled like boys, sophisticated experts of the theatre climbed on their seats and waved. When Eva appeared the noise died down. For ten seconds nothing was heard but the sound of breathing and the rustle of garments.

She looked into that gleaming sea of faces. The folds of her white Greek garment were still as marble. Then the storm of

applause burst out anew. Over the balustrade of the gallery
a girl bent and stretched out her arms, and cried with a sob in
her voice, that rose above all the plaudits: "You have understood us, little soul!"

Eva did not understand the Russian words. But it was not
necessary. She looked up, and their sense was clear to her.

IX

At midnight she appeared, as she had consented to do, in
the palace of Prince Fyodor Szilaghin.

So soon as she was seen, a respectful murmur and then a
silence surrounded her. Bearers of the most ancient names
were assembled, the most beautiful women of society and of the
court, and the representatives of foreign powers. Several
gentlemen had already formed a group about her, when Fyodor
Szilaghin approached, kissed her hand reverently, and drew her
skilfully from the group.

She passed through several rooms at his side. He did his
best to fascinate her and succeeded in holding her attention.

There was not a touch of banality about him. His gestures
and words were calculated to produce a desired effect with the
utmost coolness and subtlety. When he spoke he lowered his
eyes a little. The ease and fullness of speech that is characteristic of all Russians had something iridescent in his case.
An arrogant and almost cynical consciousness of the fact that
he was handsome, witty, aloof, mysterious, and much desired
never left him. His eyebrows had been touched with kohl,
his lips with rouge. The dull blackness of his hair threw into
striking relief the transparent pallor of his beardless face.

"I find it most remarkable, Madame," he said in a voice of
unfathomable falseness, "that your art has not to us Slavs the
oversophistication that is characteristic of most Western artists.
It is identical with nature. It would be instructive to know
the paths by which, from so different a direction, you reached
the very laws and forms on which our national dances as well

as our modern orchestral innovations are based. Undoubtedly you are acquainted with both."

" I am," Eva answered, " and what I have seen is most uncommon. It has power and character and enthusiasm."

" Enthusiasm and perhaps something more—wild ecstasy," said the prince, with a significant smile. " Without that there is no great creation in the world. Do you not believe that Christ shared such ecstasy? As for me, I cannot be satisfied with the commonly accepted figure of a gentle and gently harmonious Christ."

" It is a new point of view. It is worth thinking about," Eva said with kindly tolerance.

" However that may be," Szilaghin went on, " among us all things are still in the process of becoming—the dance as well as religion. I do not hesitate to name these two in one breath. They are related as a red rose is to a white. When I say that we are still becoming, I mean that we have yet discovered no limits either of good or evil. A Russian is capable of committing the most cruel murder, and of shedding tears, within the next hour, at the sound of a melancholy song. He is capable of all wildness, excess, and horror, but also of magnanimity and self-abnegation. No transformation is swifter or more terrible than his, from hate to love, love to hate, happiness to despair, faithfulness to treachery, fear to temerity. If you trust him and yield yourself to him, you will find him pliant, high-souled, and infinitely tender. Disappoint and maltreat him—he will plunge into darkness and be lost in the darkness. He can give, give, give, without end or reflection, to the point of fanatical selflessness. Not until he is hurled to the uttermost depths of hopelessness, does the beast in him awaken and crash into' destruction all that is about him." The prince suddenly stood still. " Is it indiscreet to ask, Madame, where you will pass the month of May? I am told you intend to go to the sea-shore." He had said these words in a changed tone, and regarded Eva expectantly.

The question came to her like an attack from ambush.

Insensibly they had left the rooms destined for the guest and passed into the extensive conservatories. Labyrinthine paths, threading innumerable flowers and shrubs, led in all directions. A dim light reigned, and where they stood in a somewhat theatrical isolation, thousands of ghostly orchids exhaled a breathless fragrance.

Skilfully and equivocally chosen as they were, the sense and purport of Szilaghin's words were very clear to Eva. Yet she was tempted to oppose her own flexibility to his eel-like smoothness of mind, despite the hidden threat of the situation. She assumed a smile, as impenetrable as Szilaghin's forehead and large pupils, and answered: " Yes; I am going to Heyst. I must rest. Life in this land of hidden madmen has wearied me. It is too bad that I must be deprived, dear Prince, of a mentor and sage like yourself."

Suddenly Szilaghin dropped on one knee, and said softly: " My master and friend beseeches you through me for the favour of being near you wherever you may elect to go. He insists on no exact time, but awaits your summons. I know neither the degree nor the cause of your hesitation, dear lady, but what pledge do you demand, what surety, for the sincerity of a feeling that avoids no test and stops at no sacrifice? "

"Please rise, prince," Eva commanded him. She stepped back a pace and stretched out her arms in a delicate gesture of unwilling intimacy. " You are a spendthrift of yourself at this moment. Please rise."

"Not until you assure me that I shall be the bearer of good news. Your decision is a grave one. Clouds are gathering and awaiting a wind that may disperse them. Processions are on the roads praying to avert an evil fate. I am but a single, but a chance messenger. May I rise now? "

Eva folded her arms across her bosom, and retreated to the very wall of hanging flowers. She became aware of the mighty

naked seriousness of fate. "Rise," she said, with lowered
and twice did fire and pallor alternate on her cheeks.
.laghin arose and smiled, swiftly breathing. Again, in
silent reverence, he carried her hand to his lips. Then he led
her, subtly chatting as before, back among the other guests.

It was twelve hours after this that Christian received the
telegram which called him to Berlin.

X

Edgar Lorm played to crowded houses in Munich. His
popularity was such that he had to prolong his stay.

It pleased Crammon enormously and puffed him up. He
walked about as though he were the sole nurse of all this
glory.

One day he was at a tea given by a literary lady. In a corner
arose laughter that was obviously directed at him. He was
amused when he discovered that the whispering group gathered
there believed firmly that he was copying Lorm's impersonation
of the Misanthrope.

Felix Imhof writhed in laughter when he heard the story.
"There's something very attractive in the notion to people who
don't really know you," he said to Crammon. "It's far more
likely that it's the other way around, and that Lorm created his
impersonation by copying you."

This interpretation was very flattering. Crammon smiled in
appreciation of it. Unconsciously he deepened the lines of misanthropy in his chubby ecclesiastical face. When Lorm had
his picture taken as Alceste, Crammon took up his stand behind
the camera, and gazed steadily at the ripe statuesqueness of the
actor's appearance.

It was his intention to learn. The rôle which had been
assigned him in the play of the actor's life—the play that
lasted from nine o'clock every morning until eleven at night
—began to arouse his dissatisfaction. He desired it to be less
episodic. It seemed to him that Lorm, the director of this

particular play, should be persuaded to change the cast. He told Lorm so quite frankly. For the actor was no longer to him, as in the days of his youth, the crown and glory of human existence and the vessel of noblest emotions, but a means to an end. Nowadays one was forced to learn of Lorm, to conceal one's true feelings impenetrably, to gather all one's energy for the moment of one's cue, to be thrifty of one's self, bravely to wear a credible mask, and thus to assure each situation of a happy ending.

So Crammon said: "I've always had rather pleasant relations with my partners. I can truly say that I'm an obliging colleague and have always stolen away into the background when it was their turn to have their monologues or great scenes in the centre of the stage. But two of them, the young lover and the heroine, have undoubtedly abused my good nature. They've gradually shoved me out of the play entirely. To their own hurt, too. The action promised to be splendid. Since I've been shoved into the wings, it threatens to be lost in the sand. It annoys me."

Edgar Lorm smiled. "It seems to me rather that the playwright is at fault than those two," he answered. "And no doubt it's a mistake in construction. No experienced man of the theatre would dispense with a character like yourself."

. "Prosit," said Crammon, and lifted his glass. They were sitting late in the Ratskeller.

"One must await developments," Lorm continued. The whole charade amused him immensely. "In the works of good authors you sometimes find unexpected turns of the action. You mustn't scold till the final curtain."

Crammon murmured morosely. "It's taking a long time. Some day soon I'm going to mount the stage and find out in which act we are. I may make an extempore insertion."

"For what particular line have you been engaged anyhow?" Lorm inquired. "Man of the world, character parts, or heavy father?"

Crammon shrugged his shoulders. The two men looked seriously at each other. A pleasant mood gleamed about the actor's narrow lips. "How long is it since we've seen each other, old boy?" he said, and threw his arm affectionately over Crammon's shoulder. "It must be years. Until recently I had a secretary who, whenever a letter came from you, would lay it on my pillow at night. He meant that action to express something like this: Look, Lorm, people aren't the filthy scamps you always call them. Well, he was an idealist who had been brought up on chicory, potatoes, and herring. You find that sort once in a while. As for you, my dear Crammon, you've put on flesh. You're comfortable and compact in that nice tight skin of yours. I'm still lean and feed on my own blood."

"My fat is only a stage property," said Crammon sadly. "The inner me is untouched."

XI

Whenever Lorm played, Judith Imhof was in the theatre. But she went neither with her husband nor with Crammon. They broke in upon her mood. She cared very little for Crammon at any time. Unless he was very jocular, he seemed to her insufferable.

She sat in the stalls, and in the entr'actes waved graciously and calmly to Felix and Crammon in their box. She was careless of the amazement of her acquaintances. If any one had the temerity to ask why she sat alone, she answered, "Imhof is annoyed when another is not pleased with something that arouses his enthusiasm. So we go on different paths."

Inevitably the curious person would ask next: "Then you don't care for Lorm?" Whereupon she would reply: "Not greatly. He forces me to take a certain interest; but I resent that. I think he's terribly overrated."

One day a lady of her acquaintance asked her whether she was happy in her marriage. "I don't know," she answered, and laughed. "I haven't any exact conception of what people mean by happiness." Her friend then asked her why she had married. "Very simply," she replied, "because being a young girl got to be such an undelightful situation that I sought to escape from it as soon as possible." The lady wanted to know whether she didn't, then, love her husband. "My dear woman," Judith said, "love! There's nothing so mischievous as the loose way in which people use that word. Most people, I believe, pretend quite shamelessly when they talk about it, and defend it simply because they don't want to admit that they've been taken in. It's exactly like the king's new clothes in the old fable. Every one acts mightily important and enthusiastic, and won't admit that the poor king is naked to the winds."

Another time she was asked whether she didn't yearn to have a child. "A child!" she cried out. "Horrors! Shall I bring forth more food for the worms?"

Once, in company, the conversation turned to the question of one's sensitiveness to pain. Judith asserted that she could bear any bodily torment without moving a muscle. She was not believed. She procured a long, golden needle, and bade one of the gentlemen pierce her whole arm with it. When he refused in horror, she asked another of stronger nerves who obeyed her. And really she did not twitch a muscle. The blood gathered in a little pool. She smiled.

Felix Imhof could weep at the least excuse. When he had a sick headache he wept. She despised this in him.

The actor took hold of her. She resisted in vain. The spell he cast over her grew ever firmer, more indissoluble. She brooded over it. Was it his transformations that attracted her so?

Although he was forty, his body was as elegent and flexible as polished steel. And like the ringing of steel was his voice. The words were sparks. Under his tread the wooden stage became a palæstra. Nothing clung or whined or crept. Everything was tension, progression, verve, the rhythm of storms. There was no inner weight or weariness. Bugles soared. She agreed with Felix when he said: " There is more of the true content of our age in this man than in all the papers, editorials, pamphlets, and plethoric three-deckers that the press has spewed forth within the past twenty years. He has crowned the living word and made it our king."

She was impatient to make the personal aquaintance of Lorm. Crammon became the intermediary, and brought the actor to her house. She was amazed at the homeliness of the man's face. She resented his insignificant, tilted nose and his mediocre forehead. But the spell was not broken. She desired to overlook these details and succeeded. They represented but another transformation of that self which she believed to be so infinitely varied.

He revealed himself as an epicure, with remnants of that greed which marks the man, who has risen from humble things. The delights of the table induced in him outbursts of noisy merriment. Over the oysters and the champagne he discussed his worst enemies with benevolence.

He was so changeable of mood that it was exhausting to associate with him. No one opposed him, and this lack of opposition had produced an empty space about him that had almost the guise of loneliness. He himself took it for the solitariness of the soul, and cherished it with a proud pain.

He discoursed only in monologues. He listened only to himself. But he did all that with the innocence of a savage. When others spoke he disappeared in an inner absorption, his eyes assumed a stony look. The part of him that remained conscious was undeviatingly courteous, but this courtesy often had an automatic air. When he came to speak again, he delighted his hearers by his wit, his paradoxes, and his masterly rendition of anecdotes.

He avoided conversation with women. Beauty and coquetry made no impression on him. When women became enthusiastic over him, his expression was one of merely courteous attention, and his thoughts were contemptuous. He had no adventures, and his name occurred in no racy stories. Once out of the theatre, he lived the life of a private gentleman of simple habits.

With cool but delicate perceptivity Judith examined the conformation of his character. She who was utterly without swift aspiration, whose dry nature perceived only the utilitarian, only the expedient, who had been stifled in mere forms from her girlhood, and esteemed nothing in others but the external, garments, jewels, display, title, name—she was like one possessed and charged with an electric fluid within three days. She was fascinated primarily by external things: his eye, his voice, his fame. But there was one deeper thing: the illusion of his art.

She knew what she was doing. Her steps were scrupulously calculated.

One day Lorm complained of the disorganization in his life, the frightful waste of his substance. It was at table, and he was answered by empty phrases. But Judith, when she succeeded in having him to herself later, took up the subject again. She persuaded him to describe the persons whom he held responsible, and expressed doubts of their trustworthiness. She disapproved of arrangements that he had made, gave him advice that he found excellent, and reproached him with the neglect of which he confessed himself guilty. "I wade in money and suffocate in debt," he sighed. "In twenty years I'll be an old man and a poor devil."

Her practical insight filled him with naïve admiration. He said to her: "I've been told once in a while that there are such women in the world as you, but I never believed in their existence. All I've ever seen were full of empty exactions and florid emotions."

"You're unjust," she replied and smiled. "Every woman has some field in which she has character and firmness, but the world pays no attention. Then, too, our relation to the world is usually a false one."

"That is a wise remark," said Lorm in a satisfied voice. He was a miser of praise.

From now on he loved to have her draw him into talk concerning his little needs and worries. She examined him in detail, and he was glad to submit. He brought her the bills rendered him by his tradespeople. "They capitalize your inexperience, and cheat you," was Judith's judgment of the situation. It made him feel ashamed.

"Have you been lending money?" she asked. It appeared that he had. For years and years he had loaned considerable sums to numerous parasites. Judith shrugged her shoulders. "You might just as well have thrown the money away."

Lorm answered: "It's such a bother when they come and beg, and their faces are so unappetizing. I give them what they ask just to be rid of them."

In this wise their conversations moved wholly within the circle of the prosaic things of daily life. But it was precisely this that Edgar Lorm had missed and needed. It was as new and as moving to him, as the discovery of a rapt and ecstatic soul to a bourgeois becoming aware of poetry and passion.

Judith had a dream. She lay quite naked beside a slippery, icy fish. And she lay with it from choice, and snuggled close to its cold body. But suddenly she began to beat it, for its cool, damp, slippery scales, which had a gleam of silver and were opaline along its back, suddenly inspired in her a witch-like fury. She beat and beat the creature, until she lost consciousness and awoke exhausted.

An excursion int the valley of the Isar was arranged. Crammon went, and Felix, a young friend of the latter, Lorm and Judith. They took their coffee in the garden of an inn, and on the way back, which led through woods, they went in couples, Lorm and Judith being the last. "I've lost my gold cigarette case," Lorm announced suddenly, examining his pocket, "I've got to go back the last part of the way. I know I had it when we were in the village." It was an object precious in itself, and to which he attached a great value because it had been given him by a king who had been devoted to him in an enthusiastic friendship in his youth, and so it was irreplaceable.

Judith nodded. "I'll wait here," she said, "I'm afraid I'm too tired to cover the distance three times."

He walked back and left Judith standing there, leaning her head against a tree and reflecting. Her forehead wrinkled and her eyes assumed a piercing look. It was silent in the wood; no breeze stirred, no bird cried, no animal rustled in the bushes. Time passed. Driven not at all by impatience, but by her thoughts, which were both violent and decisive, she finally left her place, and walked in the direction from which Lorm would have to come. When she had been walking for a while, she saw something golden gleaming in the moss. It was the cigarette case, which she picked up calmly.

Lorm came back sorely vexed. He was silent, and as he walked beside her, she quietly presented the case on her flat hand. He made a gesture of joyous surprise, and she had to tell him how she had found it.

For a while he seemed to be struggling with himself. Suddenly he said: "How much easier life would be with you."

Judith answered with a smile: "You talk of it as of something unattainable."

"I believe it to be so," he murmured, with lowered head.

"If you're thinking of my marriage," Judith said, still smiling, "I consider your expression exaggerated. The way out would be simple."

"I wasn't thinking of your marriage, but of your wealth."

"Will you tell me your meaning more clearly."

"At once." He looked about him, and went up to a tree.

"Do you see that little beetle? Look how busily he works to climb the height before him. He has probably worked his way up a considerable distance to-day. No doubt he started before dawn. When he's on top, he will have accomplished something. But if I take him between my fingers now and place him at the top, then the very path which his own labour has dug becomes a thing of no value to him. That's the way it is with beetles and also with men."

Judith considered. "Comparisons must halt. That's their prerogative, you know." She spoke with gentle mockery. "I don't understand why one should reject another, simply because that other doesn't come with empty hands. It's a funny notion."

"Between a hand that is empty, and one that commands immeasurable treasures, there is a fatal difference," Lorm said with deep earnestness. "I have worked my way up from poverty. You have no faintest notion of the meaning of that word. All that I am and have, I owe to the immediate exertions of my body and my brains. By your birth you have been accustomed all your life to buy the bodies and the brains of others. And though you had a thousand times more instinct and vision for practical things and for the necessities of a sane life than you have, yet you do not and could not comprehend the profoundly moral and rightly revered relation of accomplishment to reward. Your adventitious advantages have constantly made it possible for you to ignore this relation, and to substitute for it an arbitrary will. To me your wealth would be paralysis, a mockery and a spectre."

He looked at her with head thrown back.

"And so you think our case hopeless?" Judith asked, pale and defiant.

"Since I cannot and dare not expect you to abandon your millions and share the fate of a play-actor, it does indeed seem hopeless."

Judith's face was quite colourless. "Let us go," she said;

" the others will remark our absence, and I dislike being gos-
siped about."

Swiftly and silently they walked on. They came to a clearing
and saw beneath a black rampart of clouds the throbbing,
crimson disc of the sun. Judith stared into it with raging fury.
For the first time her will had encountered a still stronger will.
It was rage that filled her eyes with tears, rage that wrung
from her discordant laughter. When Lorm looked at her in
pained surprise, she turned away and bit her lip.

" I'm capable of doing it," she said to herself in her rage.
And the impulse hardened into a stubborn determination:
" I will!   I will! "

XII

When Christian arrived in Berlin with Amadeus Voss he
found, quite as he had expected, many people and a great
tumult about Eva. He could scarcely get to her. " I am tired,
Eidolon," she cried out, when she caught sight of him. " Take
me away from everything."

And again, when she had escaped the oppressive host of admirers, she said: " How good it is that you are here, Eidolon.
I have waited for you with an ache in my heart. We'll leave
to-morrow."

But the journey was postponed from day to day. They
planned to live alone and in retirement at the Dutch water-
ing place that was their immediate goal, but Christian had
already met a dozen people who had ordered accommodations
there, and so he doubted the seriousness of Eva's intentions.
People had become indispensable to her. When she was silent
she wanted, at least, to hear the voices of others; when she
was quiet she wanted movement about her.

When he stood before her the fragrance of her body penetrated him like a great fear. His blood flowed in such violent
waves that his pulses lost the rhythm of their beating.

He had forgotten her face, the inimitable veracity of her

gestures, her power of feeling and inspiring ecstasy, her whole powerful, delicate, flowerlike, radiant being. Everything seemed to yield to her, even the elements. When she appeared in the street, the sun shone more purely and the air was more temperate; and thus the wild turmoil about her was trans- formed into a steady and obedient tide.

Susan said to Christian: " We are to dance here, and have offers. But we don't like the Prussians. They seem an arid folk, who save their money for soldiers and barracks. I haven't seen a real face. All men and all women look alike. They may be worthy, no doubt they are; but they seem machine-made."

" Eva herself is a German," Christian rebuked the woman's spiteful words.

" Bah, if a genius is cast forth from heaven and tumbles on the earth, it is blind and cannot choose its place. Where is Herr von Crammon? " she interrupted herself. " Why doesn't he come to see us? And whom have you brought in his stead? " She poked out her chin toward Amadeus Voss, who stood timidly in a corner, and whose large spectacles made him look like an owl. " Who is that? "

Who is that? The same question appeared in the astonished faces of Wiguniewski and of the Marquis of Tavera. Amadeus was new to the world with a vengeance. The fixed expression on his features had something so silly at times, that Christian was ashamed of him and the others laughed.

Voss wandered about the streets, pushed himself into crowds, surveyed the exhibits behind the plate-glass windows of shops, stared into coffee-houses, bought newspapers and pamphlets, but found no way of calming his soul. All he could see was the face of the dancer, and the gestures with which she cut a fruit or greeted a friend or bowed or sat down in a chair or arose or smelled a flower, or the motions of her lids and lips and neck and shoulders and hips and legs. And he found all these things in her provocative and affected, and yet they had bitten into his brain as acid bites into metal.

One evening he entered Christian's room, and his face was the colour of dust.

"Who really is Eva Sorel? " he asked, with a bitter rancour. "Where does she come from? To whom does she belong? What are we doing here with her? Tell me something about her. Enlighten me." He threw himself into a chair, and stared at Christian.

When Christian, unprepared for this tempest of questions, made no answer, he went on: " You've put me into a new skin, but the old Adam writhes in it still. Is this a masquerade? If so, tell me at least what the masks represent. I seem to be disguised too, but badly. I expect you to improve my disguise."

" You aren't disguised any worse than the others," Christian said, with a soothing smile.

Voss rested his head on his two hands. " So she's a dancer, a dancer," he murmured thoughtfully. " To my way of feeling there has always been something lewd about that word and what it means. How can it help arousing images that bring the blush to one's cheek? " Suddenly he looked up, and asked with a piercing glance: " Is she your mistress? "

The blood left Christian's face. " I think I understand what disturbs you so," he said. " But now that you've gone with me, you must bear with me. I don't know how long we shall stay with this crowd, and I can't myself tell exactly why we are here. But you must not ask me about Eva Sorel. We must not discuss her either for praise or blame."

Voss was silenced.

XIII

Christian, Amadeus, Bradshaw, Tavera, and Wiguniewski went by motor. Eva used the train.

But this way of travelling agreed with her as ill as any other. All night she lay sleepless in her crumpled silks, her head buried among pillows. Susan crouched by her, giving her

perfume or a book or a glass of cold lemonade. There was a
prickling in her limbs that would not let her rest, a weight on
her bosom, an alternation of thought and fancy, of willing and
the weariness of willing in her mind. The hum of the wheels
on the rails cut into her nerves; the sable landscape, as it
glided by, irritated her like a delusion that forever changed and
melted. Malignity seemed to lurk in the fields; treacherous
forests seemed to block the way; she saw haunted houses and
terror-stricken men.

"What a torturer time is!" she whispered. "Oh, that it
stood before me, and I could have it whipped."

Susan bent nearer, and gazed at her attentively.

Suddenly she whispered tenderly: "What do you expect of
him? What is the purpose of this new game? He's the most
banal of them all. I never heard him make a polished or a
witty remark. Does he realize what you are? Not in his
wildest dreams. His head is empty. Your art means about
as much to him as the acrobatics of a circus dancer to some
dreary shop-keeper. Nations are at your feet, and he grants
you a supercilious smile. You have given the world a new
kind of delight, and this German know-it-all is untouched and
unchanged by it."

Eva said: "If the North Sea is too sinister, we must seek
a coast in the South."

Susan grew excited: "One would like to yell into his ears:
'Get on your knees! Pray!' But he wouldn't be shaken any
more than the pillar of Vendôme. Is he ever shaken by anything? I described to him how we were adored in Russia,
the ecstasy, the festivities, the outbursts of enthusiasm. He
acted as if he were hearing a moderately interesting bit of
daily news. I told him about the Grand-Duke. No, don't
frown. I had to, or I would have choked. I described that
chained barbarian, that iron soul dissolved! It's certainly
uncommon; it would make any heart beat faster. I tried to
make him visualize the situation: fifty millions of trembling

slaves and all, through his power, at your bidding. No poet could have been more impressive than I was. If you had heard me trying to penetrate his mind, you would have been astonished at my talent for sewing golden threads on sack cloth. It was all in vain. His breath came as regularly as the ticking of a clock. Once or twice he seemed to be startled. But it was due to a breeze or a mosquito."

"I wonder whether the gowns from Paris have arrived at Heyst," Eva said. The long oval of her face seemed to grow a trifle longer; her lips curled a little, and her teeth showed like pallid, freshly peeled almonds.

"Why did you refuse yourself to him?" Susan went on. "What we possess is part of our past, but a joy put off is a burden. Men are to be the rungs of your ladder—no more. Let them give you magical nights, but send them packing when the cock crows. How has he deserved a higher office? You've yielded to a whim, and made a grinning idol of him. Why did you summon him? I'm afraid you're going to commit a folly."

Eva did not answer. The tip of her tongue appeared between her lips, and she closed her eyes cunningly. Susan thought she understood those gestures, and said: "It's true, he has the marvellous diamond for which you cried. But you have but to command, and they'll trim your very shoes with such baubles."

"When did you ever see me cry for a diamond?" Eva asked indifferently. She raised herself up, and in her transparent, wavering, blossomy wrappings seemed like a spirit emerging from the dimness. "When did you ever see me cry for a diamond?" she asked again, and touched Susan's shoulder.

"You told me so yourself."

"Have you no better proof?" Eva laughed, and her laughter was her most sensuous form of expression, as her smile was her most spiritual.

Susan folded her hands and said resignedly: "Volvedme del

otro lado, que de esto ya estoy tostado! " It is a Spanish ejaculation, and means: Lay me on the other side, for I have been toasted enough on this.

XIV

The house that Eva had taken was not very far from the beach. It was an old manor, which William of Orange had built, and which had belonged to the late Duchess of Leuchtenberg until a few years ago.

The rooms, built of mighty blocks of stone, soothed Eva. By day and night she heard the long-drawn thunder of the waves. Whenever she picked up a book, she dropped it again soon and listened.

She walked through those rooms, full of ancient furniture and dark portraits, glad to possess herself, and to await without torment him who came to her. She greeted him with half-closed eyes, and with the smile of one who has yielded herself wholly.

Susan practised on a piano with muted strings. When she had finished her task, she slunk away and remained hidden.

Christian and Amadeus Voss had taken lodgings in a neighbouring villa—Voss on the ground floor, Christian above. Since Christian neither asked questions nor detained him, Voss went out in the morning and returned in the evening or even late at night. He did not say where he had been, or what he had seen or experienced.

At breakfast on the third morning, he said to Christian: " It's a thankless task to unchain a fellow like me. I breathe a different breath and sleep a different sleep. Somewhere my soul is ranging about, and I'm chasing it. I've got to catch it first, before I know how things are with me."

Christian did not look up. " We're invited to dine with Eva Sorel to-night," he said.

Voss bowed ironically. " That invitation looks damnably like charity," he said harshly. " I feel the resistance of those people to me, and their strangeness, in my very bones. What a superfluous comedy! What shall I do there? Nearly all of them talk French. I'm a provincial, a villager, and ridiculous. And that's worse than being a murderer or thief. I may make up my mind to commit arson or murder, so as not to be ridiculous any more." He opened his mouth as though to laugh, but uttered no sound.

"I'm surprised, Amadeus, that your thoughts always cling to that one point," Christian said. "Do you really believe it to be of such decisive importance? No one cares whether you're poor or rich. Since you appear in my company, no one questions your equality, or would be so vulgar as to question it. The feelings that you express orginate in yourself, and you seem to take a kind of perverse joy in them. You like to torment yourself, and then revenge yourself on others. I hope you won't take my frankness amiss."

Amadeus Voss grinned. "Sometimes, Christian Wahnshaffe, I'd like to pat your head, as though I were your teacher, and say: You did that very well. Yes, it was wonderfully well done. And yet your little arrow went astray. To hit me, you must take better aim. It is true that the morbidness is deep in my soul, far too deep to be eradicated by a few inexpensive aphorisms. When this Russian prince or this Spanish legate shake hands with me, I feel as though I had forged cheques and would be discovered in a minute. When this lady passes by me, with her indescribable fragrance and the rustling of her garments, I grow dizzy, as though I dangled high over an abyss, and my whole soul writhes in its own humiliation and slavishness. It writhes and writhes, and I can't help it. I was born that way. This is not my world, and cannot become mine. The under dogs must bleed to death, for the upper dogs consider that the order of the world. I belong to that lower kind. My place is with those who have the odour of decayed flesh, whom all avoid, who go about with an eternally festering wound. The law of my being ranges me with them. I have

no power to change that, nor has any pleasant agreement. This
is not my world, Wahnschaffe; and if you don't want me to
lose my reason and do some mischief, you had better take me
out of it so soon as possible, or else send me away."

Christian passed the tips of his fingers over his forehead.
"Have patience, Amadeus. I believe it is not my world any
longer. Give me but a little more time in which to straighten
out my own thoughts."

Voss's eyes clung to Christian's hands and lips. The words
had been quietly, almost coolly uttered, yet there was a deep
conflict in them and an expression that had power over Voss.
"I cannot imagine a man leaving this woman, if once he has
her favour," he said, with a hovering malice on his lips, "unless
she withdraws her favour."

Christian could not restrain a gesture of aversion. "We'll
meet to-night then," he said, and arose.

An hour later Amadeus Voss saw him and Eva on the beach.
He was coming down the dunes, and saw them on the flat
sands by the foam of the waves. He stopped, shaded his eyes
with his hands, and gazed out over the ocean as though watching for a sail. The other two did not see him. They walked
along in a rhythmic unity, as of bodies that have tested the
harmony of their vibrations. After a while they, too, stopped
and stood close together, and were defined like two dark,
slender shafts against the iron grey of air and water.

Voss threw himself into the sparse, stiff grass, and buried his
forehead in the moist sand. Thus he lay many hours.

Evening came. Its great event was to be the appearance
of Eva with the diamond Ignifer in her hair. She wore it in an
exquisitely wrought setting of platinum, and it shone above her
head, radiant and solitary, like a ghostly flame.

She felt its presence in every throb of her heart. It was a
part of her, at once her justification and her crown. It was no
longer an adornment but a blazing and convincing symbol of
herself.

For a while there was an almost awestruck silence. The lovely Beatrix Vanleer, a Belgian sculptress, cried out in her astonishment and admiration.

The smile of gentle intoxication faded from Eva's face, and her eyes turned far in their sockets, and she saw Amadeus Voss, whose face was of a bluish pallor.

His mouth was half open like an imbecile's, his head thrust brutally forward, his hanging arms twitched. He approached slowly, with eyes staring at the ineffable glow of the jewel. Those who stood on either side of him were frightened and made way. Eva turned her face aside, and stepped back two paces. Susan emerged beside her, and laid protective arms about her. At the same moment Christian went up to Voss, grasped his hand, and drew the quite obedient man aside.

Christian's attitude and expression had something that calmed every one. As though nothing had happened, a vivid and twittering conversation arose.

Voss and Christian stood on the balcony of stone. Voss drank the salt sea air deep into his lungs. He asked hoarsely: " Was that Ignifer? "

Christian nodded. He listened to the sea. The waves thundered like falling fragments of rock.

" I have grasped the whole secret of your race," Amadeus murmured, and the convulsion in his face melted under the influence of Christian's presence. " I have understood both man and woman. In this diamond are frozen your tears and your shudderings, your voluptuousness and your darkness too. It is a bribe and an accursed delusion, a terrible fetish! How keenly aware am I now of your days and nights, Wahnschaffe, of all that is between you and her, since I have seen the gleam of this mineral which the Lord created out of the slime, even as He created me and you and her. That stone is without pain—earthly, and utterly without pain, burned pure and merciless. My God, my God, and think of me, of me! "

Christian did not understand this outburst, but it shook

him to the soul. Its power swept aside the vexation which Voss's shameless eloquence had. aroused. He listened to the sea.

Voss pulled himself together. He went up to the balustrade, and said with unnatural self-control, " You counselled patience to-day. What was your purpose? It sounded as equivocal and as general as all you say to me. It is convenient to talk of patience. It is a luxury like any other luxury at your command, only less costly. There is no word, however, worthier of hatred or contempt. It is always false. Closely looked upon, it means cowardice and sloth. What have you in mind? "

Christian did not answer. Or, rather, he assumed having answered; and after a long while, and out of deep meditation, he asked: " Do you believe that it is of any use? "

" I don't understand," said Voss, and looked at him helplessly. " Use? To what end or how? "

Christian, however, did not enlighten him further.

Voss wanted to go home, but Christian begged him to stay, and so they went in and joined the others at dinner.

xv

When the dinner was over, the company returned to the drawing-room. The conversation began in French, but in deference to Mr. Bradshaw, who did not understand that language, changed to German.

The American directed the conversation toward the dying races of the New World, and the tragedy of their disappearance. Eva encouraged him, and he told of an experience he had had among the Navaho Indians.

The Navaho tribe had offered the longest resistance to Christianity and to its civilization. To subdue them the United States Government forbade the practice of the immemorial Yabe Chi dance, the most solemn ritual of their cult. The commissioner who was to convey this order, and on whose

staff Mr. Bradshaw had been, yielded to the passionate en-
treaty of the tribal chief, and gave permission for a final celebration of the dance. At midnight, by the light of campfires
and of pine torches, the brilliantly feathered and tattooed
dancers and singers appeared. The singers sang songs which
told of the fates of three heroes, who had been captured by a
hostile tribe and freed by the god Ya. He taught them to ride
the lightning; they fled into the cave of the Grizzly Bear, and
thence into the realm of butterflies. The dances gave a plastic
representation of these adventures. While the craggy mountains re-echoed the songs, and the contorted dances in the
tawny glow rose to an ecstasy of despair, a terrific storm broke.
Cascades of water poured from the sky and filled the dried
river-beds with roaring torrents; the fires were extinguished;
the medicine men prayed with uplifted arms; the dancers and
singers, certain now that they had incurred the anger of their
god, whose sacred ceremony they had consented to betray,
hurled themselves in their wild pain into the turbulent waters,
which carried their bodies far down into the plain.

When Mr. Bradshaw had ended, Eva said: "The gods are
vengeful; even the gentlest will defend their seats."

"That is a heathen view," said Amadeus, in a sharp and
challenging voice. "There are no gods. There are idols, to be
sure, and these must be broken." He looked defiantly about
him, and added in a dragging tone: "For the Lord saith, no
man can look upon me and live."

Smiles met his outburst. Tavera had not understood, and
turned to Wiguniewski, who whispered an explanation in
French. Then the Spaniard smiled too, compassionately and
maliciously.

Voss arose with a tormented look on his face. The merriment in those faces was like a bodily chastisement to him.
From behind his glittering eye-glasses he directed a venomous
glance toward Eva, and said in troubled tones: "In the same
context of Scripture the Lord bids Israel hurl aside its adorn-

ments that He may see what He will do with them. The meaning is clear."

"He cannot expiate the lust of the eye," Christian thought, and avoided Eva's glance.

Amadeus Voss left the company and the house. On the street he ran as though pursued, clasping his hands to his temples. He had pushed his derby hat far back. When he reached his room, he opened his box and drew out a package of letters. They were the stolen letters of the unknown woman F. He sat down by his lamp, and read with tense absorption and a burning forehead. It was not the first night that he had passed thus.

When Eva was alone with Christian, she asked: "Why did you bring that man with you?"

He laughed, and lifted her up in his arms, and carried her through many flights of rooms and out of light into darkness.

"The sea cries!" her lips said at his ear.

He prayed that all sounds might die out of the world except the thunder of the sea and that young voice at his ear. He prayed that those two might silence the disquiet that overcame him in her very embraces and made him, at the end of every ecstasy, yearn for its renewal.

That slender, passionate body throbbed toward him. Yet he heard the lamentation of an alien voice: What shall we do?

"Why did you bring this man?" Eva asked him far in the night, between sleep and sleep. "I cannot bear him. There is always sweat on his forehead. He comes from a sinister world."

There was a bluish twilight in the room that came from the blue flame of a blue lamp, and a bluish darkness lay beyond the windows.

"Why don't you answer me?" she urged, and raised herself, showing the pale face amid its wilderness of brown hair.

He had no answer for her. He feared the insufficiency of any explanation, as well as the replies that she would find.

"What is the meaning of it all? What ails you, dearest?" Eva drew him toward her, and clung to him, and kissed his eyes thirstily.

"I'll ask him to avoid your presence," said Christian. And suddenly he saw himself and Voss in the farm yard of Nettersheim, saw the kneeling men and maid servants, the old rusty lantern, the dead woman, and the carpenter who was measuring her for her coffin.

"Tell me what he means to you," whispered Eva. "It seems to me suddenly as though you were gone. Where are you really? Tell me, dear friend."

"You should have let me love you in those old days in Paris," said Christian gently, and softly rested his cheek against her bosom, "in those days when Crammon and I came to you."

"Speak, only speak," Eva breathed, seeking to hide the fright in her heart.

Her eyes gleamed, and her skin was like luminous white satin. In the darkness her face had a spiritualized thinness; the restrained charm of her gestures mastered the hour, and her smile was deep and intricate of meaning, and everything about her was play and mirroring and raptness and unexpected magic. Christian looked upon her.

"Do you remember words that you once spoke to me?" he asked. "You said: 'Love is an art like poetry or music, and he who does not understand that, finds no grace in love's sight.' Were not those your words?"

"Yes, they were. Speak to me, my darling!"

He held her in his arms, and the life of her body, its warmth, its blood that was conscious of him, and its vibration that was toward him, made speech a little easier. "You see," he said thoughtfully, and caressed her hand, "I have only enjoyed women. Nothing more. I have been ignorant of that love which is an art. It was so easy. They adored me, and I took no pains. They put no hindrances on my path, and so my

foot passed over them. Not one demanded a fulfilment of me.
They were happy enough if I was but contented. But you,
Eva, you're not satisfied with me. You look at me searchingly
and watch me; and your vigil continues even at those moments
when one floats beyond thought and knowledge. And it is because you are not satisfied with me. Or is that an error, a
deception? "

"It is so very late," said Eva, and, leaning her head back
upon the pillows, she closed her eyes. She listened to the
perished echo of her own voice, and the oppression of her
heart almost robbed her of breath.

XVI

It was in another night. They had been jesting and telling
each other amusing stories, and at last they had grown
weary.

Suddenly in the darkness outside of the window Christian
had a vision of his father and of the dog Freia; and his father
had the tread of a lonely man. Never had Christian seen loneliness so visibly embodied. The dog was his only companion.
He had sought for another friend, but there had been none to
go with him.

"How is that possible? " Christian thought.

His senses were lost in a strange drowsiness, even while he
held Eva's beautiful body, which was as smooth and cool as
ivory. And in this drowsiness visions emerged of his brother,
his sister, his mother, and about each of them was that great
loneliness and desolation.

"How is that possible? " Christian thought. "Their lives
are thronged with people."

But he answered himself, and said: "Is not your own life
likewise thronged with people to suffocation, and do you not
also feel that same loneliness and desolateness? "

Now a dark object seemed to descend upon him. It was a
coat—a wet, dripping coat. And at the same moment some

one called out to him: "Arise, Christian, arise!" But he could not arise, for those ivory arms held him fast.

Suddenly he became aware of Letitia. She uttered but one word: "Why?" It seemed to him, while he slept, if indeed he slept, that he should have chosen Letitia, who lived but for her dreams, her yearnings and imaginings, and who had been sacrificed with her dreams to the vulgar world of reality. It seemed to him as though Letitia, pointing to Eva, were saying: "What do you seek of her? She knows nothing of you, but weaves at the web of her own life. She is ambitious, and can give you no help in your suffering; and it is only to forget and deaden the pain of your soul that you are wasting yourself upon her."

Christian was astonished to find Letitia so wise. He was almost inclined to smile at her wisdom. But he knew now clearly that he was suffering. It was a suffering of an unfathomable nature, which grew from hour to hour and from day to day, like the spreading of a gangrened wound.

His head rested on the shoulder of his beloved; her little breasts rose from the violet shadows and had trembling contours. He felt her beauty with every nerve, and her strangeness and exquisite lightness. He felt that he loved her with all his thoughts and with every fibre of his flesh, and that, despite it all, he could find no help in her.

And again a voice cried: "Arise, Christian, arise!" But he could not arise. For he loved this woman, and feared life without her.

The dawn was breaking when Eva turned her face to him again: "Where are you?" she asked. "What are you gazing at?"

He answered: "I am with you."

"To the last stirrings of your thought?"

"I don't know. Who knows the last recesses of his mind?"

"I want you wholly. With every breath. And something of you escapes."

"And you," Christian asked evasively, "are you utterly with me?"

She answered passionately, and with an imperious smile, as she drew closer to him: "You are more mine than I am yours."

"Why?"

"Does it frighten you? Are you miserly in your love? Yes, you are more mine. I have broken the spell that held you and melted your soul of stone."

"Melted my soul . . .?" Christian asked in amazement.

"I have, my darling. Don't you know that I'm a sorceress? I have power over the fish in the sea, the horse on the sod, the vulture in the air, and the invisible deities that are spoken of in the books of the Persians. I can make of you what I would, and you must yield."

"That is true," Christian admitted.

"But your soul does not look at me," Eva cried, and flung her arms about him, "it is an alien soul, dark, hostile, unknown."

"Perhaps you're misusing the power you have over me, and my soul resists."

"It is to obey—that is all."

"Perhaps it is not wholly sure of you."

"I can give your soul only the assurance of the hour that is."

"What are you planning?"

"Don't ask me! Hold me fast with your thoughts. Don't let me go for a moment, or we are lost to each other. Cling to me with all your might."

Christian answered: "It seems to me as though I ought to know what you mean. But I don't want to know it. Because you see, you . . . I . . . all this . . . it's too insignificant." He shook his head in a troubled way. "Too insignificant."

"What, what do you mean by that?" Eva cried in fright,

and clung to his right hand with both hers. Tensely she looked into his face.

"Too insignificant," Christian repeated stubbornly, as though he could find no other words.

Then he reflected on all he had said and heard with his accustomed scepticism and toughmindedness, and arose and bade his friend good-night.

XVII

Edgar Lorm was playing in Karlsruhe. On a certain evening he had increased the tempo of his playing, and given vent to his disgust with his rôle, the piece, his colleagues, and his audience so obviously that there had been hissing after the last act.

"I'm a poor imbecile," he said to his colleagues at their supper in a restaurant. "Every play actor is a poor imbecile." He looked at them all contemptuously, and smacked his lips.

"We must have had more inner harmony in the days when we were suspected of stealing shirts from the housewife's line and children were frightened at our name. Don't you think so? Or maybe you're quite comfortable in your stables."

His companions observed a respectful silence. Wasn't he the famous man who filled the houses, and whom both managers and critics flattered?

Dust was whirling in the streets, the dust of summer, as he returned to his hotel. How desolate I feel, he thought, and shook himself. Yet his step was free and firm as a young huntsman's.

When he had received his key and turned toward the lift, Judith Imhof suddenly stood before him. He started, and then drew back.

"I am ready to be poor," she said, almost without moving her lips.

"Are you here on business, dear lady?" Lorm asked in a

clear, cold voice. " Undoubtedly you are expecting your husband——? "

" I am expecting no one but you, and I am alone," answered Judith, and her eyes blazed.

He considered the situation with a wrinkled face that made him look old and homely. Then with a gesture he invited her to follow him, and they entered the empty reading room. A single electric lamp burned above the table covered with newspapers. They sat down in two leather armchairs. Judith toyed nervously with her gold mesh-bag. She wore a travelling frock, and her face was tired.

Lorm began the conversation. " First of all: Is there any folly in your mind that can still be prevented? "

" None," Judith answered in a frosty tone. " If the condition you made was only a trick to scare me off, and you are cowardly enough to repudiate it at the moment of its fulfilment, then, of course, I have been self-deceived, and my business here is at an end. Don't soothe me with well-meant speeches. The matter was too serious to me for that."

" That is sharply and bitterly said, Judith, but terribly impetuous," Lorm said, with quiet irony. " I'm an old hand at living, and far from young, and a good bit too experienced to fly into the passion of a Romeo at even the most precious offers and surprises of a woman. Suppose we discuss what you've done like two friends, and you postpone for a bit any final judgment of my behaviour."

Judith told him that she had written her father, and requested him to make some other disposition of the annual income which he had settled on her at the time of her marriage, since she had determined to get a divorce from Felix Imhof, and to marry a man who had made this step a definite condition of their union. At the same time she had made a legal declaration of her renunciation before a notary, which she had brought to show Lorm, and intended thereupon to send on to her father. All this she told him very calmly. Felix had

known nothing of her intentions at the time of her departure.
She had left a note for him in the care of his valet. "Explanations are vain under such circumstances," she said. "To tell
a man whom one is leaving why one is leaving him is as
foolish as turning back the hands of the clock in the hope of
really bringing back hours that are dead. He knows where
I am and what I want. That's enough. Anyhow, it's not the
sort of thing he comprehends, and there are so many affairs
in his busy life that one more or less will make little difference."

Lorm sat quietly, his head bent forward, his chin resting on
the mother-of pearl handle of his stick. His carefully combed
hair, which was brown and still rather thick, gleamed in the
light. His brows were knit. In the lines about his nose, and
his wearied actor's mouth, there was a deep joylessness.

A waiter appeared at the door and vanished again.

"You don't know what you're letting yourself in for,
Judith," Lorm said, and tapped the floor lightly with his feet.

"Then tell me about it, so that I can adjust myself."

"I'm an actor," he said almost threateningly.

"I know it."

He laid his stick on the table, and folded his hands. "I'm an
actor," he repeated, and his face assumed the appearance of a
mask. "My profession involves my representing human nature at its moments of extreme expressiveness. The fascination of the process consists in the artificial concentration of
passion, its immediate projection, and the assigning to it of
consequences that reality rarely or never affords. And so it
naturally happens—and this deception is the fatal law of the
actor's life—that my person, this Edgar Lorm who faces you
here, is surrounded by a frame that suits him about as well as
a Gothic cathedral window would suit a miniature. A further
consequence is that I lack all power of adjustment to any
ordered social life, and all my attempts to bring myself in
harmony with such a life have been pitiable failures. I strug-

gle and dance in a social vacuum. My art is beaten foam.

"I've been told of people who have a divided personality. Well, mine is doubled, quadrupled. The real me is extinct. I detest the whole business; I practise my profession because I haven't any other. I'd like to be a librarian in the service of a king or a rich man who didn't bother me, or own a farm in some Swiss valley. I'm not talking about the accidental miseries of the theatre, disgusting and repulsive as they are— the masquerading, the lies and vanities. And I don't want you to believe either that I'm uttering the average lament of the spoiled mime, which is made up of inordinate self-esteem and of coquettish fishing for flattering contradiction.

" My suffering lies a little deeper. Its cause is, if you will try to understand me, the spoken word. It has caused a process within me that has poisoned my being and destroyed my soul. What word, you may ask? The words that pass between man and man, husband and wife, friend and friend, myself and others. Language, which you utter quite naturally, has in my case passed through all the gamuts of expression and all the temperatures of the mind. You use it as a peasant uses his scythe, the tailor his needle, the soldier his weapon. To me it is a property and a ghost, a mollusk and an echo, a thing of a thousand transformations, but lacking outline and kernel. I cry out words, whisper them, stammer them, moan, flute, distend them, and fill the meaningless with meaning, and am depressed to the earth by the sublime. And I've been doing that for five and twenty years. It has worn me thin; it has split my gums and hollowed out my chest.

"Hence all words, sincere as they may be on others' lips, are untrue on mine, untrue to me. They tyrannise over me and torment me, flicker through the walls, recall to me my powerlessness and unrewarded sacrifices, and change me into a helpless puppet. Can I ever, without being ashamed to the very marrow, say: I love? How many meanings have not those words! How many have I been forced to give them! If I utter them I practise merely the old trick of my trade, and make the pasteboard device upon my head look like a golden crown. Consider me closely and you will see the meaning of literal despair. Words have been my undoing. It sounds queer, I know; but it is true. It may be that the actor is the absolute example of hopeless despair."

Judith looked at him rather emptily. "I don't suppose that we'll torture each other much with words," she said, merely to say something.

But Edgar Lorm gave to this saying a subtle interpretation, and nodded gratefully. "What an infinitely desirable condition that would be," he answered, in his stateliest manner; "because, you see, words and emotions are like brothers and sisters. The thing that I detest saying is mouldy and flat to me in the realm of feeling too. One should be silent as fate. It may be that I am spoiled for any real experience—drained dry. I have damned little confidence in myself, and nothing but pity for any hand stretched out to save me. However that may be," he ended, and arose with elastic swiftness, "I am willing to try."

He held out his hand as to a comrade. Charmed by the vividness and knightly grace of his gesture, Judith took his hand and smiled.

"Where are you stopping?" he asked.

"In this hotel."

Chatting quite naturally he accompanied her to the door of her room.

XVIII

On the next afternoon Felix Imhof suddenly appeared at the hotel. He sent up his card to Judith, and waited in the hall. He walked up and down, swinging his little cane, carelessly whistling through his thick lips, his brain burdened with affairs, speculations, stock quotations, a hundred obligations

and appointments. But whenever he'passed the tall windows,
he threw a curious and merry glance out into the street, where
two boys were having a fight.

But now and then his face grew dark, and a quiver passed
over it.

The page returned, and bade him come up.

Judith was surprised to see him. He began to talk eagerly
·at once. " I have business in Liverpool, and wanted to see you
once more before leaving. A crowd of people came, who all
had some business with you. Invitations came for you, and
telephone calls; your dressmaker turned up, and letters, and
I was, of course, quite helpless. I can't very well receive people
with the agreeable information that my wife has just taken
French leave of me. There are a thousand things; you have
to disentangle them, or the confusion will be endless."

They talked for a while of the indifferent things which,
according to him, had brought him here. Then he added:
" I had an audience with the Prince Regent this forenoon.
He bestowed a knighthood on me yesterday."

Judith's face flushed, and she had the expression of one
who, in a state of hypnosis, recalls his waking consciousness.

Felix tapped against his faultlessly creased trousers with
his stick. " I beg your pardon for venturing any criticism,"
he said, " but I can't help observing that the whole matter
might have been better managed. To run off with that degree
of suddenness—well, it wasn't quite the proper thing, a little
beneath us, not quite fair."

Judith shrugged her shoulders. " Things that are inevitable
might as well be done quickly. And I don't see that your
equanimity is at all impaired."

" Equanimity! Nonsense! Doesn't enter the question."
He stood, as was his habit, with legs stretched far apart, rock-
ing to and fro a little, and regarding his gleaming boots.
" What has equanimity to do with it? We're cultivated people.
I'm neither a tiger nor a Philistine. Nihil humanum a me

alienum, et cetera. You simply don't know me. And
it doesn't astonish me, for what·chance have we ever had to
cultivate each other's acquaintance? Marriage gave us no
opportunity. We should retrieve our lost occasions. It is this
wish that I should like to take with me into my renewed
bachelorhood. You must promise not to avoid me as rigor-
ously in the future as you did during the eight months of our
married life."

"If it will give you any pleasure, I promise gladly," Judith
answered good-humouredly.

With that they parted.

An hour later Felix Imhof sat in the train. With protruding
eyes he stared at the passing landscape until darkness fell.
He desired conversation, argument, the relief of some projection of his inner self. With wrinkled brow he watched the·
strangers about him who knew nothing of him·or his inner
wealth, of his great, rolling ideas, or his far-reaching
plans.

At Düsseldorf he left the train. He had made up his.
mind to do so at the last possible moment. He checked his.
luggage, and huddled in his coat, walked, a tall, lean figure,
through the midnight of the dark and ancient streets.

He stopped in front of one of the oldest houses. In this.
house he had passed his youth. All the windows were dark..
"Hello, boy!" he shouted toward the window behind which
he had once slept. The walls echoed his voice. "O name-·
less boy," he said, "where do you come from?" He was accustomed to say of himself often: "I am of obscure origin like
Caspar Hauser."

But no secret weighed upon him, not even that of his own·
unknown descent. He was a man of his decade—stripped of
mystery, open to all the winds.

He entered a house, which he remembered from his student·
days. In a large room, lined with greasy mirrors, there were·
fifteen or twenty half-dressed girls. In his hat and coat he sat.

down at the piano and played with the false energy of the dilettante.

"Girls," he said, "I've got a mad rage in me!" The girls played tricks on him as he sat there. They hung a crimson shawl over his shoulders and danced.

"I'm in a rage, girls," he repeated. "It's got to be drowned out." He ordered champagne by the pailful.

The doors were locked. The girls screeched with delight.

"Do something to relieve my misery, girls," he commanded, bade half a dozen stand in a row and open their mouths. Then he rolled up hundred mark notes like cigarettes, and stuck them between the girls' teeth. They almost smothered him with their caresses.

And he drank and drank until he lost consciousness.

XIX

Christian could not be without Eva. If he left her for the shortest period, the world about him grew dark.

Yet all their relations had the pathos of farewells. If he walked beside her, it seemed to be for the last time. Every touch of their hands, every meeting of their eyes had the dark glow and pain of the irrevocable.

His love for her was in harmony with this condition. It was clinging, giving, patient, at times even obedient.

It showed its nature in the way he held her cloak for her, gave her a glass that her lips were to touch, supported her when she was weary, waited for her if she was later than he at some appointed spot.

She felt that often and questioned him; but he had no answer. He might have conveyed his sensation of an eternal farewell, but he could not have told her what was to follow it. And it became very clear to him, that not a farewell from her alone was involved, but a farewell from everything in the world that had hitherto been dear and pleasant and indispensable to him. Beyond that fact he understood nothing; he had no plans and did not make any.

He was so void of any desire or demand that Eva yielded recklessly to a hundred wishes, and was angry when none remained unfulfilled. She wanted to see the real ocean. He rented a yacht, and they cruised on the Atlantic for two weeks. She had a longing for Paris, and he took her there in his car. They had dinner at Foyot in the Rue de Tournon, where they had invited friends—writers, painters, musicians. On the following day they returned. They heard of a castle in Normandy which was said to be like a dream of the early Middle Age. She desired to see it by moonlight; so they set out while the moon was full and cloudless nights were expected. Then the cathedral at Rouen lured her; next the famous roses of a certain Baron Zerkaulen near Ghent; then an excursion into the forest of Ardennes, or a sunset over the Zuyder Zee, or a ride in the park at Richmond, or a Rembrandt at The Hague, or a festive procession in Antwerp.

"Do you never get tired?" Christian asked one day, with that unquiet smile of his that seemed a trifle insincere.

Eva answered: "The world is big and youth is brief. Beauty yearns toward me, exists for me, and droops when I am gone. Since Ignifer is mine, my hunger seems insatiable. It is radiant over my earth, and makes all my paths easy. You see, dear, what you have done."

"Beware of Ignifer," said Christian, with that same, apparently secretive smile.

Eva's lids drooped heavily. "Fyodor Szilaghin has arrived," she said.

"There are so many," Christian answered, "I can't possibly know them all."

"You see none, but they all see you," said Eva. "They all wonder at you and ask: Who is that slender, distinguished man with very white teeth and blue eyes? Do you not hear their whispering? They make me vain of you."

" What do they know of me? Let them be."

" Women grow pale when you approach. Yesterday on the promenade there was a flower-seller, a Flemish girl. She looked after you, and then she began to sing. Did you not hear? "

" No. What was the song she sang? "

Eva covered her eyes with her hands, and sang softly and with an expression on her lips that was half pain and half archness:

> " ' Où sont nos amoureuses?
> Elles sont au tombeau,
> Dans un séjour plus beau
> Elles sont heureuses.
> Elles sont près des anges
> Au fond du ciel bleu,,
> Où elles chantent les louanges
> De la Mère de Dieu.'

" It touched my very soul, and for a minute I hated you. Ah, how much beauty of feeling streams from human hearts, and finds no vessel to receive it! "

Suddenly she arose, and said with a burning glance: " Fyodor Szilaghin is here."

Christian went to the window. " It is raining," he said.

Thereupon Eva left the room, singing with a sob in her throat:

> " Où sont nos amoureuses?
> Elles sont au tombeau."

That evening they were walking down the beach. " I met Mlle. Gamaleja," Eva told him. " Fyodor Szilaghin introduced her to me. She is a Tartar and his mistress. Her beauty is like that of a venomous serpent, and as strange as the landscape of a wild dream. There was a silent challenge in her attitude to

me, and a silent combat arose between us. We talked about
the diary of Marie Bashkirtseff. She said that such creatures
should be strangled at birth. But I see from your expression,
dear man, that you have never heard of Marie Bashkirtseff.
Well, she was one of those women who are born a century
before their time and wither away like flowers in February."

Christian did not answer. He could not help thinking of the
faces of the dead fishermen which he had seen the night before.

"Mlle. Gamaleja was in London recently and brought me a
message from the Grand Duke," Eva continued; "he'll be here
in another week."

Christian was still silent. Twelve women and nineteen children had stood about the dead men. They had all been scantily
clad and absorbed in their icy grief.

They walked up the beach and moved farther away from the
tumult of the waves. Eva said: "Why don't you laugh? Have
you forgotten how?" The question was like a cry.

Christian said nothing. "To-morrow," she remarked swiftly,
and caught her veil which was fluttering in the breeze, "to-
morrow there's a village fair at Dudzeele. Come with me to
Dudzeele. Pulcinello will be there. We will laugh, Christian,
laugh!"

"Last night there was a storm here," Christian began at
last. "You know that, for we were long among the dunes up
there. Toward morning I walked toward the beach again, because I couldn't sleep. Just as I arrived they were carrying
away the bloated corpses of the fishermen. Three boats went
to pieces during the night; it was quite near Molo, but there
was no chance for help. They carried seven men away to the
morgue. Some people, all humble folk, went along, and so did
I. There in that death chamber a single lantern was burning,
and when they put down the drenched bodies, puddles gathered
on the floor. Coats had been spread over the faces of the
dead men; and of the women I saw but a single one shed tears.
She was as ugly as a rotten tree-trunk; but when she wept all

her ugliness was gone. Why should I laugh, Eva? Why should I laugh? I must think of the fishermen who earn their bread day after day out on the sea. Why should I laugh? And why to-day? "

With both hands Eva pressed her veil against her cheeks.

In that tone of his, which was never rudely emphatic, Christian continued: "Yesterday at the bar Wiguniewski and Botho Thüngen showed me a man of about fifty, a former star at the opera, who had been famous and made money in his day. The day before he had broken down on the street—from starvation. But in his pocket, they found twenty francs. When he was asked why, having the money, he had not satisfied his hunger, he answered that the money was an advance given him toward travelling expenses. He had been engaged to sing at a cabaret in Havre. It had taken him months to find this employment. But the fare to Havre is thirty-five francs, and for six days he had made frantic efforts to scrape together the additional fifteen francs. He had resisted every temptation to touch the twenty francs, for he knew that if he took but a single centime his life would be finally wrecked. But on this day the date of the beginning of his engagement had lapsed, and he returned the twenty francs to the agent. They pointed this man out to me. Leaning on his arms, he sat before an empty cup. I meant to sit down by him, but he went away. Why should I laugh, Eva, when there are such things to think about? Don't ask me to-day of all days that I should laugh."

Eva said nothing. But when they were at home, she flung herself in his arms, as though beside herself, and said: "I must kiss you."

And she kissed him and bit his lip so hard that drops of blood appeared.

"Go now," she said with a commanding gesture, "go! But don't forget that to-morrow we shall visit the fair at Dudzeele."

XX

They drove to the fair and made their way through the crowds to the little puppet-show. The benches were filled with children; the grown people stood in a semi-circle. From the harbour floated the odours of machine oil, leather, and salt herring; in the air resounded the discords of all kinds of music and of the criers' voices.

Christian made a path for Eva; half-surprised and half-morosely the people yielded. Eva followed the play with cheerful intensity. She had loved such scenes from childhood, and now they brought back to her with a poignant and melancholy glow the years of her obscure wanderings.

The Pulcinello, who played the rôle of an outwitted cheat, was forced to confess that no cunning could withstand the magic of the good fairies. His simplicity was too obvious, and his downfall too well deserved to awaken compassion. The rain of blows which were his final portion constituted a satisfying victory of good morals.

Eva applauded, and was as delighted as a child. "Doesn't it make you laugh, Christian?" she asked.

And Christian laughed, not at the follies of the rogue, but because Eva's laughter was so infectious.

When the curtain had fallen upon the tiny stage, they followed the stream of people from one amusement to another. A little line of followers was formed in their wake; a whispering passed from mouth to mouth and each pointed out Eva to the other. Several young girls seemed especially stubborn in their desire to follow the exquisitely dressed lady. Eva wore a hat adorned with small roses and a cloak of silk as blue as the sea in sunshine.

One of the maidens had gathered a bunch of lilacs, and in front of an inn she gave the flowers to Eva with a dainty courtesy. Eva thanked her, and held the flowers to her face. Five or six of the girls formed a circle about her, and took

each others' hands and danced and trilled a melody of wild
delight.

"Now I am caught," Eva cried merrily to Christian, who
had remained outside of the circle and had to endure the
mocking glances of the girls.

"Yes, now you are caught," he answered, and sought to
put himself in tune with the mood of the merrymakers.

On the steps of the inn stood a drunken fellow, who watched
the scene before him with inexplicable fury. First he exhausted himself in wild abuse, and when no one took notice of
him, he seemed overcome by a sort of madness. He picked
up a stone from the ground, and hurled it at the group. The
girls cried out and dodged. The stone, as large as a man's
fist, narrowly missed the arm of the girl who had presented
the flowers, and in its fall hit both of Eva's feet.

She grew pale and compressed her lips. Several men rushed
up to the drunken brute, who staggered into the inn. Christian
had also run in that direction; but he turned back, thinking it
more important to take care of Eva. The girls surrounded
her, sympathized and questioned.

"Can you walk?" he asked. She said yes with a determined
little air, but limped when she tried. He caught her up in his
arms, and carried her to the car, which was waiting nearby.
The girls followed and waved farewell with their kerchiefs.
Hoarse cries sounded from the inn.

"Pulcinello grew quite mad," Eva said. She smiled and
suppressed all signs of pain. "It is nothing, darling," she
whispered after a while, "it will pass. Don't be alarmed."
They drove with racing speed.

Half an hour later she was resting in an armchair in the villa.
Christian was kneeling before her, and held her naked feet
in his hands.

Susan had been quite terror stricken, when she had whisked
off her mistress's shoes and stockings, and saw to her horror
the red bruises made by the stone. She had stammered out

contradictory counsels, had summoned the servants, and excitedly cried out for a physician. At last Eva had asked her
to be quiet and to leave the room.

"The pain's almost gone," said Eva, and nestled her little
feet luxuriously into Christian's cool hands. A maid brought
in a ewer of water and linen cloths for cold bandages.

Christian held and regarded those two naked feet, exquisite
organs that were comparable to the hands of a great painter or
to the wings of a bird that soars far and high. And while he
was taking delight in their form, the clearly defined net of
muscles, the lyrical loveliness of the curves, the rosy toes
with their translucent nails, an inner monitor arose in him
and seemed to say: "You are kneeling, Christian, you are
kneeling." Silently, and not without a certain consternation,
he had whispered back: "Yes, I am kneeling, and why should
I not?" His eyes met Eva's, and the gleam of delight in hers
heightened his inner discomfort.

Eva said: "Your hands are dear physicians, and it is
wonderful to have you kneel before me, sweet friend."

"What is there wonderful about it?" Christian asked hesi-
tantly.

The twilight had fallen. Through the gently waving curtains
the evening star shone in.

Eva shook her head. "I love it. That's all." Her hair
fell open and rippled down her shoulders. "I love it," she
repeated, and laid her hands on his head, pressing it toward
her knees. "I love it."

"But you are kneeling!" Christian heard that voice again.
And suddenly he saw a water jug with a broken handle, and
a crooked window rimmed with snow, and a single boot crusted
with mud, and a rope dangling from a beam, and an oil lamp
with a sooty chimney. He saw these lowly, poverty-stricken
things.

"Have you kneeled to many as though you adored them?"
Eva asked.

He did not answer, but her naked feet grew heavy in his hands. The sensuous perception which they communicated to him through their warmth, their smoothness, their instinctive flexibility vanished suddenly, and gave way to a feeling in which fear and shame and mournfulness were blended. These human organs, these dancing feet, these limbs of the woman he loved, these rarest and most precious things on earth seemed suddenly ugly and repulsive to him, and those lowly and poverty-stricken objects—the jug with the broken handle, the crooked window with its rim of snow, the muddy boot, the dangling rope, the sooty lamp, these suddenly seemed to him beautiful and worthy of reverence.

"Tell me, have you kneeled to many?" he heard Eva's voice, with its almost frightened tenderness. And it seemed to him that Ivan Becker gave answer in his stead and said: "That you kneeled down before her—that was it, and that alone. All else was hateful and bitter; but that you kneeled down beside her —ah, that was it!"

He breathed deeply, with closed eyes, and became pale. And he relived, more closely and truly than ever, that hour of fate. He felt the breath of Becker's kiss upon his forehead, and understood its meaning. He understood the feverish transformations of an evil conscience that had caused him to identify himself with that jug, that window, that boot and rope and lamp, only to flee, only to gain time. And he understood now that despite his change from form to form, he had well seen and heard the beggar, the woman, Ivan Michailovitch, the sick, half-naked children, but that his whole soul had gathered itself together in the effort to guard himself against them for but a little while, before they would hurl themselves upon him with all their torment, despair, madness, cruelty, like wild dogs upon a piece of meat.

His respite had come to an end. With an expression of haste and firmness at once he arose. "Let me go, Eva," he said, "send me away. It is better that you send me away than that I wrench myself loose, nerve by nerve, inch by inch. I cannot stay with you nor live for you." Yet in this very moment his love for her gathered within him like a storm of flames, and he would have torn the heart from his breast to have unsaid the irrevocable words.

She sprang up swiftly as an arrow. Then she stood very still, with both hands in her hair.

He walked to the window. He saw the whole space of heaven before him, the evening star and the unresting sea. And he knew that it was all illusion, this great peace, this glittering star, this gently phosphorescent deep, that it was but a garment and a painted curtain by which the soul must not let itself be quieted. Behind it were terror and horror and unfathomable pain. He understood, he understood at last.

He understood those thousands and thousands on the shore of the Thames and their sombre silence. He understood the shipman's daughter, whose violated body had lain on coarse linen. He understood Adda Castillo and her will to destruction. He understood Jean Cardillac's melancholy seeking for help, and his sorrow over his wife and child. He understood that ancient rake who cried out behind the gates of his cloister: "What shall I do? My Lord and Saviour, what shall I do?" He understood Dietrich, the deaf and dumb lad who had drowned himself, and Becker's words concerning his dripping coat, and Franz Lothar's horror at the intertwined bodies of the Hungarian men and maids, and the panting hunger of Amadeus Voss and his saying concerning the silver cord and the pitcher broken at the fountain. He understood the stony grief of the fishermen's wives, and the opera singer who had twenty francs in his pocket.

He understood. He understood.

"Christian!" Eva cried out in a tone as though she were peering into the darkness.

"The night has come upon us," Christian said, and trembled.

"Christian!" she cried.

Suddenly he became aware of Amadeus Voss, who emerged out there from among the dark trees, and who seemed to have awaited him, for he made signs to him at the window. With a hasty good-night Christian left the room.

Eva looked after him and did not move.

A little later, forgetting the ache in her feet, she went into her dressing-room, opened her jewel case, took Ignifer out, and regarded the stone long and with brooding seriousness.

Then she put it into her hair, and went to the mirror—cool in body, pale of face, quiet-eyed. She folded her arms, lost in this vision of herself.

XXI

Christian and Amadeus walked across the dam toward Duin-bergen.

"I have a confession to make to you, Wahnschaffe," Amadeus Voss began. "I've been gambling, playing roulette, over at Ostende."

"I've heard about it," said Christian absent-mindedly. "And, of course, you lost?"

"The devil appeared to me," said Amadeus, in hollow tones.

"How much did you lose?" Christian asked.

"Maybe you think it was some refined modern devil, a hallucination, or a product of the poetic fancy," Amadeus continued in his breathless and strangely hostile way. "Oh, no, it was a regular, old-fashioned devil with a goat's beard and great claws. And he spoke to me: 'Take of their super-fluity; clothe your sensitiveness in armour; let them not intimidate you, nor the breath of their insolently beautiful world drive you into the cloudy closets of your torment.' And with his cunning fingers he guided the little, jumping ball for me. The light of the lamps seemed to cry, the rouge fell from the cheeks of the women, the spittle of poisonous greed ran down the beards of the men. I won, Christian Wahnschaffe, I won! Ten thousand, twelve thousand—I hardly remember how much.

The thousand franc notes looked like tatters of a faded flag. There were gleaming halls, stairs, gardens, white tables, champagne coolers, platters of oysters; and I breathed deep and lived and was like a lord. Strange men congratulated me, honoured me with their company, ate with me—experienced people, spick and span and respectable. In the Hotel de la Plage my goat-footed devil finally became transformed into a worthy symbol. He became a spider that had a huge egg between its feet and sucked insatiably."

"I believe you ought to go to bed and have a long sleep," said Christian drily. "How much did you lose in the end?"

"I have lost sleep," Amadeus admitted. "How much I lost? About fourteen thousand. Prince Wiguniewski advanced the money; he thought you'd return it. He's a very distinguished person, I must say. Not a muscle in his face moves when he's courteous; nothing betrays the fact that he scents the proletarian in me."

"I'll straighten out the affair with him," said Christian.

"It is not enough, Wahnschaffe," Amadeus answered, and his voice shook, "it is not enough!"

"Why isn't it enough?"

"Because I must go on gambling and win the money back. I can't remain your debtor."

"You will only increase your indebtedness, Amadeus. But I won't prevent you, if you'll make up your mind to name a limit."

Amadeus laughed hoarsely. "I knew you'd be magnanimous, Christian Wahnschaffe. Plunge the thorn deeper into my wound. Go on!"

"I don't understand you, Amadeus," Christian said calmly. "Ask as much money of me as you please. To be sure, I'd prefer to have you ask it for another purpose."

"How magnanimous again, how magnanimous!" Amadeus jeered. "But suppose that naming a limit is just what I won't do? Suppose I want to strip off my beggar's shame and become frankly a robber? Would you cast me off in that case? "

" I don't know what I should do," Christian answered. " Perhaps I should try to convince you that you are not acting justly."

These sober and simple words made a visible impression on Amadeus Voss. He lowered his head and, after a while, he said: " It crushes the heart—that interval between the hopping of the little ball and the decision of the judge. The faded bank notes rustle up, or a round roll of gold is driven up on a shovel. I invented a system. I divided eight letters into groups of three and five. Once I won seventeen hundred with my system, another time three thousand. You mustn't leave me in the lurch, Wahnschaffe. I have a soul, too. Three and five—that's my problem. I'll break the bank. I'll break the bank thrice—ten times! It is possible, and therefore it can be done. Can three and five withstand a cloudburst of gold? Would Danaë repel Perseus, or would she demand that he bring her first the head of the Gorgon Medusa? "

He fell silent very suddenly. Christian had laid an arm about his shoulder, and this familiar caress was so new and unexpected that Amadeus breathed deep as a child in its sleep. " Think of what has happened, Amadeus," said Christian. " Do think of the words you said to me: ' It is possible that you need me; it is certain that without you I am lost.' Have you forgotten so soon, dear friend? "

Amadeus started. He stood still and grasped Christian's hands: " For the love of God . . . no one has ever spoken to me thus . . . no one! "

" You will not forget it then, Amadeus? " Christian said softly.

A weakness overcame Amadeus Voss. He looked about him with unquiet eyes, and saw a low post to which the ships' hawsers were made fast. He sat down on it, and buried his face in his hands. Then he spoke through his hands: " Look you, dear brother, I am a beaten dog; that and nothing else. I feel as though I had leaned too long against a cold, hard, tinted church wall. The chill has remained in my very marrow, and I struggle because I don't want that feeling to enslave me. Often I think I should like to love a woman. I cannot live without love; and yet I live on without it, day after day. Always without love! The accursed wall is so cold. I cannot and would not and must not live without love. I am only human, and I must know woman's love, or I shall freeze to death or be turned to stone or utterly destroyed. Yet I am a Christian, and it is hard for a Christian who bears a certain image in his heart to give himself up to woman. Help me to find a woman, brother, I beseech you."

Christian looked out upon the dark sea. "How can I help him?" he thought, and felt all the coldness of the world and the confusion of mortal things.

While he stood and reflected he heard from afar across the dunes a cry, first dulled by the distance, then nearer and clearer, and then farther away again. It was such a cry as a man might utter, at his utmost need, in the very face of death. Amadeus Voss also lifted his head to listen. They looked at each other.

"We must go," said Christian.

They hurried in the direction of the cry, but the dunes and the beach were equally desolate. Thrice again they heard the cry in the same fashion, approaching and receding, but their seeking and listening and hurrying were in vain. When they were about to return Voss said: "It was not human. It came from something in nature. It was a spirit cry. Such things happen oftener than men believe. It summons us somewhere. One of us two has received a summons."

"It may be," said Christian, smiling. His sense for reality could accept such an interpretation of things only in jest.

XXII

On his way to Scotland Crammon stopped over for a day in Frankfort. He informed Christian's mother of his presence, and she begged him with friendly urgency to come to her.

It was the end of June. They had tea on a balcony wreathed in fresh green. Frau Wahnschaffe had ordered no other callers to be admitted. For a while the conversation trickled along indifferently, and there were long pauses. She wanted Crammon to give her some news of Christian, from whom she had not heard since he had left Christian's Rest. But first, since Crammon was a confidant and a witness in the suit, it was necessary to mention Judith's divorce and approaching remarriage to Edgar Lorm, and Frau Wahnschaffe's pride rebelled at touching on things that could, nevertheless, not be silently passed over.

She sought a starting point in vain. Crammon, outwardly smooth, but really in a malicious and woodenly stubborn mood, recognized her difficulty, but would do nothing to help her.

"Why do you stay at a hotel, Herr von Crammon?" she asked. "We have a right to you and it isn't nice of you to neglect us."

"Don't grudge an old tramp his freedom, dear lady," Crammon answered, "and anyhow it would give me a heartache to have to leave this magic castle after just a day."

Frau Wahnschaffe nibbled at a biscuit. "Anything is better than a hotel," she said. "It's always a bit depressing, and not least so when it's most luxurious. And it isn't really nice. You are next door to quite unknown people. And the noises! But, after all, what distinction in life is there left to-day? It's no longer in fashion." She sighed. Now she thought she had found the conversational bridge she needed, and gave herself a jolt. "What do you think of Judith?" she said in a dull, even voice. "A lamentable mistake. I thought her marriage

to Imhof far from appropriate and regretted it.   But this!
I can hardly look my acquaintances in, the face.   I always
feared the child's inordinate, ambitions, her utter lack of
restraint.   Now she throws herself at the head of an actor.
And to add to the painful complications, there is her bizarre
renunciation of her fortune.   Incomprehensible!   There's some
secret behind that, Herr von Crammon.   Does she realize clearly
what it will mean to live on a more or less limited salary?
It's incomprehensible."

"You need have no anxiety," Crammon assured ·her.
"Edgar Lorm has a princely income and is a great artist."

"Ah, artists! " Frau Wahnschaffe interrupted him, with a
touch of impatience and a contemptuous gesture.   "That means
little.   One pays them; occasionally one pays them well.   But
they are uncertain people, always on the knife's edge.   It's
customary, now to make a great deal of them, even in our
circles.   I've never understood that.   Judith will have to
pay terribly for her folly, and Wahnschaffe and I are suffering a bitter disappointment."   She sighed, and looked at
Crammon surreptitiously before she asked with apparent indifference, "Did you hear from Christian recently? "

Crammon said that he had not.'

"We have been without news of him for two months,"
Frau Wahnschaffe added.   Another shy glance at Crammon
told her that he could not give her the information she sought.
He was not sufficiently master of himself at this moment to
conceal the cause of his long and secret sorrow.

A peacock proudly passed the balcony, spread the gleaming
magnificence of his feathers in the sunlight, and uttered a
repulsive cry.

"I've been told that he's travelling with the son of the forester," said Crammon, and pulled up his eyebrows so high
that his face looked like the gargoyle of a mediæval devil.
"Where he has gone to, I can only suppose; but I have no
right to express such suppositions.   I hope our paths will cross.

We parted in perfect friendship. It is possible that we shall find each other again on the same basis."

" I have heard of the forester's son," Frau Wahnschaffe murmured. " It's strange, after all. Is it a very recent friendship? "

" Yes, most recent. I have no explanation to offer. There's nothing about a forester's son that should cause one any anxiety in itself; but one should like to know the character of the attraction."

" Sometimes hideous thoughts come to me," said Frau Wahnschaffe softly, and the skin about her nose turned grey. Abruptly she bent forward, and in her usually empty eyes there arose so sombre and frightened a glow, that Crammon suddenly changed his entire opinion of this woman's real nature.

" Herr von Crammon," she began, in a hoarse and almost croaking voice, " you are Christian's friend; at least, you caused me to believe so. Then act the part of a friend. Go to him; I expect it of you; don't delay."

" I shall do all that is in my power," Crammon answered. " It was my intention to look him up in any event. First I'm going to Dumbarton for ten days. Then I shall seek him out. I shall certainly find him, and I don't believe that there is any ground for real anxiety. I still believe that Christian is under the protection of some special deity; but I admit that it's just as well to see from time to time whether the angel in question is fulfilling his duties properly."

" You will write me whatever happens," Frau Wahnschaffe said, and Crammon gave his promise. She nodded to him when he took his leave. The glow in her eyes had died out, and when she was alone she sank into dull brooding.

Crammon spent the evening with acquaintances in the city. He returned to the hotel late, and sat awhile in the lobby, immovable, unapproachable, nourishing his misanthropy on the aspect of the passersby. Then he examined the little directory on which the names of the guests appeared. " What are these people doing here? " he asked himself. ."How important that looks: 'Max Ostertag (retired banker) and wife.' Why Ostertag of all things? Why Max? Why: and wife? "

Embittered he went up to his room. Embittered and world-weary he wandered up and down the long corridor. In front of each door, both to the right and to the left, stood two pairs of boots—one pair of men's and one pair of women's. In this pairing of the boots he saw a boastful and shameless exhibitionism of marital intimacies; for the shape and make of the boots assured him of the legal and officially blameless status of their owners. He seemed to see in those boots a morose evidence of overlong, stale unions, a vulgar breadth of tread caused by the weight of money, a commonness of mind, a self-righteous Pharisaism.

He couldn't resist the foolish temptation of creating confusion among the boots of these Philistines. He looked about carefully, took a pair of men's boots, and joined them to a pair of women's boots at another door. And he continued until the original companionship of the boots was utterly destroyed.- Then he went to bed with a pleasant sensation, comparable to that of a writer of farces who has succeeded in creating an improbable and scarcely extricable confusion amid the puppets of his plot.

In the morning he was awakened by the noise of violent and angry disputes in the hall. He raised his head, listened with satisfaction, smiled slothfully, stretched himself, yawned, and enjoyed the quarrelling voices as devoutly as though they were music.

XXIII

When on the day after his nocturnal wandering Christian came to see Eva, he was astonished to find her surrounded by a crowd of Russians, Englishmen, Frenchmen, and Belgians. Until this day she had withdrawn herself from society entirely, or else had received only at hours previously agreed upon be-

tween Christian and herself. · This unexpected change suddenly
made a mere guest of him, and pushed him from the centre
to the circumference of the circle.

The conversation turned on the arrival of Count Maidanoff,
and there was a general exchange of speculation, both in regard
to the duration and the purpose of his visit. A political setting of the stage had been feigned with conscious hypocrisy.
There was to be a visit to the king, and ministerial confer-
ences. He had first stopped at the Hotel Lettoral in Knocke,
but had soon moved to the large and magnificent Villa Her-
zynia, which his favourite and friend, Prince Szilaghin, had
rented.

Szilaghin appeared soon after Christian. Wiguniewski, obviously under orders, introduced the two men.

" I'm going to have a few friends with me to-morrow night,"
Szilaghin said, with the peculiar courtesy of a great comedian.
" I trust you will do me the honour of joining us." Coldly he
examined Christian, whose nerves grew painfully taut under
that glance. He bowed and determined not to go.

Eva was in the room that gave on the balcony, and was
posing for the sculptress, Beatrix Vanleer. The latter sat with
a block of paper and made sketches. Meantime Eva chatted
with several gentlemen. She held out her hand for Christian
to kiss, and ignored his questioning gaze.

In her cinnamon dress, with her hair high on her head and a
diadem of ivory, she seemed extraordinarily strange to him.
Her face had the appearance of delicate enamel. About her
chin there was a hostile air. Gentle vibrations about the
muscles at her temples seemed to portend an inner storm.
But these perceptions were fleeting. What Christian felt about
her was primarily a paralyzing coldness. -

When Mlle. Vanleer had finished for the day, Eva walked
up and down talking to a certain young Princess Helfersdorff.
She led her to the balcony, which was bathed in the sunlight,
and then into her boudoir, where she liked to be when she read

or rested from her exercises. Christian followed the two women, and felt, for the first time in his life, that he was being humiliated. But it did not depress him as profoundly as, an hour ago, the mere thought of such an experience would have done.

The Marquis Tavera joined him. Standing on the threshold of the boudoir, they talked of indifferent things. Christian heard Eva tell the young princess that she expected to go to Hamburg within a week. The North German Lloyd was planning a great festivity on the occasion of the launching of a magnificent ship, and she had been asked to dance. "I'm really delighted at the prospect," she added cheerfully. "I'm little more than a name to most Germans yet. Now they'll be able to see me and tell me what I amount to and where I belong."

The young lady looked at the dancer with enthusiasm. Christian thought: "I must speak to her at once." In every word of Eva's he felt an arrow of hostility or scorn aimed at him. He left Tavera, and entered the room. The decisiveness of his movement forced Eva to look at him. She smiled in surprise. A scarcely perceptible shrug marked her astonishment and censure.

Tavera had turned to the princess, and when these two moved toward the door, Eva seemed inclined to follow them. A gesture of Christian, which she saw on glancing back, determined her to wait. Christian closed the door, and Eva's expression of amazement became intense. But he felt that this was but acting. He slipped into a sudden embarrassment, and could find no words.

Eva walked up and down, touching some object here and there. "Well?" she asked, and looked at him coldly.

"This Szilaghin is an insufferable creature," Christian murmured, with lowered eyes. "I remember I once saw a manicoloured marine animal in an aquarium. It was very beautiful and also extremely horrible. I couldn't get rid of its image.

I wanted constantly to go back to it, and yet felt constantly an ugly horror of it."

"O la, la!" said Eva. Nothing else. And in this soft exclamation there was contempt, impatience, and curiosity. Then she stood before him. "I am not fond of being caged," she said in a hard voice. "I am not fond of being caught and isolated from my guests to be told trivial things. You must forgive me, but it doesn't interest me what impression Prince Szilaghin makes on you. Or, to be quite truthful, it interests me no longer."

Christian looked at her dumbly. It seemed to him that he was being chastised, beaten, and he turned very pale. The feeling of humiliation grew like a fever. "He invited me to his house to-morrow," he stammered, "and I merely wanted to tell you that I'm not going."

"You must go," Eva replied swiftly. "I beg of you to go." Avoiding the astonished question in his eyes, she added: "Maidanoff will be there. I wish you to see him."

"For what reason?"

"You are to know what I grasp at, what I do, whither I go. Can you read faces? I dare say not. Nevertheless, come!"

"What have you determined on?" he asked, awkwardly and shyly.

She gave her body a little, impatient shake. "Nothing that was not settled long ago," she answered, with a glassy coolness in her voice. "Did you think that I would drag on our lovely, wild May into a melancholy November? You might have spared us both your frankness of last night. The dream was over no moment sooner for you than for me. You should have known that. And if you did not know it, you should have feigned that knowledge. A gentleman of faultless taste does not throw down his cards while his partner is preparing to make a last bet. You do not deserve the honourable farewell that I gave you. I should have led you about, chained, like those stupid little beasts who are always whining for permission to ruin themselves for my sake. They call this thing their passion. It is a fire like any other; but I would not use it to kindle a lamp, if I needed light to unlace my shoes."

She had crossed her arms and laughed softly, and moved toward the door.

"You have misunderstood me," said Christian overwhelmed. "You misunderstand me wholly." He raised his hands and barred her way. "Do you not understand? If I had words. . . . But I love you so! I cannot imagine life without you. And yet (how shall I put it into words?) I feel like a man who owes colossal sums and is constantly dunned and tormented, and does not know wherewith to pay nor whom. Do try to understand! I was hasty, foolish. But I thought that you might help me."

It was the cry of a soul in need. But Eva did not or would not heed it. She had built of her love a soaring arch. She thought it had fallen, and no abyss seemed deep enough for its ruins to be hurled. She had neither ears now nor eyes. She had decided her fate even now; and though it frightened her, to recede was contrary to her pride and her very blood. A sovereign gesture silenced Christian. "Enough!" she said. "Of all the ugly things between two people, nothing is uglier than an explanation that involves the emotions. I have no understanding for hypochondria, and epilogues bore me. As for your creditors, see that you seek them out and pay them. It is troublesome to keep house with unpaid bills."

She went from the room.

Christian stood very still. Slowly he lowered his head, and hid his face in his hands.

XXIV

Next day Christian received a telegram from Crammon, in which the latter announced his arrival for the middle of the following week. He gazed meditatively at the slip of paper, and had to reconstruct an image of Crammon from memory, feature by feature. But it escaped him again at once.

At Fyodor Szilaghin's he found about twenty people. There were eight or ten Russians, including Wiguniewski. Then there were the brothers Maelbeek, young Belgian aristocrats, a French naval captain, Tavera, Bradshaw, the Princess Helfersdorff and her mother (a very common looking person), Beatrix Vanleer, and Sinaide Gamaleja.

Christian arrived a little later than the others, and Szilaghin was half-sitting, half-lying on a *chaise-longue.* A young wolf crouched on his knees, and on the arm of the *chaise-longue* sat a green parrot. He smiled and excused himself for not arising, pointing to the animals as though they held him fast.

From Wiguniewski's anecdotes Christian knew of Szilaghin's fondness for such trickery. At Oxford he had once gone boating alone and at night with an eagle chained to his skiff; at Rome he had once rented a palace, and given a ball to the dregs of the city's life—beggars, cripples, prostitutes, and pimps. The boastfulness of such things was obvious. But as Christian stood there and saw him with those animals, the impression he received was not only one of frantic high spirits, but also one of despair. A retroactive oppression crept over him.

The lighting of the rooms was strikingly dim and scattered. A thunderstorm was approaching, and the windows were all open on account of the sultry heat; and every flicker of lightning flashed an unexpected brightness into the rooms.

At the invitation of several guests, Sinaide Gamaleja sat down with a lute under a cluster of long-stemmed roses, and began to sing a Russian song. Over her shoulders lay a goldembroidered shawl, and her hair was held by a band of diamonds. Her figure was fragile. She had broad cheekbones, a wide mouth, and dully-glowing, heavy-lidded eyes.

The greyish-yellow wolf on Szilaghin's knees raised his head, and blinked sleepily at the singer. The melody had awakened in him a dream of his native steppes. But the parrot stirred too, and, croaking an unintelligible word, he preened himself and displayed the gorgeous plumage of his throat. Szilaghin raised a finger and bade the bird be silent; obediently it hid its beak in the feathers which a breeze lifted. A voluble old Russian kept talking to Szilaghin. The latter overheard him contemptuously, and joined in the singing of the song's second stanza.

His voice was melodious—a deep, dark baritone. But to Christian there seemed something corrupt in its music, as corrupt as the half-shut, angry, melancholy eyes with their contempt of mankind; as corrupt as the well-chiselled, waxen face, that could pass for eighteen, yet harboured all the experiences of an evil old age; as corrupt as the long, pale, sinuous, nerveless hand or the sweetish, weary, clever smile.

The Maalbeeks, Wiguniewski, the Captain, and Tavera had settled down to a game of baccarat in the adjoining room. In the pauses of the singing, one could hear the click of gold and the tap of the cards on the table. These strange noises excited the parrot; he forgot the command of his master, and uttered a discordant cry. Sinaide Gamaleja threw the animal a furious glance, and for a moment her hand twitched on the strings.

At that moment Szilaghin arose, grasped the bird's feet with one hand, its head with the other, and twisted the head of the screaming, agonizedly fluttering animal around and around as on an axis. Then he tossed the green, dead thing aside with an expression of disgust, and calmly intoned the third stanza of the song.

A flame of satisfaction appeared in Sinaide Gamaleja's eyes. The old Russian, who had visited his endless babble on the sculptress, fell suddenly silent. The wolf yawned, and, as though to confirm the fact of his own obedience, snuggled his chin against his master's arm.

Christian looked down at the dead bird, whose tattered

plumage gleamed in the lightning that flashed across the floor like a fantastic emerald. Suddenly the dead animal became to him the seal and symbol of all the corruption, vanity, unveracity, bedizenment, and danger of all he saw and felt. He looked at Szilaghin, at Sinaide, at the chattering dotard, at the gamesters, and turned away. There was an acridness in his throat and a burning in his eyes. He approached the window. The foliage rustled out there, and the thunder pealed. And the question arose within him: Whence does all this evil come? Whence does it come, and why is it so hard to separate oneself from it?

The night, the rain, and the storm drove him forth, lured him out. He ached to lose himself in the darkness, far from men. He was afraid for the first time in his life that he would shed tears. Never, in all his conscious memory, had he wept. His whole body was shaken by an emotional tumult such as he had never known, and he repressed it only by using his utmost energy. Just as he was about to touch the knob of the door, a lackey opened it, and Maidanoff and Eva appeared on the threshold. Christian stood quite still; but every vestige of colour left his face.

A vivid stir went through the company. Szilaghin jumped up to welcome these two. Maidanoff's weather-beaten leanness contrasted in a striking and sombre fashion with Eva's flower-like symmetry of form. She wore a garment diaphanous as breathing; it was held to her shoulders by ropes of pearls. Her skin had a faintly golden glow; her throat and arms and bosom pulsed with life.

The vision absorbed Christian. He stared at her. His name was spoken, with other names that were new to Maidanoff; and still he stared at that unfathomable and fatal image. His heart, in its sudden, monstrous loneliness, turned to ice; he felt both wild and stricken with dumbness; the tension of his soul became unendurable. Curious glances sought him out. He failed to move at the proper moment, and the moan that

arose from the confusion of his utter grief had made a thing
of mockery and scorn of him, before he fled past barren walls
and stupid lackeys into the open.

The rain came down in torrents. He did not call his car,
but walked along the road.

XXV

After losing twenty-eight thousand francs, the amount that
he had gradually borrowed from Mr. Bradshaw and Prince
Wiguniewski, Amadeus Voss got up from the gaming table, and
staggered into the open. He had a dim notion that he would
seek out Christian, to tell him that he would be able to settle
the debt within twenty-four hours.

He went to the telegraph office, and sent a message to
Christian. Then he stood beneath a chestnut tree in bloom,
and muttered: " Brother, brother."

A woman came along the road, and he joined her. But suddenly he burst out into wild laughter, turned down a side street,
and went on alone.

He walked and walked for six endless hours. At two o'clock
in the morning he was in Heyst. His brain seemed to have
become an insensitive lump, incapable of light or reason.

Masses of dark grey clouds that floated in the sky assumed
to him the aspect of women's bodies. The clouds, which the
hot night drove toward the north, were like cloaks over the
forms he desired. He felt an obscure yearning for all the love
in all the lands in which he had no part.

At the garden-gate of the villa he stopped and stared up at
Christian's windows. They were open and showed light.
" Brother," he muttered again, " brother! "   Christian appeared at the window. The sight of him filled Voss with a
sudden, overwhelming hatred. " Take care, Wahnschaffe! "
he cried.

Christian left the window, and soon appeared at the gate.
Amadeus awaited him with clenched fists. But when Christian

approached, he turned and fled down the street, and Christian looked after him. Then his steps became slower, and Christian followed.

After Voss had wandered about aimlessly for a time, he felt a torturing thirst. He happened to pass a sailors' tavern, considered for a moment, and entered. He ordered grog, but did not touch the glass. Five or six men sat at various tables. Three slept; the eyes of the others had a drunken stare. The tavern keeper, an obese fellow with a criminal face, sat behind the bar, and watched this elegantly attired guest, whose face was so pale and so disturbed. He concluded that the late comer was in a mood of despair, and beckoned to the bar-maid, a dark-haired, dirty Walloon, to sit down by him.

Impudently she did so, and started to talk. He did not understand her. She gave a coarse laugh, and put a hand on his knee. Behind her thin and ragged bodice her breasts stirred, like animals. She had a primitive, animal odour. He turned dizzy. Then a lust to murder stirred in him.

He drew from his pocket all the money he had left. There were seventy francs—three gold and five silver coins. " The magic numbers," he muttered, and grew a shade paler, " three and five! "

The Walloon woman turned greedy and caressing eyes upon the coins. The tavern keeper, scenting business, dragged his bulk forward.

" Strip off your clothes, and it's yours! " said Amadeus Voss.

She looked at him stupidly. The tavern keeper understood German and translated the words. She laughed shrilly, and pointed toward the door. Amadeus shook his head. " No; now; here! " He was stubborn. The girl turned to her employer, and the two consulted in whispers. Her gestures made it evident that she cared little for the presence of the drunken or snoring men. She disappeared behind a brown partition that had once been yellow. The tavern keeper

gathered the money on the table, waddled from window to
window to see that the red hangings covered all the panes,
and then stood guard at the door.

Amadeus sat there as though steeped in seething water. A
few minutes passed. Then the Walloon woman appeared
from behind the partition. The sailors looked up. One arose
and gesticulated; one uttered a wild laugh. The woman stood
with lowered eyes—stubborn, careless, rubbing one foot with
the other. She was rather fat, quite without charm, and the
lines of her body had been destroyed.

But to Amadeus Voss she was like a supernatural vision, and
he gazed upon her as though his whole soul was in that gaze.
His arms reached out, and his fingers became claws, and his
lips twitched. The fishermen and the tavern keeper no longer
saw the woman. They saw him. They felt fear. So unwonted was the sight that they did not observe the opening of
the door. The tavern keeper's whistled warning came too late.
Christian, who entered, still saw the naked woman as she hurried toward the partition.

He approached Amadeus. But the latter took no notice of
him. He stared spell-bound at the spot where the woman had
stood.

Christian laid a hand upon his shoulder. Amadeus roused
himself from his absorption, turned slow, questioning eyes upon
his friend, and strangely uttered with his quivering lips these
words: " Est Deus in nobis; agitante calescimus illo."

Then he broke down, his forehead dropped on the table, and
a shudder shook his body.

The tavern keeper muttered morosely.

" Come, Amadeus," said Christian very quietly.

The drunken fishermen and sailors stared.

Amadeus arose, and groped like a blind man for Christian's
hand.

" Come, Amadeus," Christian repeated, and his voice seemed
to make a deep impression on Voss, for he followed him without

hesitation. The tavern keeper and the sailors accompanied
them into the street.

The tavern keeper said to the men with him: "Those are
what you call gentlemen. Look how they behave! It shows
you why the world is ruled so ill."

"The dawn is breaking," said one of the fishermen, and
pointed to a purple streak in the eastern heaven.

Christian and Amadeus likewise stared at the purple seam
of the east, and Amadeus spoke again: "Est Deus in nobis;
agitante calescimus illo."

KAREN ENGELSCHALL

I

On the appointed hour of the appointed day Crammon arrived. He had prepared himself to stay and to be festive; but he was disappointed. Eva and her train were on the point of leaving. Maidanoff had proceeded to Paris, whither Eva was to follow him.

Crammon had been informed of this new friendship of his idol. All other news came to him too, and so he was aware that a quarrel had arisen between Christian and Eva. He was the more astonished to see Christian determined to follow Eva to Hamburg.

They had exchanged but a few words, when the transformation in Christian struck him. He laid his hand on the young man's shoulder, and asked sympathetically: "Have you nothing to confide?"

He spent the evening with Wiguniewski. "It isn't possible," he said; "you're mistaken. Or else the world is topsy-turvy and I can no longer tell a man from a woman."

"I had no special liking for Wahnschaffe from the start," Wiguniewski confessed. "He's too impenetrable, mysterious, spoiled, cold, and, if you will, too German. Nevertheless I knew from the first that he was the very man for Eva Sorel. You couldn't see the two together without a sense of delight—the sort of delight that a beautiful composition gives you, or anything that is spiritually fitting and harmonious."

Crammon nodded. "He has a strange power over women," he said. "I've just had another instance which is the more remarkable as it developed from a mere sight of his picture. At the Ashburnhams' in Yorkshire, where I've been staying, I made the acquaintance of a Viennese girl, a banker's daughter, rather ugly,. to be frank, but with a peculiar little sting and, charm and wit of her own. Not a bad figure, though rather— shall we say scanty? Yes. Her name is Johanna Schöntag, though that matters little. I called her nothing but Rumpel- stilzkin. That fitted her like a glove. God knows how she got there. Her sister, a russet-haired person who looks as though she'd jumped out of a Rubens, is married to an attaché of some minor legation, Roumanian or Bulgarian or something like that. The big capitalists fit their daughters into society that way. Well, anyhow, this Rumpelstiezkin and I agreed to amuse each other in the murky boredom of Lord and Lady Ashburn- ham's house. So one day I showed the girl a miniature of Christian which Gaston Villiers painted for me in Paris. She looked at the picture and her merry face grew grave, ab- sorbed, and she handed it back to me silently. A couple of days later she asked to see it again, and it had the same effect on her. She asked me about the man, and I, of course, became very eloquent, and happened to remark, too, that I expected to meet Christian here. She insisted at once that she must meet him, and that I must plan to have her do so. Remember she's rather unapproachable as a rule, fastidious, turning up her nose—her worst feature by the way—at things that please most people. The request was unexpected and rather a nui- sance. One mustn't, as you know, bring the wrong people together and land one's self in difficulties. So I said at once: ' The Almighty forbid! ' I admonished her gently to change her mind, and painted the danger in its darkest hues. She laughed at me, and asked me whether I'd grown strait-laced; then she at once developed a most cunning plan. She had time enough. She wasn't expected home till the first of November, which gave her seven weeks. So she would announce her intention of studying the Dutch galleries, the pursuit of culture being always respectable. She had a companion and chaperone, as it was, and her sister, who was broad-minded in such matters, could be taken into her confidence. Her energy and astute-

ness made me feel weak, and forced me into the conspiracy.
Well, she arrived yesterday. She's at the Hotel de la Plage,
a little scared, like a bird that's dropped out of its nest, a
little dissatisfied with herself, vexed by little attacks of mo-
rality; and I, for my part, don't know what to do with her. I
bethought me too late that Christian isn't to be caught by
such tricks, and now I've got to make it clear to the girl. All
this is by the way, prince—a sort of footnote to your discourse, which I did not intend to interrupt."

Wiguniewski had listened with very slight sympathy. · He
began again: " These past months, as I've said, have given
us all an unforgettable experience. We have seen two free
personalities achieving a higher form of union than any of the
legitimized ones. But suddenly this noble spectacle turns into
a shabby farce; and it is his fault. For such a union has its
organic and natural close. A man of subtle sensitiveness knows
that, and adjusts himself accordingly. Instead of that, he
actually lets it get to the point of painful scenes. He seeks
meetings that humiliate him and make him absurd. When
she is out he waits in her rooms for her return, and endures
her passing him by with a careless nod. Once he sat waiting
all night and stared into a book. He lets the Rappard woman
treat him insolently, and doesn't seem to mind that the fruits
and flowers he sends daily are regularly refused. What is it?
What does it mean? "

" It points to some sorrow, and assuredly to a great sorrow
for me," Crammon sighed. " It's incomprehensible."

" She entertained at dinner day before yesterday,"
Wiguniewski continued. " As though to mock him he was
placed at the lower end of the table. I didn't even know the
people who sat by him. It seems to arouse a strange cruelty
in her that he doesn't refuse to bear these humiliations; he, on
the other hand, seems to find some inexplicable lure in his
suffering. He sat down that evening in silence. Afterwards a
curious thing happened. Groups had been formed after dinner.

He stood a few feet from Eva and gazed at her steadily. His face had a brooding look as he observed her. She wore Ignifer, which is his gift, and looked like Diana with a burning star above her forehead."

"That's excellently well put, prince," Crammon exclaimed.

"The conversation touched upon many subjects without getting too shallow. You know her admirable way of checking and disciplining talk. Finally there arose a discussion of Flemish literature, and some one spoke of Verhaeren. She quoted some verses of a poem of his called 'Joy.' The sense was somewhat as follows: My being is in everything that lives about me; meadows and roads and trees, springs and shadows, you become me, since I have felt you wholly. There was a murmur of appreciation. She went to a shelf and took down a volume of Verhaeren's poems. She turned the pages, found the poem she sought, and suddenly turned to Wahnschaffe. She gave him the book with a gesture of command; he was to read the poem. He hesitated for a moment, then he obeyed. The effect of the reading was both absurd and painful. He read like a schoolboy, low, stammering, and as though the content were beyond his comprehension. He felt the absurdity and painfulness of the incident himself, for his colour changed as the ecstatic stanzas came from his lips like an indifferent paragraph in a newspaper; and when he had finished the reading, he laid the book aside, and left without a glance at any one. But Eva turned to us, and said as though nothing had happened: 'The verses are wonderful, aren't they?' Yet her lips trembled with fury. But what was her purpose? Did she want to prove to us his inability to feel things that are beautiful and delicate? Did she want to put him to shame, to punish him and publicly expose the poverty of his nature? Or was it only an impatient whim, the annoyance at his dumb watchfulness and his searching glances? Mlle. Vanleer said later: 'If he had read the verses like a divine poet, she would have forgiven him.' 'Forgiven him what?' I asked. She smiled,

and answered: 'Her own faithlessness.' There may be something in that. At all events, you should get him out of this
situation, Herr von Crammon."

" I shall do all in my power," said Crammon, and the lines
of care about his mouth grew deeper. He wiped his forehead.
"Of course I don't know how far my influence goes. It would
be empty boastfulness to guarantee anything. I've been told
too that he frequents all sorts of impossible dives with impossible people. I could weep when I think of it. He was the
flower of modern manhood, the pride of my lengthening years,
the salt of the earth! Unfortunately he had, even when I left
him, certain attacks of mental confusion, but I put those down
to the account of that suspicious fellow, Ivan Becker."

" Don't speak of him! Don't speak of Becker! " Wiguniewski interrupted sharply. " Not at least in that manner, I
must beg and insist."

Crammon opened his eyes very wide, and the tip of his
tongue became visible, like a red snail peering out of its shell.
He choked down his discomfort and shrugged his shoulders.

Wiguniewski said: " At all events you've given me an indi-
cation. I never considered such a possibility. It throws a
new light on many things. It's true, by the way, that Wahnschaffe associates with questionable people. The queerest of
them all is Amadeus Voss, a hypocrite and a gambler. One
must not couple such persons with Ivan Becker. Becker may
have set him upon a certain road. If we assume that, a number of incidents become clear. But anything really baneful
comes from Voss. Save your friend from him! "

" I haven't seen the fellow yet," Crammon murmured. " What
you tell me, Prince, doesn't take me quite unawares. Nevertheless, I'm grateful. But let that scoundrel beware! May
I never drink another drop of honest wine, if he escape me!
Let me never again glance at a tempting bosom, if I don't
grind this infamous cur to pulp. So help me! "

Wiguniewski arose, and left Crammon to plan his revenge.

II

The morning sun of late September was gilding sea and land, when Crammon entered Christian's room. Christian was sitting at his curved writing table. The bright blue tapestries on the walls gleamed; chairs and tables were covered by a hundred confused objects. Everything pointed to the occupant's departure.

"Don't let me disturb you, dear boy; I have time enough," said Crammon. He swept some things from a chair, sat down, and lit his pipe.

But Christian put down his pen. "I don't know what's the matter with me," he said angrily, without looking at Crammon, "I can't get two coherent sentences down on paper. However carefully I think it out, by the time it's written it sounds stiff and silly. Have you the same experience?"

Crammon answered: "There are those who have the trick. It takes, primarily, a certain impudence. You must never stop to ask: Is that correct? Is it true? Is it well-founded? Scribble ahead, that's all. Be effective, no matter at what cost. The cleverest writers are often the most stupid fellows. But to whom are you writing? Is the haste so great? Letters can usually be put off."

"Not this time. It is a question of haste," Christian answered. "I have a letter from Stettner and I can't make out his drift. He tells me that he's quitting the service and leaving for America. Before he goes he wants to see me once more. He takes ship at Hamburg on October 15. Now it fortunately happens that I'll be in Hamburg on that date, and I want to let him know."

"I don't see any difficulty there," Crammon said seriously. "All you need say is: I'll be at such a place on such a day, and expect or hope, et cetera. Yours faithfully or sincerely or cordially, et cetera. So he's going to quit? Why? And run off to America? Something rotten in the state of Denmark?"

" He was challenged to a duel, it appears, and refused the challenge. That's the only reason he gives. He adds that matters shaped themselves so that he is forced to seek a new life in the New World. It touches me closely; I was always fond of him. I must see him."

" I'd be curious too to know what really happened," said Crammon. " Stettner didn't strike me as a chap who'd lightly run away and risk his honour. He was an exemplary officer. I'm afraid it's a dreary business. But I observe that it gives you a pretext for going to Hamburg."

Christian started. " Why a pretext? " He was a little embarrassed. " I need no pretext."

Crammon bent his head far forward, and laid his chin on the ivory handle of his stick. His pipe remained artfully poised in one corner of his mouth, and did not move as he spoke. " You don't mean to assert, my dearest boy, that your conscience doesn't require some additional motive for the trip," he began, like a father confessor who is about to use subtle arguments to force a confession from a stubborn malefactor, " and you're not going to try to make a fool of an old boon-companion and brother of your soul. One owes something to a friend. You should not forget under whose auspices and promises you entered the great world, nor what securities *he* offered—securities of the heart and mind—who was the author and master of your radiant entry. Even Socrates, that rogue and revolutionary, recalled such obligations on his death bed. There was a story about a cock—some sort of a cock, I believe. Maybe the story doesn't fit the case at all. No matter. I always thought the ancients rather odious. What does matter is that I don't like your condition, and that others who love you don't like it. It rends my very heart to see you pilloried, while people who can't tell a stud-horse from a donkey shrug their shoulders at you. It's not to be endured. I'd rather we'd quarrel and exchange shots at a distance of five paces. What has happened to you? What has come over you? Have you stopped gathering scalps to offer your own head? The hares and the hounds, I tell you, are diverse creatures. I understand all things human, but the divine order must be kept intact. It's flying in the face of providence that you should stand at the gate like a beggar. You used to be the one who showed others the door; they whined and moaned after you—and that was proper. I had an uncle who was something of a philosopher, and he used to say: when a woman, a lawyer, and a stove are at their hottest—turn your back to them. I've always done that, and kept my peace of mind and my reputation. There are extenuating circumstances in your case, I admit. There is but one such woman in a century, and whoever possesses her may well lose his reason. But even that should not apply to you, Christian. Splendour is your natural portion: it is for you to grant favours; at your board the honey should be fresh each day. And now tell me what you intend to do."

Christian had listened to this lengthy though wise and pregnant discourse with great patience. At times there was a glint of mockery or anger in his eyes. Then again he would lower them and seem embarrassed. Sometimes he grasped the sense of Crammon's words, sometimes he thought of other things. It cost him an effort to recall clearly by what right this appar-ently complete stranger interfered in his life and sought to influence his decisions. And then again he felt within himself a certain tenderness for Crammon in the memory of common experiences and intimate talks; but all that seemed so far away and so estranged from the present.

He looked out of the window, from which the view was free to the horizon where sea and sky touched. Far in the distance a little white cloud floated like a white, round pillow. The same tenderness that he felt for Crammon, he now felt for that little cloud.

And as Crammon sat before him and waited for an answer, there suddenly came into his mind the story of the ring which Amadeus had told him. He began: " A young candidate for

Holy Orders, who was tutor to the children of a banker, fell under the suspicion of having stolen a costly ring. He told me the story himself, and from his words I knew that the ring, when he saw it on the hand of his employer's wife, aroused his desire. In addition he loved this woman, and would have been happy to have had something by which to remember her. But he was utterly innocent of the disappearance of the ring, and some time after he had left that house, his innocence received the most striking confirmation. For the lady sent him the ring as a gift. He was wretchedly poor, and the ring would have meant much to him; but he went and threw it into a well, a deep old-fashioned well. The costliest thing he had ever possessed in life, he threw without hesitation or reflection into a well—that's what this man did."

"Oh, well, very well. Although . . . no, I don't quite see your meaning," said Crammon, discontentedly, and shifted his pipe from the right to the left corner of his mouth. "What good did the ring do the poor fool? How absurd to take something that reaches you in a manner so delicate and discreet, and throw it into a well? Would not a box have served, or a drawer? There at least it could have been found. It was a loutish trick."

Crammon's way of sitting there with his legs crossed, showing his grey silk socks, had something about it so secure and satiated, that it reminded one of an animal that basks in the sun and digests its food. Christian's disgust at his words quieted, and was replaced by a gentle, almost compassionate tenderness. He said: "It is so hard to renounce. You can talk about it and imagine it; you can will it and even believe yourself capable of it. But when the moment of renunciation comes, it is hard, it is almost impossible to give up even the humblest of things."

"Yes, but why do you want to renounce?" Crammon murmured in his vexation. "What do you mean exactly by renunciation? What is it to lead to?"

Christian said almost to himself: "I believe that one must cast one's ring into a well."

"If you mean by that that you intend to forget our wonderful Queen Mab, all I have to say is—the Lord help you in your purpose," Crammon answered.

"One holds fast and clings because one fears the step into the unknown," Christian said.

Crammon was silent for a few minutes and wrinkled his forehead. Then he cleared his throat and asked: "Did you ever hear about homœopathy? I'll explain to you what is meant by it. It means curing like with like. If for instance some food has disagreed with you violently, and I give you a drug that would, in a state of health, have sickened you even more violently than your food—that would be a homœopathic treatment."

"So you want to cure me?" Christian asked, and smiled. "From what and with what?"

Crammon moved his chair nearer to Christian's, laid a hand on his knees, and whispered astutely: "I've got something for you, dear boy. I've made an exquisite find. There's a woman in your horoscope, as the sooth-sayers put it. Some one is yearning for you, is immensely taken with you, and dying of impatience to know you. And it's something quite different, a new type, something prickling and comical, indeterminate, sensitive, a little graceless and small and not beautiful, but enormously charming. She comes from the bourgeoisie at its most obese, but she struggles with both hands and feet against the fate of being a pearl in a trough. There's your chance for employment, distraction, and refreshment. It won't be a long affair,—an interlude of her holidays, but instructive, and, in the homœopathic sense, sure to work a cure. For look you: Ariel, she is a miracle, a star, the food of the gods. You can't live on such nourishment; you need bread. Descend, my son, from the high tower where you still grasp after the *miraculum cœli* that once flamed on your bosom. Put it out of your mind;

descend, and be contented with mortality. To-night at seven in the dining-room of the Hotel de la Plage. Is it a bargain? "

Christian laughed, and got up. On the table stood a vase filled with white pinks. He took out one of the flowers, and fastened it into Crammon's button-hole.

"Is it a bargain or not? " Crammon asked severely.

"No, dear friend, there's nothing in that for me," Christian answered, laughing more heartily. "Keep your find to yourself."

The veins on Crammon's forehead swelled. "But I've promised to bring you, and you mustn't leave me in the lurch." He was in a rage. "I don't deserve such treatment, after all the slights which you have put on me for months. You give rights to an obscure vagabond that astonish the whole world, and you cast aside heartlessly an old and proved friend. That does hurt and embitter and enrage one. I'm through."

"Calm yourself, Bernard," said Christian, and stooped to pick up some blossoms that had fallen on the floor. And as he put back the flowers into the vase, there came to him the vision of Amadeus Voss' white face, showing his bleeding soul and paralyzed by desire and renunciation, even as it was turned toward the fat, morose Walloon woman. "I don't comprehend your stubbornness," he continued. "Why won't you let me be? Don't you know that I bring misfortune to all who love me? "

Crammon was startled. Despite Christian's equivocal smile, he felt a sudden twinge of superstitious fear. "Idiotic! " he growled. He arose and took his hat, and still tried to wring from Christian a promise for the evening. At that moment a knock sounded at the door, and Amadeus Voss entered.

"I beg your pardon," he stammered, and looked shyly at Crammon, who had at once assumed an attitude of hostility. "I merely wanted to ask you, Christian, whether we are going to leave. Shall the packing be done? We must know what to do."

Crammon was furious. "Fancy the scoundrel taking such a tone," he thought. He could hardly force himself to assume the grimace of courtesy that became inevitable when Christian, quite hesitatingly, introduced them to each other.

Amadeus bowed like an applicant for some humble office. His eyes behind their lenses clung to Crammon, like the valves of an exhaust pump. He found Crammon repulsive at once; but he thought it advisable not only to hide this feeling but to play the part of obsequiousness. His hatred was so immediate and so violent, that he was afraid of showing it too soon, and stripping himself of some chance of translating it into action.

Crammon sought points of attack. He treated Voss with contempt, looked at him as though he were a wad of clothes against the wall, neither answered him nor listened to what he said, deliberately prolonged his stay, and paid no attention to Christian's nervousness. Voss continued to play the part he had selected. He agreed and bowed, rubbed the toe of one of his boots against the sole of the other, picked up Crammon's stick when the latter dropped it; but as he seemed determined not to be the first to yield, Crammon at last took pity on the silent wonder and torment in Christian's face. He waved his well-gloved left hand and withdrew. He seemed to swell up in his rage like a frog. "Softly, Bernard," he said to himself; "guard your dignity, and do not step into the ordure at your feet. Trust in the Lord who said: Vengeance is mine." He met a little dog on his path, and administered a kick to it, so that the beast howled and scurried into an open cellar.

Across the table Christian and Voss faced each other in silence. Voss pulled a flower from the vase, and shredded its calyx with his thin fingers. "So that was Herr von Crammon," he murmured. "I don't know why I feel like laughing. But I can't help it. I do." And he giggled softly to himself.

"We leave to-morrow," said Christian, held a handkerchief

to his mouth, and breathed the delicate perfume that aroused in him so many tender and slowly fading images.

Voss took a blossom, tore it in two, gazed tensely at the parts, and said: " Fibre by fibre, cell by cell. I am done with this life of sloth and parasitism. I want to cut up the bodies of men and anatomize corpses. Perhaps one can get at the seat of weakness and vulgarity. One must seek life at its source and death at its root. The talent of an anatomist stirs within me. Once I wanted to be a great preacher like Savonarola; but it's a reckless thing to try in these days. One had better stick to men's bodies; their souls would bring one to despair."

" I believe one must work," Christian answered softly. " It does not matter at what. But one must work." He turned toward the window. The round, white cloud had vanished; the silver sea had sucked it up.

" Have you come to that conclusion? " Voss jeered. " I've known it long. The way to hell is paved with work; and only hell can burn us clean. It is well that you have learned that much."

III

Crammon and Johanna Schöntag were sitting in a drawing-room of the hotel. They had had dinner together. Johanna's companion, Fräulein Grabmeier, had already retired.

" You must be patient, Rumpelstilzkin," said Crammon. " I'm sorry to say that he hasn't bitten yet. The bait is still in the water."

" I'll be patient, my lord," said Johanna, in her slightly rough, boyish voice, and a gleam of merriment, in which charm and ugliness were strangely blended, passed over her face. " I don't find it very hard either. Everything is sure to go wrong with me in the end. If ever unexpectedly a wish of mine is fulfilled, and something I looked forward to does happen, I'm as wretched as I can be, because it's never as nice as I thought it would be. The best thing for me, therefore, is to be disappointed."

"You're a problematic soul," said Crammon musingly.

Johanna gave a comical sigh. " I advise you, dear friend and protector, to get rid of me by return post." She stretched her thin little neck with an intentionally bizarre movement. " I simply interfere with the traffic. I'm a personified evil omen. At my birth a lady by the name of Cassandra appeared, and I needn't tell you the disagreeable things that have been said of her. You remember how when we were at target practice at Ashburnhill I hit the bull's-eye. Everybody was amazed, yourself included; but I more so than any one, because it was pure, unadulterated chance. The rifle had actually gone off before I had taken aim. Fate gives me such small and worthless gifts, in order to seem friendly and lull me into security. But I'm not to be deceived. Ugh! A nun, a nun! " she interrupted herself. Her eyes became very large, as she looked into the garden where an Ursuline nun was passing by. Then she crossed her arms over her bosom, and counted with extraordinary readiness: "Seven, six, five, four, three, two, one." Then she laughed, and showed two rows of marvellous teeth.

"Is it your custom to do that whenever a nun appears?" Crammon asked. His interest in superstitions was aroused.

" It's the proper ritual to follow. But she was gone before I came to one, and that augurs no good. By the way, dear baron, your sporting terminology sounds suspicious. What does that mean: ' he hasn't bitten yet; the bait is still in the water ' ? I beg you to restrain yourself. I'm an unprotected girl, and wholly dependent on your delicate chivalry. If you shake my tottering self-confidence by any more reminiscences of the sporting world, I'll have to telegraph for two berths on the Vienna train. For myself and Fräulein Grabmeier, of course."

She loved these daring little implications, from which she

could withdraw quite naïvely. Crammon burst into belated laughter, and that fact stirred her merriment too.

She was very watchful, and nothing escaped her attentive eyes. She took a burning interest in the characters and actions of people. She leaned toward Crammon and they whispered together, for he could tell a story about each form and face that emerged from the crowd. The chronicle of international biography and scandal of which he was master was inexhaustible. If ever his memory failed him, he invented or poetized a little. He had everything at his tongue's end—disputes concerning inheritances, family quarrels, illegitimate descent, adulteries, relationships of all sorts. Johanna listened to him with a smile. She peered at all the tables and carefully observed every uncommon detail. She picked up and pinned down, as an entomologist does his beetles, any chance remark or roguish expression, any silliness or peculiarity of any of these unconscious actors of the great world or the half world.

Suddenly the pupils of her greyish blue eyes grew very large, and her lips curved in a bow of childlike delight. "Who is that?" she whispered, and thrust her chin out a little in the direction of a door at Crammon's back. But she at once knew instinctively who it was. She would have known it without the general raising of heads and softening of voices, of which she became aware.

Crammon turned around and saw Eva amid a group of ladies and gentlemen. He arose, waited until Eva glanced in his direction, and then bowed very low. Eva drew back a little. She had not seen him since the days of Denis Lay. She thought a little, and nodded distantly. Then she recognized him, kicked back her train with an incomparable grace, and, speaking in every line before her lips moved, went up to him.

Johanna had arisen too. Eva remarked the little figure. She gave Crammon to understand that he had a duty toward his companion, and that she would not refuse an introduction to the unknown girl, on whose face enthusiasm and homage were

so touchingly to be seen. Crammon introduced Johanna in his
most ceremonious manner. Johanna grew pale and red and
curtsied. She seemed to herself suddenly so negligible that she
was overcome with shame. Then she tore off the three yellow
roses at her corsage, and held them out to Eva with a sudden
and yet timid gesture. Eva liked this impulse. She felt its
uniqueness and veracity, and therefore knew its value.

IV

Christian and Amadeus wandered across the Quai Kokerill
in Antwerp.

A great transatlantic liner lay, silent and empty, at the
pier. The steerage passengers waited at its side for the hour
of their admission. They were Polish peasants, Russian Jews,
men and women, young ones and aged ones, children and suck-
lings. They crouched on the cold stones or on their dirty
bundles. They were themselves dirty, neglected, weary, dully
brooding—a melancholy and confused mass of rags and human
bodies.

The mighty globe of the sun rolled blood-red and quivering
over the waters.

Christian and Amadeus stopped. After a while they went on,
but Christian desired to turn back, and they did so. At a
crossing near the emigrants' camp, a line of ten or twenty
donkey-carts cut off the road. The carts looked liked bisected
kegs on wheels, and were filled with smoked mackerels.

"Buy mackerels!" the cart-drivers cried. "Buy mackerels!" And they cracked their whips.

A few of the emigrants approached and stared hungrily;
they consulted with others, who were already looking for coins
in their pockets, until finally a few determined ones proceeded
to make a purchase.

Then Christian said to Voss: "Let us buy the fish and
distribute them. What do you think?"

Amadeus was ill pleased. He answered. "Do as you wish. Great lords must have their little pleasures." He felt uncomfortable amid the gathering crowd.

Christian turned to one of the hucksters. It was difficult to make the man understand normal French, but gradually he succeeded. The huckster summoned the others, and there followed excited chatter and gesticulations. Various sums were named and considered and rejected. This process bored Christian; it threatened to be endless. He offered a sum that represented a considerable increase over the highest price named, and handed his wallet to Amadeus that the men might be paid. Then he said to the increasing throng of emigrants in German: "The fish are yours."

A few understood his words, and conveyed their meaning to the others. Timidly they ventured forward. A woman, whose skin was yellow as a lemon from jaundice, was the first to touch a fish. Soon hundreds came. From all sides they brought baskets, pots, nets, sacks. A few old men kept the crowd in order. One of these, who wore a flowing white beard and a long Jewish coat, bowed down thrice before Christian. His forehead almost touched the earth.

A sudden impulse compelled Christian to see in person to the just distribution of the fish. He turned up his sleeves, and with his delicate hands threw the greasy, malodourous fish into the vessels held out for them. He laughed as he soiled his fingers. The hucksters and some idle onlookers laughed too. They thought him a crazy, young Englishman out for a lark. Suddenly his gorge rose at the odour of the fish, and even more at the odour of these people. He smelled their clothes and their breath, and gagged at the thought of their teeth and fingers, their hair and shoes. A morbid compulsion forced him to think of their naked bodies, and he shuddered at the idea of their flesh. So he stopped, and slipped away into the twilight.

His hands still reeked of the smoked fish. He walked

through the streets that had had nothing to do with his adventure and the night seemed empty.

Amadeus Voss had escaped. He waited in front of the hotel. There the line of motor cars had gathered that was to accompany Eva on her journey to Germany. Among the travellers were Crammon and Johanna Schöntag.

V

In October the weather turned hot on the Rio de la Plata. All day one had to stay in the house. If one opened a window, living fire seemed to stream in. Once Letitia fainted, when she wanted to air her stuffy room, and opened one of the wooden shutters.

The only spot that offered some shade and coolness toward evening was an avenue of palms beside the river. Sometimes, during the brief twilight, Letitia and her young sister-in-law Esmeralda would steal away to that place. Their road passed the ranchos, the wretched cave-like huts in which the native workmen lived.

Once Letitia saw the people of the ranchos merrily feasting and in their best garments. She asked for the reason, and was told that a child had died. "They always celebrate when some one dies," Esmeralda told her. "How sad must their lives be to make them so in love with death."

The avenue of palms was forbidden ground. When darkness came, the bushes rustled, and furtive men slipped back and forth. Not long before the mounted police had caught a sailor here who was wanted for a murder in Galveston. Somehow Letitia dreamed of him. She was sure he had killed his man through jealousy and bore the marks of a beautiful tragedy.

One evening she had met in this spot a young naval officer, who was a guest on a neighbouring estate. Letitia exchanged glances with him, and from that time on he sought some way of approaching her. But she was like a prisoner, or like a Turkish woman in a harem. So she determined to outwit her guards; she really fell in love with the young officer. Her imagination made an heroic figure of him, and she began to long for him.

The heat increased. Letitia could not sleep at night. The mosquitoes hummed sweetishly, and she cried like a little child. By day she locked herself in her room, stripped off her clothes, and lay down on the cold tiles.

Once she was lying thus with arms outstretched. "I'm like an enchanted princess," she thought, "in an enchanted castle."

Some one knocked at the door, and she heard Stephen's voice calling her. Idly she raised her head, and from under her heavy lids gazed down at her naked body. "What a bore it is," she thought, "what a terrible bore always to be with the same man. I want others too." She did not answer, and let her head droop, and rubbed her glowing cheek against the warm skin of her upper arm. It pleased the master of the harem out there to beg for admission; but Letitia did not open the door.

After a while she heard a tumult in the yard—laughter, the cracking of whips, the report of rifles, and the cries of beasts in torment. She jumped up, slipped into a silk dressing gown, opened the window that gave on the verandah, and peered out.

Stephen had tied together the tails of two cats by means of a long fuse. Along the fuse were fastened explosive bits of firework. The hissing little rockets singed the cats' fur, and the glowing cord burned into their flesh. The cats tumbled about in their agony and howled. Stephen goaded them and followed them. His brothers, bent over the balustrade, roared with delight. Two Indians, grave and silent, watched from the gate.

Stephen had, of course, counted on Letitia's opening the door in her curiosity. A few great leaps, and he was beside

her. Esmeralda, who was in the plot, had at once faced
Letitia and prevented her from locking the door. White with
rage, and with raised fist, he stormed across the threshold.
She fell to her knees, and hid her face in her hands.

"Why do you beat me?" she moaned, in horror and surprise. But he did not touch her.

His teeth gnashed. "To teach you to obey.".

She sobbed. "Be careful! It's not only me you're hurting now!"

"Damnation, what are you saying?" He stared at her
crouching figure.

". You're hurting two now." Letitia enjoyed fooling him.
Her tears were now tears of pity for herself.

"Woman, is that true?" he asked. Letitia peered furtively between her fingers, and thought mockingly: "It's like
the last act of a cheap opera." She nodded with a gesture of
pain, and determined to deceive him with the naval officer.

Stephen gave a howl of triumph, danced about, threw himself down beside her, and kissed her arms, her shoulders, and
her neck. At the windows and doors appeared Doña Barbara, Esmeralda, Stephen's brothers, and the servants. He
lifted Letitia on his strong shoulders, and carried her about
on the verandah. He roared his orders: a feast was to be
prepared, an ox slaughtered, champagne to be put on ice.

Letitia had no qualms of conscience. She was glad to
have made a fool of him.

When old Gunderam learned the cause of the rejoicing
in his house, he chuckled to himself. "Fooled all the same,
my sly lawyer man. In spite of the written agreement, you
won't get the Escurial, not for a good while, even if she has
a whole litter." With an unappetizing, broken little comb
he smoothed his iron grey beard, and poured eau de Cologne
on his head, until his hair, which was still thick, dripped.

But, strangely enough, the lie that Letitia had told
in her terror turned out to be the truth. In a few days she

was sure. Secretly she was amazed. Every morning she stood before the mirror, and looked at herself with a strange respect and a subtle horror. But she was unchanged. Her mood became gently melancholy, and she threw a kiss to her image in the glass.

Since they were now afraid of crossing her wishes, she was permitted to attend a ball given by Señor and Señora Küchelbäcker, and it was there that she made the formal acquaintance of the naval lieutenant, Friedrich Pestel.

VI

Felix Imhof and the painter Weikhardt met at the exhibition of the "secessionists" in Munich. For a while they strolled through the rooms, and looked at the paintings; then they went out on the terrace, and sat down at a table that commanded a view of the park.

It was in the early afternoon, and the odours of oil and turpentine from within blended with the fragrance of the sun-warmed plants.

Imhof crossed his long legs, and yawned affectedly. "I'm going to leave this admirable home of art and letters for some months," he declared. "I'm going to accompany the minister of colonial affairs to South West Africa. I'm anxious to see how things are going there. Those people need looking after. Then, too, it's a new experience, and there will be hunting."

Weikhardt was utterly self-absorbed. He was full of his own annoyances, his inner and outer conflicts, and therefore spoke only of himself. "I am to copy a cycle by Luini for the old Countess Matuschka," he said. "She has several blank walls in her castle in Galicia, and she wants tapestries for them. But the old creature is close as the bark on the tree, and her bargaining is repulsive."

Imhof also pursued his own thoughts. "I've read a lot about Stanhope recently," he said. "A tremendous fellow, modern through and through, reporter and conquistador at the same time. The blacks called him the 'cliff-breaker.' It makes one's mouth water. Simply tremendous! "

Weikhardt continued: " But I dare say I'll have to accept the commission. I've come to the end of my tether. It'll be good to see the old Italians again, too. In Milan there's a Tintoretto that's adorable. I'm on the track of a secret. I'm doing things that will count. The other day I finished a picture, a simple landscape, and took it to an acquaintance of mine. He has a rather exquisite room, and there we hung it. The walls had grey hangings, and the furnishings were in black and gold. He's a rich man and wanted to buy the picture. But when I saw how much he liked it, and saw, too, the delicate, melancholy harmony of its colours with the tints of the room, I felt a sudden flash of encouragement. I couldn't bear to talk money, and I simply gave him the thing. He accepted it quietly enough, but he continued saying: 'How damned good it is! ' "

" It'll take my thoughts off myself, this little trip to the Southern Hemisphere," said Imhof. " I'm not exactly favoured of fortune just now. To be frank—everything's in the deuce of a mess. My best horse went to smash, my favourite dog died, my wife took French leave of me, and my friends avoid me—I don't know why. My business is progressing backward, and all my speculations end in losses. But, after all, what does it matter? I say to myself: Never say die, old boy! Here's the great, beautiful world, and all the splendour and variety of life. If you complain, you deserve no better. My sandwich has dropped into the mud. All right; I must get a fresh one. Whoever goes to war must expect wounds. The main thing is to stick to your flag. The main thing is faith—quite simple faith."

It was still a question which of the two would first turn his attention from himself, and hear his companion's voice. Weikhardt, whose eyes had grown sombre, spoke again: " O this dumb loneliness in a studio, with one's hundred failures, and the ghosts of one's thousand hours of despair! I have a chance to marry, and I'm going to take it, too. The girl has no money, to be sure, but she has a heart. She's not afraid of my poverty, and comprehends the necessary quixotism of an artist's life. She comes of a Protestant family of very liberal traditions, but two years ago she became a Catholic. When I first met her I was full of suspicion, and assumed all sorts of reasons for her step except the simple and human ones. It's very difficult to see the simple and the human things, and still more difficult to do them. Gradually I understood what it means—to believe! and I understood what is to be reverenced in such faith. It is faith itself that is sacred, not that in which the faith is placed. It doesn't matter what one has faith in—a book, a beast, a man, a star, a god. But it must be pure faith—immovable and unconquerable. Yes, I quite agree with you—we need simple faith."

So they had found each other through a word. "When do I get my picture, your Descent from the Cross?" Imhof inquired.

Weikhardt did not answer the question. As he talked on, his smooth, handsome, boyish face assumed the aspect of a quarrelsome old man's. Yet his voice remained gentle and slow, and his bearing phlegmatic. "Humanity to-day has lost its faith," he continued. "Faith has leaked out like water from a cracked glass. Our age is tyrannised by machinery: it is a mob rule without parallel. Who will save us from machinery and from business? The golden calf has gone mad. The spirit of man kowtows to a warehouse. Our watchword is to be up and doing. We manufacture Christianity, a renaissance, culture, et cetera. If it's not quite the real thing, yet it will serve. Everything tends toward the external—toward expression, line, arabesque, gesture, mask. Everything is stuck on a hoarding and lit by electric lamps.

Everything is the very latest, until something still later begins to function. Thus the soul flees, goodness ceases, the form breaks, and reverence dies. Do you feel no horror at the generation that is growing up? The air is like that before the flood."

"Create, O artist, and don't philosophize," Imhof said gently.

Weikhardt was shamed a little. "It's true," he said, "we have no means of knowing the goal of it all. But there are symptoms, typical cases that leave little room for hope. Did you hear the story of the suicide of the German-American Scharnitzer? He was pretty well known among artists. He used to go to the studios himself, and buy whatever took his fancy. He never bargained. Sometimes he would be accompanied by a daughter of eighteen, a girl of angelic beauty. Her name was Sybil, and he used to buy pictures for her. She was especially fond of still-life and flower pieces. The man had been in California and made millions in lumber. Then he returned to the fatherland to give the girl an atmosphere of calm and culture. Sybil was his one thought, his hope, his idol and his world. He had been married but a short time. His wife, it is said, ran away from him. All that a life of feverish activity had left him of deep feeling and of hope for the future was centred in this child. He saw in her one girl in a thousand, a little saint. And so indeed she seemed—extraordinarily dainty, proud and ethereal. One would not have dared to touch her with one's finger. When the two were together, a delightful sense of harmony radiated from them. The father, especially, seemed happy. His voluntary death caused all the more consternation. No one suspected the motive; it was assumed that he had suffered a moment of madness. But he left behind him a letter to an American friend which explained everything. He had been indisposed one day, and had had to stay in bed. Sybil had invited several girl friends to tea, and the little com-

pany was in a room at the other end of their suite. But
all the doors between were open, even the last was slightly
ajar, so that the murmur of the girls' voices came to him
inarticulately. A sudden curiosity seized him to know what
they were saying.. He got up, slipped into a dressing gown,
went softly through the intervening rooms, and listened at
the door. The conversation was about the future of these
girls—the possibilities of love, happiness, and marriage. Each
gave her ideas. Finally it was Sybil's turn to speak her
thoughts. At first she refused; but they urged her again
and again. She said she took no interest in emotions of any
sort; she didn't yearn for love; she wasn't able to feel even
gratitude to any one. What she expected of marriage was
simply liberation from a galling yoke. She wanted a man
who could give her all that life held—boundless luxury and
high social position—and who, moreover, would be abjectly
at her feet. That, she said, was her program, and she
intended to carry it out too. The other girls fell silent.
None answered. But that hour poisoned the father's soul.
This cynicism, uttered by the pure and spiritual voice of
the child he adored and thought a miracle of depth and
sweetness, the child on whom he had wasted all he was and
had, plunged him into an incurable melancholy, and caused
him finally to end his life."

"My dear fellow," cried Imhof, and waved his arm, "that
man wasn't a lumber merchant, he was a minor poet."

"It's possible that he was," Weikhardt replied, and smiled;
"quite possible. What does it alter? I admire a man who
cannot survive the destruction of all his ideals. It's better
than to be a cliff-breaker, I assure you. Most people haven't
any ideals to be destroyed. They adapt themselves end-
lessly, and become vulgar and sterile." Again his eyes grew
sombre, and he added, half to himself: "Sometimes I dream
of one who neither rises nor falls, of one who walks on

earth whole and unchangeable, unswerving and unadaptable.
Perfectly unadaptable. It is 'of such an one that I
dream."

Imhof jumped up, and smoothed his coat. "Talk, talk! "
he rattled, in the disagreeable military tone that he assumed
in his moments of pseudo-virility. "Talk won't improve
things." He passed his arm through Weikhardt's, and as
they left the terrace, which had been gradually filling with
other guests, he recited, boldly, unashamed, and in the same
tone, the alcaic stanza of Hölderlin:

"Still man will take up arms against all who breathe;
Compelled by pride and dread he consumes himself
    in conflict, and destroys the lovely
        Flower of his peace that is brief of blooming."

VII

On their first evening in Hamburg, Crammon rented a
box in the playhouse, and invited Christian, Johanna Schöntag, and Herr Livholm, one of the directors of the Lloyd,
to be his guests. He had made the latter's acquaintance in
the hotel where he had gone to pay Eva a visit of welcome.
He had liked the man, who cut a good figure, and so he had
added him to the party in order, as he put it, to keep the
atmosphere normal by the presence of an entirely neutral
person.

"Social skill," he was accustomed to say, "is not unlike
skill in cookery and serving. Between two heavy, rich dishes
there must be one like foam that stimulates the palate quite
superficially. Otherwise the meal has no style."

The play was a mediocre comedy, and Christian was frankly
bored. Crammon thought it his duty to show a condescending and muffled amusement, and now and then he gave Christian a gentle poke, to persuade him also to show some appreciation of the performance. Johanna was the only one who
was genuinely amused. The source of her amusement was

an actor to whom a serious rôle had been assigned, but who talked with such silly affectation and false importance that every time he appeared she had to hold her lacy handkerchief to her lips to smother her laughter.

Occasionally Christian gave the girl a far and estranged glance. She wasn't either agreeable or the reverse; he did not know what to make of her. This feeling of his had not changed since he had first seen her during the journey in Eva's company.

She felt the coldness of his glance. Her merriment did not vanish; but on the lower part of her face appeared a scarcely perceptible shadow of disappointment.

As though seeking for help, she turned to Christian. " The man is terribly funny, don't you think so? " It was characteristic of her to end a question with a negative interrogation.

" He's certainly worth seeing," Christian agreed politely.

The door of the box opened, and Voss entered. He was faultlessly dressed for the occasion; but no one had expected or invited him. They looked at him in astonishment. He bowed calmly and without embarrassment, stood quite still, and gave his attention to the stage.

Crammon looked at Christian. The latter shrugged his shoulders. After a while Crammon arose, and with sarcastic courtesy pointed to his seat. Voss shook his head in friendly refusal, but immediately thereafter assumed once more his air of humility and abjectness. He stammered: " I was in the stalls and looked up. I thought there was no harm in paying a visit." Suddenly Crammon went out, and was heard quarrelling with the usher. Johanna had become serious, and looked down at the audience. Christian, as though to ward off disagreeable things, ducked his shoulders a little. The people in the near-by seats became indignant at the noise Crammon was making. Herr Livholm felt that the proper atmosphere had hardly been preserved.

Amadeus Voss alone showed himself insensitive to the situation.

He stood behind Johanna, and thought: " The hair of this
woman has a fragrance that turns one dizzy." At the end
of the act he withdrew, and did not return.

Late at night, when he had him alone, Crammon vented
his rage on Christian. " I'll shoot him down like a mad
dog, if he tries that sort of thing again! What does the
fellow think? I'm not accustomed to such manners. Damned
gallow's bird—where'd he grow up? Oh, my prophetic soul!
I always distrusted people with spectacles. Why don't you
tell him to go to hell? In the course of my sinful life, I've
come in contact with all kinds of people; I know the best
and I know the dregs; but this fellow is a new type. Quite
new, by God! I'll have to take a bromide, or I won't be able
to sleep."

" I believe you are unjust, Bernard," answered Christian,
with lowered eyes. But his face was stern, reserved, and
cold.

VIII

Amadeus Voss submitted the following plan to Christian:
to go to Berlin, first as an unmatriculated student, and
later to prepare himself for the state examination in medicine.

Christian nodded approvingly, and added that he intended
to go to Berlin shortly too. Voss walked up and down in
the room. Then he asked brusquely: ." What am I to live
on? Am I to address envelopes? Or apply for stipends? If
you intend to withdraw your friendship and assistance, say
so frankly. I've learned to wade through the mud. The
new kind won't offer more resistance than the old."

Christian was thoroughly surprised. A week ago, in Holland, he had given Amadeus ten thousand francs. " How
much will you need? " he asked.

"Board, lodging, clothes, books . . ." Voss went over the items, and his expression was that of one who formulates demands and uses the tone of request only as a matter of courtesy. "I'll be frugal."

"I shall order two thousand marks a month to be sent you," Christian said, with an air of aversion. The impudent demand for money pained him. Possession weighed upon him like a mountain. He could not get his arms free nor lift his chest, and the weight grew heavier and heavier.

In a bowl of chrysolite on the table lay a scarf-pin with one large, black pearl. Voss, whose hands always groped for some occupation, had taken it up, and held it between his thumb and index finger against the light. "Do you want the pin?" Christian asked. "Take it," he persuaded Amadeus, who was hesitating. "I really don't care about it."

Voss approached the mirror, and with a curious smile stuck the pin into his cravat.

When Christian was left alone, he stood for a while quite lost in thought. Then he sat down, and wrote to his manager at Christian's Rest. He wrote in his lanky script and his no less awkward style. "My dear Herr Borkowski:— I have determined to sell Christian's Rest, together with all furnishings and objects of art, as well as the park, woods, and farms. I herewith commission you to find a capable and honest real estate dealer, who might telegraph me any favourable offers. You know people of that sort, and need merely drive over to Frankfort. Have the kindness to settle the matter as quietly as possible. No advertisements are to appear in the press."

Then he wrote a second letter to the manager of his racing stable at Waldleiningen. To write this he had to do more violence to his heart than the first had cost him, for he saw constantly fixed upon him the gentle or spirited eyes of the noble animals. He wrote: "My dear Herr Schaller:—

I have determined to discontinue my racing stable. The horses are to be sold at auction or quietly to fanciers. I should prefer the latter method, and I suppose you share that feeling. Baron Deidinger of Deidingshausen was at one time much interested in Columbus and the mare Lovely. Inquire of him whether he wants them. Admirable and Bride o' the Wind could be offered either to Prince Pless or Herr von Strathmann. Have my friend Denis Lay's Excelsior sent to Baden-Baden, and boarded temporarily in the stables of Count Treuberg. I don't wish him to remain at Waldleiningen alone."

When he had sealed the letters, he sighed with relief. He rang, and gave the letters to his valet. The latter had turned to go, when Christian called him back. "I'm very sorry to have to give you notice, Wilhelm," he said. "I'm going to attend to myself hereafter."

The man could not trust his ears. He had been with Christian for three years, and was genuinely devoted to him.

"I'm sorry, but it's necessary," said Christian, looked past the man, and had almost the same strange smile with which he had watched Amadeus Voss at the mirror putting the black pearl pin into his cravat.

IX

Crammon asserted that Amadeus Voss was paying his attentions to Johanna Schöntag. Johanna was annoyed, and tapped him with her long gloves. "I congratulate you on your conquest, Rumpelstilzkin," Crammon teased her. "To have a monster like that in leash is no small achievement. I should advise muzzling the monster, however. What do you think, Christian, wouldn't you - advise a muzzle, too?"

"A muzzle?" answered Christian. "Yes, if it would keep people from talking. So many talk too much."

Crammon bit his lips. The reproof struck him as harsh.

Somewhere beneath the downs of life on which he lay and enjoyed himself, there was, evidently, a stone. The stone hurt. He sought for it, but the softness of the down calmed him again, and he forgot his pain.

"I was sitting in the breakfast room, and waiting for Madame Sorel," Johanna began in a voice whose every shading and inflection sought to woo Christian's ear, "when Herr Voss came in and marched straight up to me. 'What does that bad man want of me?' I asked myself. He asked me, as though we'd been bosom friends for years, whether I didn't want to go with him to St. Paul's to hear the famous itinerant preacher Jacobsen. I couldn't help laughing, and he stalked away insulted. But this afternoon, as I was leaving the hotel, he seemed suddenly to spring from the earth, and invited me to a trip around the harbour. He had rented a motor launch, and was looking for a companion. He had the same gruff familiarity, and when he left he was quite as insulted as before. And you call that paying attentions? I felt much more as though he were going to drag me off and murder me. But perhaps that's only his manner." She laughed.

"You're the only person, at all events, whom he distinguishes by observing at all," Crammon said, with the same mockery.

"Or the only one whom he considers his equal," Johanna said, with a childlike frown.

Christian was wondering: "Why does she laugh so often? Why are her hands so pudgy and so very pink?" Johanna felt his disapproval, and was as though paralysed. And yet Christian felt himself drawn toward her by some hidden power.

Why should he resist? Why be so ceremonious? Such was his thought, as Johanna arose, and he, with unobtrusive glances, observed her graceful form that still possessed the flexibility of immaturity. He saw the nape of her slender neck, in which were expressed both the weakness of her will and the fineness of her temper. He knew these signs; he had often been guided by them and used them.

Crammon, massive and magnificent in a great easy chair, spoke with some emphasis of Eva's appearance on the morrow. The whole city was in a state of expectancy. But Christian and Johanna had suddenly become truly aware of one another.

"Are you coming along?" Christian turned carelessly, and with a sense of boredom, to Crammon.

"Yes, my boy, let us eat!" Crammon cried. He called Hamburg the Paradise of Saint Bernard, concerning whom, as his patron saint and namesake, he had instituted especial investigations, and who, according to him, had been a mighty trencherman during his lifetime at Tours.

A frightened, subtle, and very feminine smile hovered about Johanna's lips. As she preceded the two men, the motions of her dainty body expressed a vague oppression of the spirit, and at the same time a humorous rebellion against her own un-freedom.

X

Amadeus Voss knew that he had no one's sympathy, no one's except Christian's. And him he suspected, watching him, weighing and analysing his words and actions. In his terror of hypocrisy and treachery, he practised both himself. Nothing healed or convinced or reconciled him. Least of all did he pardon Christian the fact that the latter's glance and presence had the effect of subduing him. His bitterness moaned from his very dreams.

He read in the Scriptures: "There was a certain house-holder, which planted a vineyard, and hedged it round about, and digged a winepress in it, and built a tower, and let it out to husbandmen, and went into a far country: and when the time of the fruit drew near, he sent his servants to the husbandmen that they might receive the fruits of it. And the husbandmen took his servants, and beat one, and killed another, and stoned another. Again he sent other servants, more than the first, and they did unto them likewise. But last of all, he sent unto them his son, saying, They will reverence my son. But when the husbandmen saw the son, they said among themselves, This is the heir; come, let us kill him, and let us seize on his inheritance. And they caught him, and cast him out of the vineyard, and slew him."

Sometimes he would not leave Christian's side for hours. He would study his gestures and the expressions of his countenance, and all these perceptions fed the corrosive fire in his brain. For this was the heir! Then he would flee and bruise and stamp upon his very soul, until his consciousness of guilt cast him down into the very dust. He would return, and his demeanour would be a silent confession: " I can thrive only in your presence." It seemed to him that this silence of his was like a cry; but it was not heard, and so his brother seemed again to become his foe. Thus he kept passing from darkness, through fires and fumes, back into the darkness.

He suffered from his own embarrassment and importunateness. In the midst of luxury and plenty, into which he had been transferred by a fabulous turn of fortune, he suffered from the memories of his former poverty, still felt how it had bound and throttled him, and still rebelled against what was gone. He could not freely take what was given him, but closed his eyes, and shuddered with both desire and a pang of conscience. He would not look upon the pattern of his web of life. He turned its texture around, and brooded over the significance of the intricately knotted threads. And there was no human relationship which did not rouse his suspicion, no harmless conversation in which he did not seek a sting directed toward himself, no face that did not feed his hatred, no beauty whose counter part of ugliness he did not see. To him everything turned to poison and decay, all blossoms became noxious weeds, all velvet a Nessus shirt, all light an evil smouldering, every stimulus a wound: on every wall he saw the flaming letters, *mene tekel upharsim.*

He could not yield himself or conquer the stubbornness of his heart. With the object of his desire in his very hands, his envy burned on. Whatever had once humiliated him spurred his vengefulness through retrospection. Chastisements which his father had inflicted distorted the old man's image beyond the grave; his fellow pupils in the seminary had once strewn pepper into his coffee, and he could not forget it; he could not forget the expression on the face of Adeline Ribbeck with which she had given him his first month's salary in a closed envelope; he remembered the contempt and contumely of hundreds, who had inflicted upon him their revenge for the oppression or degradation which they themselves had endured. He could not conquer these things nor forgive fate. The marks that had been burned into his flesh throbbed like new wounds.

But at other times he would cast himself into the dust in prayer and in great need of forgiveness. Religious scruples plagued him into remorse; he panted for an hour's release from consciousness, judged himself with cruel severity, and condemned himself to ascetic practices.

And these hurled him into the other extreme of a wild, undiscriminating, and senseless dissipation and a mad waste of money. He could no longer resist the excitement of gambling, and fell into the hands of sharpers, drifted into loathsome dives, where he acted the part of a wealthy man and an aristocrat in incognito, for he desired to test this human mask, and prove its worthlessness to himself. Since his companions took him seriously in this rôle, which filled his own mind with shame and despair, he took his high losses with apparent calm, and overlooked the open cheating. One evening the den in which he happened to be was raided by the police, and he escaped by a hair's breadth. One creature clung to him, frightened him with possible dangers ahead, threatened exposure, and wrung from him a considerable sum of hush money.

He became the prey of cocottes. He bought them jewels and frocks and instituted nightly revels. In his eyes they were outcasts that he used as a famishing man might slake his thirst at a mud puddle with no clean water within reach. And he was brutally frank with them. He paid them to endure his contempt. They were surprised, resisted only his most infamous abuses, and laughed at his unconquerable traits of the churchly hypocrite. Once he remained alone with a girl who was young and pretty. He had blindfolded himself. But suddenly he fled as though the furies were at his heels.

Thrice he had set the date for his departure and as many times had put it off. The image of Johanna had joined that of Eva in his soul, and both raged in his brain. Both belonged to an unattainable world. Yet Johanna seemed less alien; she might conceivably hear his plea. Eva and her beauty were like a strident jeer at all he was. He had heard so much and read so much of her art that he determined to await her appearance, in order (as he told Christian) to form a judgment of his own, and be no longer at the mercy of those who fed her on mere adulation and brazen flattery.

The audience was in full evening dress. Amadeus sat next to Christian in the magnificent and radiant hall, in which had gathered royal and princely persons, the senators of the free city, the heads of the official and financial world, and representatives of every valley and city of Germany. Christian had bought seats near the stage. Crammon, who was an expert in matters of artistic perspective, had preferred the first row in the balcony. With him were Johanna and Botho von Thüngen, to whom he had emphatically explained that the play of the dancer's feet and legs was interfered with by the dark line of the stage below, while from their present position its full harmony would be visible.

Amadeus Voss had almost determined to remain rigid in mind. He hardly resisted actively, for he did not expect anything powerful enough to make resistance worth while.

He was cold, dull, unseeing. Suddenly, there floated upon the stage a bird-like vision, a being miraculously eased of human heaviness, one who was all rhythm, and turned the rhythm of motion into music. She broke the chains of the soul, and made every emotion an image, every action a myth, every step a conquest over space and matter. But the face of Amadeus seemed to say: How can that serve me? How does that serve you? Filled by the fury of sex, he saw only a scabrous exhibition, and when the thunder of applause burst out, he showed his teeth.

Eva's last number was a little dramatic episode, a charming *jeu d'esprit*, which she had invented and worked out, to be accompanied by a composition of Delibes. It was very simple. She was Pierrot playing with a top. She regulated and guided the whimsical course of the toy. In ever new positions, turns, and rhythms, she finally drove the top toward a hole into which it disappeared. But this trivial action was so filled with life by the wealth and variety of her rhythmic gestures, so radiant with spirit and swiftest grace, so fresh in inspiration, so heightened in the perfection of its art, that the audience watched breathlessly, and released its own tensity in a fury of applause.

In the foyer Crammon rushed up to Christian, and drew him through the crowd along the dim passage way that led back of the stage. Amadeus Voss, unnoticed by Crammon, followed them unthinkingly and morosely. The sight of the wings, of cliffs and trees, of discarded drops, electrical apparatus and pulleys and of the hurrying stage-hands, stirred in him a dull and hostile curiosity.

An excited crowd thronged toward Eva's dressing-room. She sat in the silken Pierrot costume of black and white, the dainty silver whip still in her hand, amid a forest of flowers. Before her kneeled Johanna Schöntag with an adoring moisture in her eyes. Susan gave her mistress a glass of cool champagne. Then in a mixture of five or six languages she tried to make it clear to the unbidden guests that they were in the way. But each wanted a look, a word, a smile of Eva for himself.

Next to the room in which Eva sat, and separated from it by a thin partition with an open door, was a second dressing-room, which contained only her costumes and a tall mirror. Accidentally pushed in that direction, and not through any will of his own, Amadeus Voss suddenly found himself alone in this little chamber. Having entered it, his courage grew, and he ventured a little farther in.

He looked around and stared at the garments that lay and hung here—the shimmering silks, the red, green, blue, white, and yellow shawls and veils, the fragrant webs of gauze, batiste, and tulle. There were wholly transparent textures and the heaviest brocades. One frock glowed like pure gold, another gleamed like silver; one seemed made of rose-leaves, another knitted of spun glass, one of white foam and one of amethyst. And there stood dainty shoes—a long row of them, shoes of Morocco leather and of kid and silk; and there were hose of all colours, and laces and ribands and antique beads and brooches. The air was drenched with a fragrance that stung his senses—a fragrance of precious creams and unguents, of a woman's skin and hair. His pulses throbbed and his face turned grey. Involuntarily he stretched out his hand, and grasped a painted Spanish shawl. Angrily, greedily, beside himself, he crushed it in his hands, and buried his mouth and nose in it and trembled in every limb.

At that moment Susan Rappard saw him, and pointed to him with a gesture of astonishment. Eva saw him too, gently thrust Johanna aside, arose, and approached the threshold. When she saw the man in his strange and absorbed ecstasy, she felt as though she had been spattered with filth, and uttered a soft, brief cry. Amadeus Voss twitched and dropped the shawl. His eyes were wild and guilty. With a light laugh and an expression of transcendent contempt, which summed up a long dislike, Eva raised the little silver whip and struck him full in the face. His features grew very white, in a contortion of voluptuousness and terror.

In the tense silence Christian went up to Eva, took the silver whip from her hand, and said in a tone scarcely distinguishable from his habitual one: "Oh, no, Eva, I shall not let you do that." He held the handle of the whip firmly at both ends, and bent it until the fragile metal snapped. Then he threw the two pieces on the floor.

They gazed at each other. Disgust at Amadeus still flamed in Eva's face. It yielded to her astonishment at Christian's temerity. But Christian thought: "How beautiful she is!" And he loved her. He loved her in her black and white Pierrot's costume with the black velvet buttons, he loved her with that little cap and its impudent little tassel on her head; he loved her, and she seemed incomparable to him, and his blood cried out after her as in those nights from which she had driven him forth. But he also asked himself: "Why has she grown evil?" And a strange compassion for her stole over him, and a stranger sense of liberation. And he smiled. But to all who were watching, this smile of his seemed a little empty.

Again Amadeus Voss read in the Scripture: "What mean ye that ye beat my people to pieces, and grind the faces of the poor? Because the daughters of Zion are haughty, and walk with stretched forth necks and wanton eyes, walking and mincing as they go, and making a tinkling with their feet: Therefore the Lord will strike with a scab the crown of the head of the daughters of Zion, and the Lord will discover their secret parts. In that day will the Lord take away the bravery of their tinkling ornaments about their feet, and their cauls, and their round tires like the moon, the chains, and the bracelets, and the mufflers, the bonnets, and the ornaments of the legs, and the headbands, and the tablets, and the earrings, the rings, and nose jewels, the changeable suits of apparel, and the mantles, and the wimples, and the crisping pins, the glasses, and the fine linen, and the hoods and the veils. And it shall come to pass, that instead of sweet smell there shall be stink; and instead of a girdle a rent; and instead of well set hair baldness; and instead of a stomacher a girding of sackcloth; and burning instead of beauty. Thy men shall fall by the sword, and thy mighty in the war. And her gates shall lament and mourn; and she being desolate shall sit upon the ground."

On the same evening he left for Berlin.

XI

Lorm and Judith had a magnificent apartment near the Tiergarten in Berlin.

Edgar Lorm flourished. Order and regularity ruled his life. With childlike boastfulness he spoke of his home. His manager and friend, Dr. Emanuel Herbst, congratulated him on his visible rejuvenation.

He introduced to Judith the people whom he had long valued; but she judged most of them sharply and without sympathy. Her characteristic arrogance drove away many who meant well. But under the sway of his new comforts Lorm submitted to her opinions.

But he would not give up Emanuel Herbst. When Judith mocked at his waddling gait, his homeliness, his piping voice, his tactless jokes, Lorm grew serious. "I've known him for over twenty years. The things that annoy you endear him to me quite as much as those precious qualities in him which I know well, and which you've had no chance to discover."

"No doubt he's a monster of virtue," Judith replied, "but he bores me to extinction."

Lorm said: "One should get used to the idea that other people don't exist exclusively for our pleasure. Your point of view is too narrowly that of use and luxury. There are human qualities that I value more highly than a handsome face or polished manners. One of these is trustworthiness. People with whom one has professional dealings often refuse to honour the demands of common decency—especially in regard to the keeping of their given word—with a calm frivolity that makes one's gorge rise. So I'm intensely grateful to Herbst, since it means so infinitely much to me, for this—that our relations have never been shadowed by distrust, and that our simplest verbal agreements are as firm and as valid as a written contract."

Judith recognized that in this case she would have to change her tactics. She was amiable, as though she were convinced of his virtues, and sought to gain his favour. Dr. Herbst saw through her, but showed no consciousness of his insight. He treated her with an elaborate courtesy that seemed a trifle old-fashioned, and effectually concealed his reservations.

Sometimes in the evening she would sit with the two men, and join in their shop talk of playwrights and plays, actors and actresses, successes and failures. And while she seemed attentive, and even asked an occasional question, she thought of her dressmaker, of her cook, of her weekly account, or of her old life, that was so different and had perished so utterly. And her eyes would grow hard.

It would happen that she would pass through the rooms with a bitter expression on her face and a hostile glance for the things about her. She hated the many mirrors which Lorm required, the rugs that had been recently bought, the pretentious furniture and paintings, the countless bibelots, photographs, ornaments, books, and piously guarded souvenirs.

She had never before lived in a house where other tenants above and below reminded her of their repulsive and unfamiliar lives. She listened to the slightest noises, and felt that she had fallen into a slum.

It was hardly in harmony with her nature to wait each morning until her husband happened to rise, to see that the breakfast was complete, to stand aside while the barber, the masseur, the chauffeur, the messenger of the theatre, and the secretary had completed their tasks or received their instructions; to wait again until he returned from rehearsal, tired, annoyed, and hungry, and then to watch him at luncheon—a meal that he required to be both rich and exquisite—gobble his food; to guard him from noise and interruption when he memorized his lines; to answer strange voices on the telephone, to give information, refuse invitations, to send the troublesome away and to soothe the impatient. She was wholly out of her natural element, but she forced herself to endure even as she had endured bodily pain when the long needle had been thrust through her arm.

Emanuel Herbst, who was a keen observer and a learned student of human nature, quietly analysed the relations of this husband and this wife. He said to himself: "Lorm is not fulfilling her expectations; so much is clear. She fancied she could peel him the way one peels an onion, and that the removal of each layer would reveal something so new and surprising as to make up to her for all she has renounced. She will soon discover her miscalculation, for Lorm is always the same. He can't be stripped. He wears his costumes and puts on make-up. She will soon reproach him for this very ability to fill empty forms with a beautiful content, and to remain, in his own person, but a humble servitor of his art. And the more guilty he becomes in her eyes, the more power over him will she gain. For he is tired—tired to death of the affected, the flatterers and sentimentalists, of the sweets and easements of his daily life. Terribly spoiled as he is, he yearns unconsciously for chains and a keeper."

The result of his reflection filled Emanuel Herbst with anxious apprehension.

But Judith remembered her dream—how she had lain beside a fish because it pleased her, and then beaten it in sudden rage over its cool, moist, slippery, opalescent scales. And she lay beside the fish and struck it, and the fish became more and more subservient and her own.

Her constant terror was this thought: "I am poor, impoverished, dependent, without security." The thought tormented her to such a degree that she once expressed it to the house-keeper. The latter was astonished and replied: " But in addition to your pin money, the master gives you two thousand marks a month for the house. Why should you yield to morbid fancies? "

Judith looked at the woman suspiciously. She distrusted all whom she paid. The moment they mentioned money she fancied herself robbed.

One day the cook gave notice. She was the fourth since the establishment of the household. A quantity of sugar was missing. There was a quarrel, an ugly one, and Judith was told things that no one had ever dared to tell her before.

The secretary mislaid a key. When at last it was found Judith rushed to the drawer which it fitted to see whether the stationery, the pencils, and the pen-points were intact.

The housekeeper had bought twenty yards of linen. Judith thought the price paid too high. She drove to the shop herself. The taxi-fare amounted to more than she could possibly have saved on the purchase. Then she chaffered with the clerk for a reduction, until it was granted her through sheer weariness. She told Lorm the story with a triumphant air. He neglected to praise her. She jumped up from the table, locked herself in her room, and went to bed. Whenever she thought that she had some reason for anger, she went to bed.

Lorm came to her door, knocked softly, and asked her to open it. She let him stand long enough to regret his conduct, and then opened the door. She told her story all over, and he listened with a charming curiosity on his face. " You're a jewel," he said, and stroked her cheek and hand.

But it would also happen, if she really wanted something, that she would spend sums out of all proportion to her wretched little economies. She would see a hat, a frock, an ornament in a show window, and not be able to tear herself away. Then she would go into the shop, and pay the price asked at once.

One day she visited an auction sale, and happened to come
in just as an old Viennese bon-bon dish was offered for sale.
It was one of those objects that make little show, but which
delight the collector's heart. At first the dish didn't tempt her
at all. Then the high bidding for it excited her, and she herself began to bid for it. It kindled something in her, and she
made bid after bid, and drove all competitors from the field.

Hot and excited, she came home and rushed into Lorm's
study. Emanuel Herbst was with him. The two men sat
by the fire in familiar talk. Judith disregarded Herbst. She
stood before her husband, unwrapped the dish, and said: " Look
at this exquisite thing I bought, Edgar."

It was toward evening, but no lights had been lit. Lorm
loved the twilight and the flicker of the fire in his chimney,
which was, alas, only a metropolitan imitation of a log fire.
In the rich, red, wavering reflection of the glow, Judith looked
charming in her delight and mobility.

Lorm took the dish, regarded it with polite interest, drew up
his lips a little, and said: " It's pretty." Herbst's face puckered
into innumerable ironical little wrinkles.

Judith grew angry. " Pretty? Don't you see that it's magical, a perfect little dream, the sweetest and rarest thing imagin-
able? The connoisseurs were wild after it! Do you know
what it cost? Eighteen hundred marks. And I had six or
seven rabid competitors bidding against me. Pretty! " She
gave a hard little laugh. " Give it to me. You handle it too
clumsily."

" Calm yourself, sweetheart," said Lorm gently. " I suppose
its virtues are subtle."

But Judith was hurt, more by Herbst's silent mockery than
by Lorm's lack of appreciation. She threw back her head,
rustled through the room, and slammed the door behind her.
When she was angry, her own manners had, at times, a touch
of commonness.

For a while the two men were silent. Then Lorm, embar-

rassed and with a deprecating smile, said: "A little dream
. . . for eighteen hundred marks. . . . Oh, well! There's
something childlike about her."

Emanuel Herbst rubbed his tongue up and down between his
teeth and his upper lip. It made him look like an ancient baby.
Then he ventured: "You ought to make it clear to her that
eighteen hundred marks are one thousand eight hundred times
one mark."

"She won't get that far," answered Lorm. "Somebody who
has always lived on the open sea, and is suddenly transported
to a little inland lake, finds it hard to get the new measure-
ments and perspectives. But women are queer creatures." He
sighed and smiled. "Have a nip of whiskey, old man?".

Sorrowfully Herbst rocked his Cæsarean head. "Why
queer? They are as they are, and one must treat them accordingly. Only one ·mustn't be under any mistaken impression,
as to what one has. For instance: A horseshoe is not birch
wood. It looks like a bow, but you can't bend it—not with all
your might. If you string it, the string droops slackly and will
never propel your arrow. All right, let's have your whiskey."

"But occasionally," Lorm replied cheerfully, and filled the
tiny glasses, "you can turn a horseshoe into the ·finest
Damascene steel."

"Bravo! A good retort! You're as ready as Cardinal
Richelieu. Your health!"

"If you'll let me be Richelieu, I'll appoint you to be my
Father Joseph. A great rôle, by the way. Your health, old
man!"

XII

Crammon and Johanna Schöntag planned to drive to Stel-
lingen to see Hagenbeck's famous zoological gardens, and Crammon begged Christian to lend them his car. They were just
about to start when Christian issued from the hotel. "Why
don't you come along?" Crammon asked. "Have you any-

thing better to do? The three of us can have a very amusing time."

Christian was about to refuse, when he caught Johanna's urgent and beseeching look. She had the art of putting her wishes into her eyes in such a way that one was drawn by them, and lost the power to resist. So he said: "Very well, I'll come along," and took the seat next to Johanna's. But he was silent on the whole drive.

It was a sunny day of October.

They wandered through the park, and Johanna made droll comments on the animals. She stopped in front of a seal; and exclaimed: "He looks quite like Herr Livholm, don't you think so?" She talked to a bear as though he were a simple sort of man, and fed him bits of sugar. She said that the camels were incredible, and only pretended to look that way to live up to the descriptions in the books of natural history. "They're almost as ugly as I am," she added; and then, with a crooked smile: "Only more useful. At least I was told at school that their stomachs are reservoirs of water. Isn't the world a queer place?"

Christian wondered why she spoke so contemptuously of herself. She bent over a stone balustrade, and the sight of her neck somehow touched him. She seemed to him a vessel of poor and hurt things.

Crammon discoursed. "It is very curious about animals. Scientists declare they have a great deal of instinct. But what is instinct? I've usually found them to be of an unlimited stupidity. On the estate where I passed my childhood, we had a horse, a fat, timid, gentle horse. It had but one vice: it was very ticklish. I and my playmates were strictly enjoined from tickling it. Naturally we were constantly tempted to tickle it. There were five of us little fellows—no higher than table legs. Each procured a little felt hat with a cock's feather in it. And as the horse stood dull-eyed in front of the stable, we marched in single file under the belly of the stupid beast, tickling it with our feathers as we passed. The feathers tickled so frightfully that he kicked with all fours like a mule. It's a riddle to me to this day how one of us, at least, failed to be killed. But it was amusing and grotesque, and there was no sign of instinct anywhere."

They went to the monkey house. A crowd stood about a little platform, on which a dainty little monkey was showing off its tricks under the guidance of a trainer. " I have a horror of monkeys," said Crammon. " They annoy me through memory. Science bids me feel a relationship with them; but after all one has one's pride. No, I don't acknowledge this devilish atavism." He turned around, and left the building in order to wait outside.

Alone with Christian, a wave of courage conquered Johanna's timidity. She took Christian's arm and drew him nearer to the platform. She was utterly charmed, and her delight was childlike. " How dear, how sweet, how humble! " she cried. A spiritual warmth came from her to Christian. He yielded himself to it, for he needed it. Her boyish voice, however, stirred his senses and aroused his fear. She stood very close by him; he felt her quiver, the response to the hidden erotic power that was in him, and the other voices of his soul were silenced.

He took her hand into his. She did not struggle, but a painful tension showed in her face.

Suddenly the little monkey stopped in its droll performance and turned its lightless little eyes in terror toward the spectators. Some shy perception had frightened it; it seemed, somehow, to think and to recollect itself. As it became aware of the many faces, the indistinctness of its vision seemed to take on outline and form. Perhaps for a second it had a sight of the world and of men, and that sight was to it a source of boundless horror. It trembled as in a fever; it uttered a piercing cry of lamentation; it fled, and when the trainer tried to grasp it, it leaped from the platform and frantically sought a hiding-place. Tears glittered in its eyes and its teeth chattered, and in spite of the animal characteritsics of these gestures and expressions, there was in them something so human and soulful that only a few very coarse people ventured to laugh.

To Christian there came from the little beast a breath from an alien region of earth and forests and loneliness. His heart seemed to expand and then to contract. "Let us go," he said, and his own voice sounded unpleasantly in his ears.

Johanna listened to his words. She was all willingness to listen, all tension and all sweet humility.

XIII

Randolph von Stettner had arrived. There were still several days before the date of his sailing, and he was on his way to Lübeck, where he wished to say good-bye to a married sister. Christian hesitated to promise to be in Hamburg on his friend's return. Only after much urging did he consent to stay.

They dined in Christian's room, discussed conditions in their native province, and exchanged reminiscences. Christian, laconic as usual, was silently amazed at the distance of all these things from his present self.

When the waiter had removed the dishes, Stettner gave an account of all that had driven him to the determination to expatriate himself. While he talked he stared with an un-changing look and expression at the table cover.

"You know that for some years I've not been comfortable in my uniform. I saw no aim ahead except the slow and distant moments of advancement. Some of my comrades hoped for war. Well, the life makes that hope natural. In war one can prove one's self in the only way that has any meaning to a pro-fessional soldier in any army. But personally I couldn't share that hope. Others marry money, still others go in for sports and gambling. None of these things attracted me. The service itself left me utterly dissatisfied. I seemed to myself in reality an idler who lives pretentiously on others.

"Imagine this: you stand in the barracks yard; it's raining, the water makes the sand gleam; the few wretched trees drip and drip; the men await some command with the watchfulness of well-trained dogs; the water pours from their packs, the sergeant roars, the corporals grit their teeth in zeal and rage; but you? With a monotony like that of the drops that trickle from your cap, you think: 'What will to-night be like? And to-morrow morning? And to-morrow night?' And the whole year lies ahead of you like a soaked and muddy road. You think of your desolate room with its three dozen books, the meaningless pictures, and the carpet worn thin by many feet; you think of the report you've got to hand in, and the canteen accounts you've got to audit, and the stable inspection, and the next regimental ball, where the arrogant wives of your superior officers will bore you to the point of illness with their shallow talk; you think your way through the whole circle of your life, and find nothing but what is trivial and cheerless as a rainy day. Is that endurable?

"One day I put the question to myself: What was I really accomplishing, and what was the nature of my reward? The answer was that, from a human and intellectual point of view, my accomplishment was an absolute zero. My reward consisted of a number of privileges, the sum of which raised me very high in the social scale, but gave me this position only at the cost of surrendering my personality wholly. I had to obey my superiors and to command my inferiors. That was all. The power to command was conditioned in the duty to obey. And each man in the service, whatever his station, is bound in the identical way, and is simply a connective apparatus in a great electrical circuit. Only the humblest, the great mass of privates, were confined to obedience. The ultimate responsibility at the very top was lost in the vague. In spite of its ultimate primitiveness, the structure of every military

organization has a mystery at its core. But between the
arbitrary will of a very few and the touching and incomprehensible humility of the great mass, the parts function according to iron laws. Whoever refuses to function, or rebels, is
crushed.

"There are those who assert that this compulsion has a
moral effect and subserves a higher conception of freedom.
I was myself of that opinion for a long time; but I did not find
it permanently tenable. I felt myself weakening, and a rebellion seething in my blood. I pulled myself together, and fought
against criticism and doubt. In vain. Something had gone
out of me. I lost the readiness to obey and the security to
command. It was torment. Above me I saw implacable idols,
below me defenceless victims. I myself was both idol and
victim, implacable and defenceless at once. It seemed to me
that humanity ceased where the circle of my activity began. My
life seemed to me no longer a part of the general life of mankind, but a fossilized petrefaction conditioned in certain formu-
læ of command and obedience.

"This condition could, of course, not remain hidden. My
comrades withdrew their confidence from me. I was observed
and distrusted. Before I had time to clarify either my mind
or my affairs, an incident occurred which forced me to a
decision. A fellow officer in my regiment, Captain von Otto,
was engaged to the daughter of an eminent judge. The wedding, although the date had been set, could not take place.
Otto had a slight attack of pulmonary trouble and had to go
South for cure. About four weeks after his departure, there
was a celebration in honour of the emperor's birthday, and
among the ladies invited was the captain's betrothed. Everybody was rather gay and giddy that evening, especially a dear
friend of mine, Georg Mattershausen, a sincere, kindly chap
who had just received a promotion in rank. The captain's
betrothed, who had been his neighbour at table, was infected
by his merriment, and on the way home he begged her for a

kiss. She refused, and he was going to steal one. She now grew very serious; he at once came to his senses, apologized with the utmost sincerity, and, at the very door of her paternal house, received her solemn promise to mention the incident to no one. When, however, seventeen weeks later, Captain von Otto returned, the girl was seized by some queer scruple, and thought it her duty to tell him of the incident between herself and Mattershausen. The result was a challenge. The conditions were extraordinarily severe: ten paces distance, drawn revolvers, half a minute to aim, exchange of shots to the disablement of either combatant. I was Mattershausen's second. Otto, who had held himself to be affronted and had sent the challenge, had the first shot. He aimed carefully at the head of his adversary. I saw that. But the bullet whistled past my friend's ear. Mattershausen aimed, but his revolver did not go off. This was counted a shot. New pistols were brought. Otto aimed as carefully as before and this time shot Mattershausen straight through the heart. Death was immediate.

"I wonder whether you, too, think that that was a harsh punishment for a moment of youthful thoughtlessness and impropriety. To me it seemed terribly harsh. I felt profoundly that a crime had been committed against my friend. Our fossilized caste had perpetrated a murder. Two days later, in the officers' mess, I expressed this opinion quite frankly. There was general astonishment. One or two sharp replies were made. Some one asked me what I would have done in such a situation. I answered that I would certainly not have sent a challenge, that I could never approve a notion of honour so morbid and self-centred as to demand a human life for a trifle. Even if the young girl's over-tender conscience had persuaded her to break her promise, I would have caused no further trouble, and let the little incident glide into forgetfulness. At that there was general indignation—a great shaking of heads, angry or troubled faces, an exchange of significant

glances. But I kept on. Mattershausen's wretched end had
hit me damned hard, and I relieved my whole mind. So I
added that, if I had been in Mattershausen's place, I would
have refused the challenge, quite regardless of consequences.
That statement fell among them like a bomb, and a painful
silence followed. 'I imagine you would have reconsidered,'
said the ranking major, 'I don't think you would have disregarded all the consequences.' 'All,' I insisted, 'certainly, all!'
At that moment Captain von Otto, who had been sitting at
another table, arose, and asked frostily: 'You would have
risked the odium of cowardice?' I too arose, and answered:
'Under such circumstances I would have risked that too.'
Captain von Otto smiled a contorted smile, and said with an
emphasis that could not be misinterpreted: 'Then I don't
understand your sitting at the same table with officers of His
Majesty.' He bowed stiffly, and went out.

"The die had been cast. No one was curious as to what
I would do; no one doubted but that there was only one thing
left for me to do. But I was determined to push the matter to
its logical conclusion. That super-idol, known as the code of
honour, had issued its decree; but I was determined to refuse
obedience and take the consequences upon myself. That very
evening, when I came home, two comrades were awaiting me
to offer me their services. I refused courteously. They looked
at me as though I had gone mad, and went off in absurd haste.

"The inevitable consequences followed. You can understand that I could no longer breathe in that air. You cannot
outrage the fetishes of your social group and go unpunished.
I had to avoid insult, and learned what it was to be an outcast.
And that is bad. The imagination alone cannot quite grasp the
full horror of it. I saw clearly that there was no place left for
me in my fatherland. The way out was obvious."

Christian had listened to his friend's story with unmoved
countenance. He got up, took a few turns through the room,
and returned to his seat. Then he said: " I think you did the

right thing. I am sorry you must leave us, but you did right."

Stettner looked up. How strange that sounded: You did right. A question hovered on his lips. But it was not uttered. For Christian feared that question, and silenced it by a sudden conventionality of demeanour.

XIV

Christian, the brothers Maelbeek, who had followed Eva from Holland, Botho von Thüngen, a Russian councillor of state named Koch, and Crammon sat at luncheon in the dining hall of the hotel.

They were talking about a woman of the streets who had been murdered. The police had already caught the murderer. He was a man who had once belonged to good society, but had gradually gone to the dogs. He had throttled the woman and robbed her in a sailor's tavern.

Now all the prostitutes in the city had unanimously determined to show their sister, who had sacrificed her life to her calling, a last and very public mark of respect, and to follow her coffin to the grave. The respectable citizens of Hamburg felt this to be a sort of challenge and protested. But there was no legal provision by which the demonstration could be stopped.

"We ought to see the spectacle," said Crammon, "even if we have to sacrifice our siesta."

"Then there's no time to be lost," the elder Maelbeek declared, and looked at his watch. "The friends will assemble at the house of mourning at three sharp." He smiled, and thought this way of putting the matter rather witty.

Christian said that he would go too. The motor took them to a crossing that had been closed by the police. Here they left the car, and Herr von Thüngen persuaded the police captain to let them pass.

They were at once surrounded by a great throng of humble folk—sailors, fishermen, workingmen, women, and children.

The windows of the houses were thronged with heads. The
Maelbeeks and Koch stopped here, and called Thüngen to join
them. Christian walked farther. Somehow the behaviour of his
companions irritated him. He felt the kind of curiosity which
filled them as something disagreeable. He was curious too,
but in another way. Or, at least, it seemed different to him.

Crammon remained by his side., But the throng grew rowdy.
"Where are you going?" Crammon asked peevishly. "There
is no use in going farther. Let us wait here."

Christian shook his head.

"Very well. I take my stand here," Crammon decided, and
separated from Christian.

The latter made his way up to the dirty, old house at the
door of which the hearse was standing. It was a foggy day.
The black wagon was like a dark hole punched into the grey.
Christian wanted to go a little farther, but some young fellows
purposely blocked his way. They turned their heads, looked
him over, and suspected him of being a "toff." Their own
garb was cheap and flashy; their faces and gestures made it
clear what trade they drove. One of them was a young giant.
He was half a head taller than Christian, and his brows joined
over the bridge of his nose. On the index finger of his left
hand he wore a huge carnelian ring.

Christian looked about him quite unintimidated. He saw
hundreds of women, literally hundreds, ranging in age from
sixteen to fifty, and in condition from bloom to utter decay, and
from luxury to rags and filth.

They had all gathered—those who had passed the zenith of
their troubled course, and those who had barely emerged from
childhood, frivolous, sanguine, vain, and already tainted with
the mire of the great city. They had come from all streets;
they were recruited from all nations and all classes; some had
escaped from a sheltered youth, others had risen from even
direr depths; there were those who felt themselves pariahs
and had the outcast's hatred in their eyes, and there were others

who showed a certain pride in their calling and held themselves aloof. He saw cynical and careworn faces, lovely and hardened ones, indifferent and troubled, greedy and gentle faces. Some were painted and some pallid; and the latter seemed strangely naked.

He was familiar with them from the streets and houses of many cities, as every man is. He knew the type, the unfailing stamp, the acquired gesture and look—this hard, rigid, dull, clinging, lightless look. But he had never before seen them except when they were exercising their function behind the gates of their calling, dissembling their real selves and under the curse of sex. To see many hundreds of them separated from all that, to see them as human beings stripped of the stimulus and breath of a turbid sexuality—that was what seemed to sweep a cloud from his eyes.

Suddenly he thought: " I must order my hunting lodge to be sold, and the hounds too."

The coffin was being carried from the house. It was covered with flowers and wreaths; and from the wreaths fluttered ribands with gilt inscriptions. Christian tried to read the inscriptions, but it was impossible. The coffin had small, silver-plated feet that looked like the paws of a cat. By some accident one of these had been broken off, and that touched Christian, he hardly knew why, as unbearably pitiful. An old woman followed the coffin. She seemed more vexed and angry than grief-stricken. She wore a black dress, but the seam under one arm was ripped open. And that too seemed unbearably pitiful.

The hearse started off. Six men carrying lighted candles walked in front of it. The murmur of voices became silent. The women, walking by fours, followed the hearse. Christian stood still close pressed against a wall, and let the procession pass him by. In a quarter of an hour the street was quite desolate. The windows of the houses were closed. He remained alone in the street, in the fog.

As he walked away he reflected: "I've asked my father to take care of my collection of rings. There are over four thousand of them, and many are beautiful and costly. They could be sold too. I don't need them. I shall have them sold."

He wandered on and on, and lost all sense of the passing of time. Evening came, and the city lights glowed through the fog. Everything became moist, even to the gloves on his hands.

He thought of the missing foot on the coffin of the murdered harlot, and of the torn seam of the old woman's dress.

He passed over one of the great bridges of the Elbe, and then walked along the river bank. It was a desolate region. He stopped near the light of a street lamp, gazed into the water, drew forth his wallet, took out a bank note of a hundred marks, turned it about in his hands, shook his head, and then, with a gesture of disgust, threw it into the water. He took a second and did the same. There were twenty bank notes in his wallet. He took them out one by one, and with that expression half of disgust, half of dreaminess, he let them glide into the river.

The street lamps illuminated the inky water for a short distance, and he saw the bank notes drift away.

And he smiled and went on.

XV

When he reached the hotel he felt an urgent need of warmth. By turns he entered the library, the reception hall, the dining-room. All these places were well heated, but their warmth did not suffice him. He attributed his chill to walking so long in the damp.

He took the lift and rode up to his own rooms. He changed his clothes, wrapped himself warmly, and sat down beside the radiator, in which the steam hissed like a caged animal.

Yet he did not grow warm. At last he knew that his shivering was not due to the moisture and the fog, but to some inner cause.

Toward eleven o'clock he arose and went out into the corridor. The stuccoed walls were divided into great squares by gilt moulding; the floor was covered by pieces of carpet that had been joined together to appear continuous. Christian felt a revulsion against all this false splendour. He approached the wall, touched the stucco, and shrugged his shoulders in contempt.

At the end of the long corridor was Eva's suite. He had passed the door several times. As he passed it again he heard the sound of a piano. Only a few keys were being gently touched. After a moment's reflection he knocked, opened the door, and entered.

Susan Rappard was alone in the room. Wrapped in a fur coat, she sat at the piano. On the music rack was propped a book that she was reading. Her fingers passed with ghostly swiftness over the keys, but she struck one only quite rarely. She turned her head and asked rudely: "What do you want, Monsieur?"

Christian answered: "If it's possible, I should like to speak to Madame. I want to ask her a question."

"Now? At night?" Susan was amazed. "We're tired. We're always tired at night in this hyperborean climate, where the sun is a legend. The fog weighs on us. Thank God, in four days we have our last performance. Then we'll go where the sky is blue. We're longing for Paris."

"I should be very happy if I could see Madame," Christian said.

Susan shook her head. "You have a strange kind of patience," she said maliciously. "I hadn't suspected you of being so romantic. You're pursuing a very foolish policy, I assure you. Go in, if you want to, however. Ce petit laideron est chez elle, demoiselle Schöntag. She acts the part of a court fool. Everything in the world is amusing to her—herself not least. Well, that is coming to an end too."

Voices and clear laughter could be heard. The door of

Eva's rooms opened, and she and Johanna appeared on the threshold. Eva wore a simple white garment, unadorned but for one great chrysoprase that held it on the left shoulder. Her skin had an amber gleam, the quiver of her nostrils betrayed a secret irritation. The beautiful woman and the plain one stood there side by side, each with an acute feminine consciousness of her precise qualities: the one vital, alluring, pulsing with distinction and freedom; the other all adoration and yearning ambition for that vitality and that freedom.

Tenderly and delicately Johanna had put her arm about Eva and touched her friend's bare shoulder with her cheek. With her bizarre smile she said: "No one knows how it came that Rumpelstilzkin is my name."

They had not yet observed Christian. A gesture of Susan's called their attention to him. He stood in the shadow of the door. Johanna turned pale, and her shy glance passed from Eva to Christian. She released Eva, bowed swiftly to kiss Eva's hand, and with a whispered good-night slipped past Christian.

Although Christian's eyes were cast down, they grasped the vision of Eva wholly. He saw the feet that he had once held naked in his hands; under her diaphanous garment he saw the exquisite firmness of her little breasts; he saw the arms that had once embraced him and the perfect hands that had once caressed him. All his bodily being was still vibrantly conscious of the smoothness and delicacy of their touch. And he saw her before him, quite near and hopelessly unattainable, and felt a last lure and an ultimate renunciation.

"Monsieur has a request," said Susan Rappard mockingly, and preparing to leave them.

"Stay!" Eva commanded, and the look she gave Christian was like that she gave a lackey.

"I wanted to ask you," Christian said softly, "what is the meaning of the name Eidolon by which you used to call me. My question is belated, I know, and it may seem foolish to-

day." He smiled an embarrassed smile. "But it torments me
not to know when I think about it, and I determined to ask
you."

Susan gave a soundless laugh. In its belated and unmotivated
urgency, the question did, indeed, sound a little foolish. Eva
seemed amused too, but she concealed the fact. She looked
at·her hands and said: "It is hard to tell you what it means
—something that one sacrifices, or a god to whom one sacrifices,
a lovely and serene spirit. It means either or perhaps both at
once. Why remind ourselves of it? There is no Eidolon any
more. Eidolon was shattered, and one should not exhibit the
shards to me. Shards are ugly things."

She shivered a little, and her eyes shone. She turned to
Susan. "Let me sleep to-morrow till I wake. I have such
evil dreams nowadays, and find no rest till toward morning." ·

XVI

Passing back through the corridor Christian saw a figure
standing very still in the semi-darkness. He recognized
Johanna, and he felt that this thing was fated—that she should
be standing here and waiting for him.

She did not look at him; she looked at·the floor. Not until
he came quite close to her did she raise her eyes, and then she
looked timidly away. Her lips quivered. A question hovered
on them. She knew all that had passed between Eva and
Christian. That they had once been lovers only increased her
enthusiastic admiration for them both. But what happened
between them now—her brief presence made her sure of its
character—seemed to her both shameful and incomprehensible.

She was imaginative and sensitive, and loved those who were
nobly proud; and she suffered when such noble pride and
dignity were humbled. Her whole heart was given over to her
ideal of spiritual distinction. Sometimes she would misunderstand her own ideal, and take external forms and modes as
expressions of it. And this division in her soul, to which she

•was not equal, sometimes delivered her into the power of mere
frivolity. ";It is late," she whispered timidly. It was not a
statement; it was an attempt to save herself. Each time that
Christian had been mentioned, three things had struck her
mind: his elegance, his fine pride, his power over all hearts.
That was the combination that called to her and stirred her and
filled her days with longing.

Thus she had followed Crammon in search of the great adventure, although she had said of him but an hour after she had
met him: " He is grandiosely and grotesquely comic." She had
followed him like a slave to a market of slaves, hoping to catch
the eye of the khalif.

But she had no faith in her own power. Voluntarily and
intentionally she crumbled the passions of her being into small
desires. She suffered from that very process and jeered at
herself. She was too timid to take greatly what she wanted.
She nibbled at life and had not the adventurousness of great
enjoyments. And she mocked at her own unhappy nature, and
suffered the more.

And now he stood before her. It frightened and surprised
her, even though she had waited for him. Since he stayed,
she wanted to think him bold and brave. But she could not,
and at once she shrank into self-contempt. " It is late," she
whispered again, nodded a good-night, and opened the door of
her room.

But Christian begged silently with an expression that was
irresistible. He crossed the threshold behind the trembling
girl. Her face grew hard. But she was too fine to play a
coquettish game. Before her blood was stirred her eyes had
yielded. The pallor of her face lit it with a new charm. There
was no hint of plainness any more. The stormy expectation
of her heart harmonized the lines of her features and melted
them into softness, gentleness, and delicacy.

Of her power over the senses of men she was secure. She
had tested her magnetism on those whom one granted little

and who gave less. Flirtations had been used as anodynes in her social group. One had played with false counters, and by a silent compact avoided serious moments. But her experience failed her to-night, for here there was not lightness but austerity. She yielded herself to this night, oblivious of the future and its responsibilities.

' XVII

Stephen Gunderam had to go to Montevideo. In that city there was a German physician who had considerable skill in the treatment of nervous disorders; and the bull-necked giant suffered from insomnia and nocturnal hallucinations. Furthermore, there was to be a yacht race at Montevideo, on the results of which Stephen had bet heavily.

He appointed Demetrios and Esmeralda as Letitia's guardians. He said to them: " If anything happens to my wife or she does anything unseemly, I'll break every bone in your bodies." Demetrios grinned. Esmeralda demanded that he bring her a box of sweets on his return.

Their leave-taking was touching. Stephen bit Letitia's ear, and said: " Be true to me."

Letitia immediately began to play upon the mood of her guardians. She gave Demetrios a hundred pesos and Esmeralda a gold bracelet. She corresponded secretly with the naval lieutenant, Friedrich Pestel. An Indian lad, of whose secrecy and reliability she was sure, served as messenger. Within a week Pestel's ship was to proceed to Cape Town, so there was little time to be lost. He did not think he would be able to return to the Argentine until the following winter. And Letitia loved him dearly.

Two miles from the estate there was an observatory in the lonely pampas. A wealthy German cattle-man had built it, and now a German professor with his two assistants lived there and watched the firmament. Letitia had often asked to see the observatory, but Stephen had always refused to let her visit it. Now she intended to make it the scene of her meeting with Friedrich Pestel. She yearned for a long talk with him.

To use an observatory as a refuge for forlorn lovers—it was a notion that delighted Letitia and made her ready to run any risk. The day and the hour were set, and all circumstances were favourable. Riccardo and Paolo had gone hunting; Demetrios had been sent by his father to a farm far to the north; the old people slept. Esmeralda alone had to be deceived. Fortunately the girl had a headache, and Letitia persuaded her to go to bed. When twilight approached, Letitia put on a bright, airy frock in which she could ride. She did not hesitate in spite of her pregnancy. Then, as though taking a harmless walk, she left the house and proceeded to the avenue of palms, where the Indian boy awaited her with two ponies.

It was beautiful to ride out freely into the endless plain. In the west there still shone a reddish glow, into which projected in lacy outline the chain of mountains. The earth suffered from drought; it had not rained for long, and crooked fissures split the ground. Hundreds of grasshopper traps were set up in the fields, and the pits behind them, which were from two to three metres deep, were filled with the insects.

When she reached the observatory, it was dark. The building was like an oriental house of prayer. From a low structure of brick arose the mighty iron dome, the upper part of which rotated on a movable axis. The shutters of the windows were closed, and there was no light to be seen. Friedrich Pestel waited at the gate; he had tethered his horse to a post. He told her that the professor and his two assistants had been absent for a week. She and he, he added, could enter the building nevertheless. The caretaker, an old, fever-stricken mulatto, had given him the key.

The Indian boy lit the lantern that he had carried tied to his saddle. Pestel took it, and preceded Letitia through a desolate brick hallway, then up a wooden and finally up a spiral iron stairway. " Fortune is kind to us," he said. " Next week there's going to be an eclipse of the sun, and astronomers are arriving in Buenos Ayres from Europe. The professor and his assistants have gone to receive them."

Letitia's heart beat very fast. In the high vault of the observatory, the little light of the lantern made only the faintest impression. The great telescope was a terrifying shadow; the drawing instruments and the photographic apparatus on its stand looked like the skeletons of animals; the charts on the wall, with their strange dots and lines, reminded her of black magic. The whole room seemed to her like the cave of a wizard.

Yet there was a smile of childlike curiosity and satisfaction on Letitia's lips. Her famished imagination needed such an hour as this. She forgot Stephen and his jealousy, the eternally quarrelling brothers, the wicked old man, the shrewish Doña Barbara, the treacherous Esmeralda, the house in which she lived like a prisoner—she forgot all that completely in this room with its magic implements, in this darkness lit only by the dim flicker of the lantern, beside this charming young man who would soon kiss her. At least, she hoped he would.

But Pestel was timid. He went up to the telescope, unscrewed the gleaming brass cover, and said: " Let us take a look at the stars." He looked in. Then he asked Letitia to do the same. Letitia saw a milky mist and flashing, leaping fires. " Are those the stars? " she asked, with a coquettish melancholy in her voice.

Then Pestel told her about the stars. She listened with radiant eyes, although it didn't in the least interest her to know how many millions of miles distant from the earth either Sirius or Aldebaran happened to be, and what precisely was the mystery which puzzled scientists in regard to the southern heavens.

" Ah," she breathed, and there was indulgence and a dreamy scepticism in that sound.

The lieutenant, abandoning the cosmos and its infinities,

talked about himself and his life, of Letitia and of the impression she had made on him, and of the fact that he thought only of her by day and by night.

Letitia remained very, very still in order not to turn his thoughts in another direction and thus disturb the sweet suspense of her mood.

As befitted a man with a highly developed conscience, Pestel had definitely laid his plans for the future. When he returned at the end of six months, ways and means were to be found for Letitia's divorce from Stephen and her remarriage to him. He thought of flight only as an extreme measure.

He told her that he was poor. Only a very small capital was deposited in his name in Stuttgart. He was a Suabian—simplehearted, sober, and accurate.

"Ah," Letitia sighed again, half-astonished and half-saddened. "It doesn't matter," she said with determination. "I'm rich. I own a great tract of forest land. My aunt, the Countess Brainitz, gave it to me as a wedding present."

"A forest? Where?" Pestel asked, and smiled.

"In Germany. Near Heiligenkreuz in the Rhön region. It's as big as a city, and when it's sold it will bring a lot of money. I've never been there, but I've been told that it contains large deposits of some ore. That would have to be found and exploited. Then I'd be even richer than if I sold the forest." These facts had grown in Letitia's imagination; they were the children of the dreams and wishes she had harboured since her slavery in this strange land. She was not lying; she had quite forgotten that she had invented it all. She wished this thing to be so, and it had taken on reality in her mind.

"It's too good, altogether too good to be true," Pestel commented thoughtfully.

His words moved Letitia. She began to sob and threw herself on his breast. Her young life seemed hard to her and ugly and surrounded by dangers. Nothing she had hoped for had become reality. All her pretty soap-bubbles had burst in the wind. Her tears sprang from her deep realization of this fact and out of her fear of men and of her fate. She yearned for a pair of strong arms to give her protection and security.

Pestel was also moved. He put his arms about her and ventured to kiss her forehead. She sobbed more pitifully, and so he kissed her mouth. Then she smiled. He said that he would love her until he died, that no woman had ever inspired such feelings in him.

She confessed to him that she was with child by the unloved husband to whom she was chained. Pestel pressed her to his bosom, and said: "The child is blood of your blood, and I shall regard it as my own."

The time was speeding dangerously. Holding each other's hands they went down the stairs. They parted with the promise to write each other daily.

"When he returns from Africa I'll flee with him on his ship," Letitia determined, as she rode home slowly across the dark plain. Everything else seemed ugly and a bore to her. "Oh, if only it were to be soon," she thought in her anxiety and heart-ache. And curiosity stirred in her to know how Pestel would behave and master the dangers and the difficulties involved. She believed in him, and gave herself up to tender and tempting dreams of the future.

In the house her absence had finally been noticed, and servants had been sent out to look for her. She slipped into the house by obscure paths, and then emerged from her room with an air of innocence.

XVIII

Stettner had returned to Hamburg. His ship was to sail on that very evening. He had several errands in the city, and Christian and Crammon waited for him in order to accompany him to the pier.

Crammon said: "A captain of Hussars who suddenly turns up in mufti—I can't help it, there's something desperate about

it to me. I feel as though I were on a perpetual visit of con-
dolence. After all, he's déclassé, and I don't like people in that
situation. Social classes are a divine institution; a man who
interferes with them wounds his own character. One doesn't
throw up one's profession the way one tosses aside a rotten
apple. These are delicate and difficult matters. Common
sense may disregard them; the higher intelligence reverences
them. What is he going to do among the Yankees? What
good can come of it?"

"He's a chemist by inclination, and scholarly in his line,"
Christian answered. "That will help."

"What do the Yankees care about that? He's more likely to
catch consumption and be trodden under. He'll be stripped of
pride and dignity   It's a country for thieves, waiters, and
renegades. Did he have to go as far as all this?'"

"Yes," Christian answered, "I believe he did."

An hour later they and Stettner arrived at the harbour.
Cargoes and luggage were still being stowed, and they strolled,
Stettner between Crammon and Christian, up and down a narrow alley lined with cotton-bales, boxes, barrels, and baskets.
The arc lamps cast radiant light from the tall masts, and a
tumult of carts and cranes, motors and bells, criers and whistles
rolled through the fog. The asphalt was wet; there was no
sky to be seen.

"Don't forget me wholly here in the old land," said Stettner.
A silence followed.

"I don't know whether we shall be as well off in the old
country in the future as we have been in the past," said Crammon, who occasionally had pessimistic attacks and forebod-
ings. "Hitherto we haven't suffered. Our larders and cellars
have been well-stocked, nor have the higher needs been neglected. But times are getting worse, and, unless I mistake,
clouds are gathering on the political horizon. So I can't call it
a bad idea, my dear Stettner, to slip away quietly and amiably.
I only hope that you'll find some secure position over there

from which you may calmly watch the spectacle of our débâcle. And when the waves rise very high, you might think
of us and have a mass said for us, that is for me, because
Christian has been expelled from the bosom of Holy
Church."

Stettner smiled at this speech. But he became serious again
at once. " It seems to me too that, in a sense, we're all trapped
here. Yet I have never felt myself so deeply and devotedly a
German as at this moment when I am probably leaving my
fatherland forever. But in that feeling there is a stab of pain.
It seems to me as though I should hurry from one to another
and sound a warning. But what to warn them of, or why warn
them at all—I don't know."

Crammon answered weightily. " My dear old Aglaia wrote
me the other day that she had dreamed of black cats all night
long. She is deep, she has a prophetic soul, and dreams like
that are of evil presage. I may enter a monastery. It is
actually within the realm of the possible. Don't laugh, Christian; don't laugh, my dearest boy! You don't know all my
possibilities."

It had not occurred to Christian to laugh.

Stettner stopped and gave his hands to his friends. " Good-
bye, Crammon," he said cordially. " I'm grateful that you
accompanied me. Good-bye, dear Christian, good-bye." He
pressed Christian's hand long and firmly. Then he tore himself
away, hastened toward the gang-plank, and was lost in the
crowd.

" A nice fellow," Crammon murmured. " A very nice fellow.
What a pity! "

When the car met them Christian said: " I'd like to walk a
bit, either back to the hotel or somewhere else. Will you
come, Bernard? "

" If you want me, yes. Toddling along is my portion."

Christian dismissed his car. He had a strange foreboding, as
though something fateful were lying in wait for him.

"Ariel's days here are numbered," said Crammon. "Duty calls me away. I must look after my two old ladies. Then I must join Franz Lothar in Styria. We'll hunt heath-cocks. After that I've agreed to meet young Sinsheim in St. Moritz. What are your plans, my dear boy?"

"I leave for Berlin to-morrow or the day after."

"And what in God's name are you going to do there?"

"I'm going to work."

Crammon stopped, and opened his mouth very wide. "Work?" he gasped, quite beside himself. "What at? What for, O misguided one?"

"I'm going to take courses at the university, under the faculty of medicine."

Horrified, Crammon shook his head. "Work . . . courses . . . medicine . . . Merciful Providence, what does this mean? Is there not enough sweat in the world, not enough bungling and half-wisdom and ugly ambition and useless turmoil? You're not serious."

"You exaggerate as usual, Bernard," Christian answered, with a smile. "Don't always be a Jeremiah. What I'm going to do is something quite simple and conventional. And I'm only going to try. I may not even succeed; but I must try it. So much is sure."

Crammon raised his hand, lifted a warning index finger, and said with great solemnity: "You are upon an evil path, Christian, upon a path of destruction. For many, many days I have had a presentiment of terrible things. The sleep of my nights has been embittered; a sorrow gnaws at me and my peace has flown. How am I to hunt in the mountains when I know you to be among the Pharisees? How shall I cast my line into clear streams when my inner eye sees you bending over greasy volumes or handling diseased bodies? No wine will glitter beautifully in my glass, no girl's eyes seem friendly any more, no pear yield me its delicate flavour!"

"Oh, yes, they will," Christian said, laughing. "More than

that: I hope you'll come to see me from time to time, to convince yourself that you needn't cast me off entirely."

Crammon sighed. "Indeed I shall come. I must come and soon, else the spirit of evil will get entire control of you. Which may God forbid! "

XIX

Johanna told Eva, whom she adored, about her life. Eva thus received an unexpected insight into the grey depths of middle-class existence. The account sounded repulsive. But it was stimulating to offer a spiritual refuge to so much thirst and flight.

She herself often seemed to her own soul like one in flight. But she had her bulwarks. The wind of time seemed cold to her, and when she felt a horror of the busy marionettes whose strings were in her hands, she felt herself growing harder. The friendship which she gave to this devoted girl seemed to her a rest in the mad race of her fate.

They were so intimate that Susan Rappard complained. The latter opened her eyes wide and her jealousy led her to become a spy. She became aware of the relations that had developed between Johanna and Christian.

At dinner there had been much merriment. Johanna had bought a number of peaked, woollen caps. She had wrapped them carefully in white paper, written some witty verses on each bundle, and distributed them as favours to Eva's guests. No one had been vexed. For despite her mockery and gentle eccentricity, there was a charm about her that disarmed every one.

"How gay you are to-day, Rumpelstilzkin," Eva said. She, too, used that nickname. The word, which she pronounced with some difficulty, had a peculiar charm upon her lips.

"It is the gaiety that precedes tears," Johanna answered, and yielded as entirely to her superstitious terror as she had to her jesting mood.

A wealthy ship-owner had invited Eva to view his private picture gallery. His house was in the suburbs. She drove there with Johanna.

Arm in arm they stood before the paintings. And in that absorbed union there was something purifying. Johanna loved it as she loved their common reading of poetry, when they would sit with their cheeks almost touching. Extinguished in her selfless adoration, she forgot what lay behind her—the anxious, sticky, unworthily ambitious life of her family of brokers; she forgot what lay before her—oppression and force, an inevitable and appointed way.

Her gestures revealed a gentle glow of tenderness.

On their way back she seemed pale. "You are cold," Eva said, and wrapped the robe more firmly about her friend.

Johanna squeezed Eva's hand gratefully. "How dear of you! I shall always need some one to tell me when I'm hot or cold."

This melancholy jest moved Eva deeply. "Why do you act so humble?" she cried. "Why do you shrink and hide and turn your vision away from yourself? Why do you not dare to be happy?"

Johanna answered: "Do you not know that I am a Jewess?"

"Well?" Eva asked in her turn. "I know some very extraordinary people who are Jews—some of the proudest, wisest, most impassioned in the world."

Johanna shook her head. "In the Middle Ages the Jews were forced to wear yellow badges on their garments," she said. "I wear the yellow badge upon my soul."

Eva was putting on a tea gown. Susan Rappard was helping her. "What's new with us, Susan?" Eva asked, and took the clasps out of her hair.

Susan answered: "What is good is not new, and what is new is not good. Your ugly little court fool is having an affair with M. Wahnschaffe. They are very secretive, but there are whispers. I don't understand him. He is easily and

quickly consoled. I have always. said/ that he has neither
a mind nor a heart. Now it is plain that he has no eyes
either."

Eva had flushed very dark. Now she became very pale.
" It is a lie," she said.

، Susan's voice was quite dry. " It is the truth. Ask her. I
don't think she'll deny it."

Shortly thereafter Johanna slipped into the room. She had
on a dress of simple, black velvet which set off her figure
charmingly. Eva sat before the mirror. Susan was arranging
her hair. She had a book in her hand and read without looking
up.

On a chair near the dressing-table lay an open jewel case.
Johanna stood before it, smiled timidly, and took out of it a
beautifully cut cameo, which she playfully fastened to her
bosom; she looked admiringly at a diadem and put it in her
hair; she slipped on a few rings and a pearl bracelet over her
sleeve. Thus adorned she went, half hesitatingly, half with an
air of self-mockery, up to Eva.

Slowly Eva lifted her eyes from the book, looked at Johanna,
and asked: " Is it true? " She let a few seconds pass, and
then with wider open eyes she asked once more: " Is it
true? "

Johanna drew back, and the colour left her cheeks. She
suspected and knew and began to tremble.

Then Eva arose and went close up to her and stripped the
cameo from the girl's bosom, the diadem from her hair, the
rings from her fingers, the bracelet from her arm, and threw
the things back into the case. Then she sat down again, took
up her book, and said: ".Hurry, Susan! I want to rest a
little."

Johanna's breath failed her. She looked like one who has
been struck. A tender blossom in her heart was crushed forever, and from its sudden withering arose a subtle miasma.
Almost on the point of fainting she left the room.

As though to seal the end of a period in her life and warn her of evil things to come, she received within two hours a telegram from her mother which informed her of a catastrophe and urgently summoned her home. Fräulein Grabmeier began packing at once. They were to catch the train at five o'clock in the morning.

From midnight on Johanna sat waiting in Christian's room. She lit no light. In the darkness she sat·beside a table, resting her head in her hands. She did not move, and her eyes were fixed on vacancy.

XX

In the course of their talk Christian and Crammon had wandered farther and farther into the tangled alleys around the harbour. "Let us turn back and seek a way out," Crammon suggested. "It isn't very nice here. A damnable neighbourhood, in fact."

He peered about, and Christian too looked around. When they had gone a few steps farther, they came upon a man lying flat on his belly on the pavement. He struggled convulsively, croaked obscene curses, and shook his fist threateningly toward a red-curtained, brightly lit door.

Suddenly the door opened, and a second man flew out. A paper box, an umbrella, and a derby hat were pitched out after him. He stumbled down the steps with outstretched arms, fell beside the first man, and remained sitting there with heavy eyes.

Christian and Crammon looked in through the open door. In the smoky light twenty or thirty people were crouching. The monotonous crying of a woman became audible. At times it became shriller.

The glass door was flung shut.

I shall see what goes on in there," said Christian, and mounted the steps to the door. Crammon had only time to utter a horrified warning. But he followed. The reek of cheap whiskey struck him as he entered the room behind Christian.

Beside tables and on the floor crouched men and women. In every corner lay people, sleeping or drunk. The eyes which were turned toward the newcomers were glassy. The faces here looked like lumps of earth. The room, with its dirty tables, glasses, and bottles had a colour-scheme of scarlet and yellow. Two sturdy fellows stood behind the bar.

The woman whose crying had penetrated to the street sat on a bench beside the wall. Blood was streaming down her face, and she continued to utter her monotonous and almost bestial whine. In front of her, trying hard to keep erect on legs stretched far apart, stood the huge fellow whom Christian had observed at the public funeral of the murdered harlot. In a hoarse voice, in the extreme jargon of the Berlin populace, he was shouting: " Yuh gonna git what's comin' to yuh! I'll show yuh what's what! I'll blow off yer dam' head-piece'n yuh cin go fetch it in the moon! "

On the threshold of an open door in the rear stood a stout man with innumerable watch-charms dangling across his checked waistcoat. A fat cigar was held between his yellow teeth. He regarded the scene with a superior calm. It was the proprietor of the place. When he saw the two strangers his brows went up. He first took them to be detectives, and hastened to meet them. Then he saw his mistake and was the more amazed. " Come into my office, gentlemen," he said in a greasy voice, and without removing the cigar. " Come back there, and I'll give you a drink of something good." He drew Christian along by the arm. A woman with a yellow head-kerchief arose from the floor, stretched out her arms toward Christian, and begged for ten pfennigs. Christian drew back as from a worm.

An old man tried to prevent the gigantic lout from maltreating the bleeding woman any more. He called him Mesecke and fawned upon him. But Mesecke gave him a blow under the

chin that sent him spinning and moaning. Murmurs of pro-
test sounded, but no one dared to offend the giant. The proprietor whispered to Christian: "What he wants is brass;
wants her to go on the street again and earn a little. Nothing
to be done right now."

He grasped Crammon by the sleeve too, and drew them both
through the door into a dark hall. " I suppose you gentlemen
are interested in my establishment? " he asked anxiously. He
opened a door and forced them to enter. The room into which
they came showed a tasteless attempt at such luxury as is
represented by red plush and gilt frames. The place was
small, and the furniture stood huddled together. Crossed
swords hung above a bunch of peacock feathers, and above the
swords the gay cap of a student fraternity. Between two windows stood a slanting desk covered with ledgers. An emaciated
man with a yellowish face sat at the desk and made entries in
a book. He quivered when the proprietor entered the room,
and bent more zealously over his work.

The proprietor said: " I've got to take care of you gents
or something might happen. When that son of a gun is quiet
you can go back and look the place over. I guess you're
strangers here, eh? " From a shelf he took down a bottle.
" Brandy," he whispered. " Prime stuff. You must try it.
I sell it by the bottle and by the case. A number one! Here
you are! " Crammon regarded Christian, whose face was without any sign of disquiet. With a sombre expression he went
to the table and, as though unseeing, touched his lips to the
glass which the proprietor had filled. It was a momentary
refuge, at all events.

In the meantime a frightful noise penetrated from the outer
room. " Fighting again," said the proprietor, listened for a
moment, and then disappeared. The noise increased furiously
for a moment. Then silence fell. The book-keeper, without
raising his waxy face, said: " Nobody can stand that. It's
that way every night. And the books here show the profits.

That man Hillebohm is a millionaire, and he rakes in more and more money without mercy, without compassion. Nobody can stand that."

The words sounded like those of a madman.

"Are we going to permit ourselves to be locked up here?" Crammon asked indignantly. "It's rank impudence."

Christian opened the door, and Crammon drew from his back pocket the Browning revolver that was his constant companion. They passed through the hall and stopped on the threshold of the outer room. Mesecke had vanished. Many arms had finally expelled him. The woman from whom he had been trying to get money was washing the blood from her face. The old man who had been beaten when he had pleaded for her said consolingly: "Don't yuh howl, Karen. Things'll get better. Keep up, says I!" The woman hardly listened. She looked treacherous and angry.

A tangle of yellow hair flamed on her head, high as a helmet and unkempt. While she was bleeding she had wiped the blood with her naked hand, and then stained her hair with it.

"You go home now," the proprietor commanded. "Wash your paws and give our regards to God if you see him. Hurry up, or your sweetheart'll be back and give you a little more."

She did not move. "Well, how about it, Karen," a woman shrilled. "Hurry. D'yuh want some more beating?"

But the woman did not stir. She breathed heavily, and suddenly looked at Christian.

"Come with us," Christian said unexpectedly. The bartenders roared with laughter. Crammon laid a hand of desperate warning on Christian's shoulder.

"Come with us," Christian repeated calmly. "We will take you home."

A dozen glassy eyes stared their mockery. A voice brayed: "Hell, hell, but you're gettin' somethin' elegant." Another hummed as though scanning verses: "If that don't kill the

bedbugs dead, I dunno what'll do instead!   Don't yuh be
scared, Karen.   Hurry!   Use your legs! "

Karen got up.   She had not taken her shy and sombre eyes
from Christian.   His beauty overwhelmed her.   A crooked,
frightened, cynical smile glided over her full lips.

She was rather tall.   She had fine shoulders and a well-
developed bosom.   She was with child—perhaps five months;
it was obvious when she stood.   She wore a dark green dress
with iridescent buttons, and at her neck a flaming red riband
fastened by a brooch that represented in silver, set with garnets,
a Venetian gondola, and bore the inscription: *Ricordo di Venezia.*   Her shoes were clumsy and muddy.   Her hat—made of
imitation kid and trimmed with cherries of rubber—lay beside
her on the bench.   She grasped it with a strange ferocity.

Christian looked at the riband and at the silver brooch with
its inscription: *Ricordo di Venezia.*

Crammon sought to protect their backs.   For new guests
were coming in—fellows with dangerous faces.   He had simply
yielded to the inevitable and incomprehensible, and determined
to give a good account of himself.   He gritted his teeth over the
absence of proper police protection, and said to himself: " We
won't get out of this hole alive, old boy."   And he thought of
his comfortable hotel-bed, his delicious, fragrant bath, his excellent breakfast, and of the box of chocolates on his table.
He thought of young girls who exhaled the fresh sweetness of
linen, of all pleasant fragrances, of Ariel's smile and Rumpelstilzkin's gaiety, and of the express train that was to have
taken him to Vienna.   He thought of all these things as though
his last hour had come.

Two sailors came in dragging between them a girl who was
pale and stiff with drunkenness.   Roughly they threw her on
the floor.   The creature moaned, and had an expression of
ghastly voluptuousness, of strange lasciviousness on her face.
She lay there stiff as a board.   The sailors, with a challenge in
their voices, asked after Mesecke.   He had evidently met them

and complained to them. They wanted to get even with the
proprietor. One of them had a scarlet scratch across his forehead; the other's arms were naked up to his shoulders and
tattooed until they were blue all over. The tattooing represented a snake, a winged wheel, an anchor, a skull, a phallus, a
scale, a fish, and many other objects.

· Both sailors measured Christian and Crammon with impudent glances. The one with the tattooed arms pointed to the
revolver in Crammon's hand, and said: " If you don't put up
that there pistol I'll make you, by God! "

The other went up to Christian and stood so close to him
that he turned pale. Vulgarity had never yet touched him,
nor had the obscene things of the gutter splashed his garments.
Contempt and disgust arose hotly in him. These might force
him to abandon his new road; for they were more terrible than
the vision of evil he had had in the house of Szilaghin.

But when he looked into the man's eyes, he became aware
of the fact that the latter could not endure his glance. Those
eyes twitched and flickered and fled. And this perception gave
Christian courage and a feeling of inner power, the full effec-
tiveness of which was still uncertain.

" Quiet there! " the proprietor roared at the two sailors.
" I want order. You want to get the police here, do you?
That'd be fine for us all, eh? You're a bit crazy, eh? The
girl can go with the gentlemen, if they'll pay her score. 'Two
glasses champagne—that's one mark fifty. And that ends it."

Crammon laid a two-mark piece on the table. Karen Engelschall had put on her hat, and turned toward the door. Christian and Crammon followed her, and the proprietor followed
them with sarcastic courtesy, while the two sturdy bar-tenders
formed an additional bodyguard. A few half-drunken men
sent the strains of a jeering song behind them.

The street was empty. Karen gazed up and down it, and
seemed uncertain in which direction she should go. Crammon
asked her where she lived. She answered harshly that she

didn't want to go home. "Then where shall we take you?"
Crammon asked, forcing himself to be patient and considerate.
She shrugged her shoulders. "It don't matter," she said.
Then, after a while, she added defiantly. "I don't need you."

They went toward the harbour, Karen between the two men.
For a moment she stopped and murmured with a shudder of
fear: "But I mustn't run into him. No, I mustn't."

"Will you suggest something then?" Crammon said to her.
His impulse was simply to decamp, but for Christian's sake,
and in the hope of saving him uninjured from this mesh of
adventures, he played the part of interest and compassion.

Karen Engelschall did not answer, but hurried more swiftly
as she caught sight of a figure in the light of a street lamp.
Until she was beyond its vision she gasped with terror.

"Shall we give you money?" Crammon asked again.

She answered furiously: "I don't need your money. I want
no money." Surreptitiously she gazed at Christian, and her
face grew malicious and stubborn.

Crammon went over beside Christian, and spoke to him in
French. "The best thing would be to take her to an inn where
she can get a room and a bed. We can deposit a sum of money
there, so that she is sheltered for a while. Then she can help
herself."

"Quite right. That will be best," Christian replied. And, as
though he could not bear to address her, he added: "Tell her
that."

Karen stopped. She lifted her shoulders as though she were
cold, and said in a hoarse voice: "Leave me alone. What are
you two talking about? I won't walk another step. I'm tired.
Don't pay no attention to me!" She leaned against the wall
of a house, and her hat was pushed forward over her forehead.
She was as sorry and dissipated a looking object as one could
possibly imagine.

"Isn't that the sign of an inn?" Crammon asked and pointed
to an illuminated sign at the far end of the street.

Christian, who had very keen eyes, looked and answered:
" Yes. It says ' King of Greece.' Do go and inquire."

".A lovely neighbourhood and a lovely errand," Crammon
said plaintively. "I am paying for my sins." But he
went.

Christian remained with the woman, who looked down
silently and angrily. Her fingers scratched at her riband.
Christian listened to the beating of the tower-clock. It struck
two. At last Crammon reappeared. He beckoned from a distance and cried: " Ready."

Christian addressed the girl for the first time. " We've found
a shelter for you," he said, a little throatily, and, quite contrary to his wont, blinked his eyes. His own voice sounded dis-
agreeably in his ears. " You can stay there for some days."

She looked at him with eyes that glowed with hatred. An
indescribable but evil curiosity burned in her glance. Then
she lowered her eyes again. Christian was forced to speak
again: " I think you will be safe from that man there. Try
to rest. Perhaps you are ill. We could summon a physician."

She laughed a soft, sarcastic laugh. Her breath smelt of
whiskey.

Crammon called out again.

" Come on then," Christian said, mastering his aversion with
difficulty.

His voice and his words made the same overwhelming impression on her that his appearance had done. She started to
go as though she were being propelled from behind.

A sleepy porter in slippers stood at the door of the inn. His
servile courtesy proved that Crammon had known how to treat
him. " Number 14 on the second floor is vacant," he said.

" Send some one to your lodgings to-morrow for your things,"
Crammon advised the girl.

She did not seem to hear him. Without a word of thanks
or greeting she followed the porter up the soiled red carpet of
the stairs. The rubber cherries tapped audibly against the

brim of her hat. Her clumsy form disappeared in the blackness.

Crammon breathed a sigh of relief. " My kingdom for a four-wheeler," he moaned. At a nearby corner they found a cab.

XXI

When Christian entered his room and switched on the electric light, he was surprised to find Johanna sitting at the table. She shaded her eyes from the sudden glare. He remained at the door. His frown disappeared when he saw the deadly pallor of the girl's face.

" I must leave," Johanna breathed. " I've received a telegram and I must start for Vienna at once."

" I am about to leave, too," Christian answered.

For a while there was silence. Then Johanna said: " Shall I see you again? Will you want me to? Dare I? " Her timid questions showed the old division of her soul. She smiled a smile of patience and renunciation.

" I shall be in Berlin," Christian answered. " I don't know yet where I shall live. But whenever you want to know, ask Crammon. He is easily reached. His two old ladies send him all letters."

" If you desire it, I can come to Berlin," Johanna said with the same patient and resigned smile. " I have relatives there. But I don't think that you do desire it." Then, after a pause, during which her gentle eyes wandered aimlessly, she said: " Then is this to be the end? " She held her breath; she was taut as a bow-string.

Christian went up to the table and rested the index finger of one hand on its top. With lowered head he said slowly: " Don't demand a decision of me. I cannot make one. I should hate to hurt you. I don't want something to happen again that has happened so often before in my life. If you feel impelled to come—come! Don't consider me. Don't think, above all, that I would then leave you in the lurch. But just now is a critical time in my life. More I cannot say."

Johanna could gather nothing but what was hopeless for herself from these words. Yet through them there sounded a note that softened their merely selfish regretfulness. With a characteristically pliant gesture, she stretched out her arm to Christian. Her pose was formal and her smile faint, as she said: " Then, au revoir—perhaps! "

XXII

When the girl had gone, Christian lay down on the sofa and folded his hands beneath his head. Thus he lay until dawn. He neither switched off the light nor did he close his eyes.

He saw the paintless stairs that led to the den where he had been and the red carpet of the inn soiled by many feet; he saw the lamp in the desolate street and the watch charms on the proprietor's waistcoat; he saw the brandy bottle on the shelf, and the green shawl of one of the drunken women, and the tattooed symbols on the sailor's naked arm: the anchor, the winged wheel, the phallus, the fish, the snake; he saw the rubber cherries on the prostitute's hat and the silver brooch with the garnets and the foolish motto: *Ricordo di Venezia*.

And more and more as he thought of these things they awakened in him an ever surer feeling of freedom and of liberation, and seemed to release him from other things that he had hitherto loved, the rare and precious things that he had loved so exclusively and fruitlessly. And they seemed to release him likewise from men and women whose friendship or love had been sterile in the end.

As he lay there and gazed into space, he lived in these poor and mean things, and all fruitless occupations and human relationships lost their importance; and even the thought of Eva ceased to torment him and betray him into fruitless humiliation. That radiant and regal creature allured him no more, when he thought of the blood-stained face of the harlot. For the latter aroused in him a feeling akin to curiosity that gradually filled his soul so entirely that it left room for nothing else.

Toward dawn he slumbered for an hour. Then he arose, and bathed his face in cold water, left the hotel, hired a cab, and drove to the inn called " The King of Greece."

The nightwatchman was still at his post. He recognized this early guest and guided him with disagreeable eagerness up two flights of stairs to the room of Karen Engelschall.

Christian knocked. There was no answer. " You just go in, sir," said the porter. " There ain't no key and the latch don't work. All kinds of things will happen, and it's better for us to have the doors unlocked." .

Christian entered. It was a room with ugly brown furnishings, a dark-red plush sofa, a round mirror with a crack across its middle, an electric bulb at the end of a naked wire, and a chromo-lithograph of the emperor. Everything was dusty, worn, shabby, used-up, poor and mean.

Karen Engelschall lay in the bed asleep. She was on her back, and her dishevelled hair looked like a bundle of straw; her face was pale and a little puffy. Recent scars showed on her forehead and right cheek. Her full, but flaccid breasts protruded above the coverings.

His old and violent dislike of sleeping people stirred in Christian, but he mastered it and regarded her face. He wondered from what social class she had come, whether she was a sailor's or a fisherman's daughter, a girl of the lower middle-classes, of the proletariat or the peasantry. Thus his curiosity employed his mind for a while until he became fully aware of the indescribable perturbation of that face. It was as void of evil as of good; but as it lay there it seemed distraught by the unheard of torment of its dreams. Then Christian thought of the carnelian on Mesecke's hand, and the repulsively red stone which was like a beetle or a piece of raw flesh became extraordinarily vivid to him.

He made a movement and knocked against a chair; the noise

awakened Karen Engelschall. She opened her lids, and fear and horror burned in her eyes when she observed a figure in her room; her features became distorted with fury, and her mouth rounded itself for a cry. Then she saw who the intruder was, and with a sigh of relief slid back among the pillows. Her face reassumed its expression of stubbornness and of enforced yielding. She watched, not knowing what to make of this visit, and seemed to wonder and reflect. She drew the covers up under her chin, and smiled a shallow, flattered smile.

Involuntarily Christian's eyes looked for the red riband and the silver brooch. The girl's garments had been flung pell-mell on a chair. The hat with the rubber cherries lay on the table.

"Why do you stand?" Karen Engelschall asked in a cheerful voice. "Sit down." Again, as in the night, his splendour and distinction overwhelmed her. Smiling her empty smile, she wondered whether he was a baron or a count. She had slept soundly and felt refreshed.

"You cannot stay in this house very long," Christian said courteously. "I have considered what had better be done for you. Your condition requires care. You must not expose yourself to the brutality of that man. It would be best if you left the city."

Karen Engelschall laughed a harsh laugh. "Leave the city? How's that going to be done? Girls like me have to stay where they are."

"Has any one a special claim on you?" Christian asked.

"Claim? Why? How do you mean? Oh, I see. No, no. It's the way things are in our business. The feller to whom you give your money, he protects you, and the others mind him. If he's strong and has many friends you're safe. They're all rotten, but you got no choice. You get no rest day or night, and your flesh gets tired, I can tell you."

"I can imagine that," Christian replied, and for a second looked into Karen's round and lightless eyes, "and for that reason I wanted to put myself at your disposal. I shall leave

Hamburg either to-day or to-morrow, and probably stay in Berlin for some months. I am ready to take you with me. But you must not delay your decision, because I have not yet any address in Berlin, I don't know yet where I shall live, and if a plan like this is delayed it is usually not carried out at all. At the moment you have eluded your pursuer, and so the opportunity to escape is good. You don't need to send for your things. I can get you whatever you need when we arrive."

Those words, spoken with real friendliness, did not have the effect which Christian expected. Karen Engelschall could not realize the simplicity and frankness of their intention. A mocking suspicion arose in her mind. She knew of Vice Crusaders and Preachers of Salvation; and these men her world as a rule fears as much as it does the emissaries of the police. But she looked at Christian more sharply, and àn instinct told her that she was on the wrong track. Clumsily considering, she drifted to other suppositions that had a tinge of cheap romance. She thought of plots and kidnapping and a possible fate more terrible than that under the heel of her old tormentor. She brooded over these thoughts in haste and rage, with convulsed features and clenched fist, passing from fear to hope and from hope to distrust, and yet, even as on the day before, compelled by something irresistible, a force from which she could not withdraw and which made her struggles futile.

"What do you want to do with me?" she asked, and gave him a penetrating glance.

Christian considered in order to weigh his answer carefully. "Nothing but what I have told you."

She became silent and stared at her hands. "My mother lives in Berlin," she murmured. "Maybe you'd want me to go back to her. I don't want to."

"You are to go with me." Christian's tone was firm and almost hard. His chest filled with breath and exhaled the air painfully. The final word had been spoken.

Karen looked at him again. But now her eyes were serious

and awake to reality. "And what shall I do when I'm with you?"

Christian answered hesitatingly: "I've come to no decision about that. I must think it over."

Karen folded her hands. "But I've got to know who you are."

He spoke his name.

"I am a pregnant woman," she said with a sombre look, and for the first time her voice trembled, "a street-walker who's pregnant. Do you know that? I'm the lowest and vilest thing in the whole world! Do you know that?"

"I know it," said Christian, and cast down his eyes.

"Well, what does a fine gentleman like you want to do with me? Why do you take such an interest in me?"

"I can't explain that to you at the moment," Christian answered diffidently.

"What am I to do? Go with you? Right away?"

"If you are willing, I shall call for you at two, and we can drive to the station."

"And you won't be ashamed of me?"

"No, I shall not be ashamed."

"You know how I look? Suppose people point their fingers at the whore travelling with such an elegant gentleman?"

"It does not matter what people do."

"All right. I'll wait for you." She crossed her arms over her breast and stared at the ceiling and did not stir. Christian arose and nodded and went out. Nor did Karen move when he was gone. A deep furrow appeared on her forehead, the fresh scars gleamed like burns upon her earthy skin, a dull and primitive amazement turned her eyes to stone.

XXIII

When Christian crossed the reception room of the hotel he saw Crammon sitting sadly in a chair. Christian stopped and

smiled and held out his hand. " Did you sleep well, Bernard? "
he asked.

" If that were my only difficulty I should not complain,"
Crammon answered. " I always sleep well. The troubles begin
when I'm awake. Age with his stealing steps! The old pleasures no longer sting, the old delights are worn out. One counts
on gratitude and affection, and gets care and disappointment.
I think a monastery would be the best place for me. I must
look into that plan more closely."

` Christian laughed. " Come now, Bernard, you would be a
very unsuitable person in a monastery. Drive the black
thoughts away and let us have breakfast."

" All right, let us have breakfast." Crammon arose. " Have
you any idea why poor Rumpelstilzkin suddenly fled by night?
She had bad news from home, I am told, but that's no reason
why she should have gone without a word. It was not nice or
considerate. And in a few hours Ariel too will be lost to us.
Her rooms are filled with cases and boxes, and M. Chinard is
bursting with self-importance. Black clouds are over us, and
all our lovely rainbows fade. This caviare, by the way, is
excellent. I shall withdraw into an utterly private life. Perhaps I shall hire a secretary, either a man or a fat, appetizing,
and discreet woman, and begin to dictate my memoirs. You,
my dear fellow, seem in more excellent spirits than for a long
time."

" Yes, excellent," Christian said, and his smile revealed his
beautiful teeth. " Excellent! " he repeated, and held out his
hand to his astonished friend.

" So you have finally become reconciled to your loss? "
he winked, and pointed upward with a significant gesture.

Christian guessed his meaning. " Entirely," he said cheerily.
" I'm completely recovered."

" Bravo! " said Crammon, and, comfortably eating, he phi-
losophized: " It would be saddening were it otherwise. I re-

peat what I have often said: Ariel was born for the stars.
There are blessed stars and fateful stars. Some are inhabited
by good spirits, others by demons. We have known that
from times immemorial. Let them wage their battles among
themselves. If it comes to collisions and catastrophes, it is a
cosmic matter in which we mortals have no share. When all
is said and done, you are but a mortal too, though one so
blessed that you were even granted a stay in the happy hunting grounds of the gods. But excesses are evil. You cannot
compete with Muscovite autocrats. Siegfried can conquer the
dragons in the end; were Lucifer to attack him with fire-
breathing steeds, the hero would but risk his skin in vain.
Your renunciation is as wise as it is delightful. I drink to
your pleasant future, dearest boy! "

Christian went to a buffet where magnificent fruit was exposed for sale. He knew Crammon's passionate delight in rare
and lovely fruit. He selected a woven basket and placed in the
middle a pine-apple cut open so that its golden inside showed.
He surrounded it with a wreath of flawless apples and of great,
amber-coloured peaches from the South of France. They were
elastic and yet firm. He added seven enormous clusters of
California grapes. He arranged the fruit artistically, carried
the basket to Crammon, and presented it to him with jesting
solemnity.

They separated. When, late that afternoon, Crammon returned to the hotel, he learned to his bitter amazement that
Christian had left.

He could not compose himself. It seemed to him that he
was the victim of some secret cabal. " They all leave me in the
lurch," he murmured angrily to himself; " they make a mock of
me. It's like an epidemic. You are through with life, Bernard
Gervasius, you are in every one's way. Go to your cell and
bemoan your fate."

He ordered his valet to pack, and to secure accommodations
on the train to Vienna. Then he placed the basket of fruit on

the table, and in his sad reflections plucked berry after berry of
the grape.

XXIV

In his quiet little house, furnished in the style of the age of
Maria Theresa, he forgot what he had suffered. He lived an
idyl.

He accompanied the two pious ladies to church, and out of
considerateness and kindness to them even prayed occasionally.
His chief prayer was: Lord, forgive those who have trespassed
against me and lead me not into temptation. On sunny after-
noons the carriage appeared and took the three for a ride
through the parks. In the evening the bill of fare for the
following day was determined on, and the national and traditional dishes were given the preference. Then he read to the
devoutly attentive Misses Aglaia and Constantine classical
poems: a canto of Klopstock's " Messiah," Schiller's " Walk,"
or something by Rückert. And he still imitated the voice and
intonation of Edgar Lorm. Also he related harmless anecdotes
connected with his life; and he adorned and purified them so
that they would have been worthy of a schoolgirl's library.

Not till the two ladies had retired did he light his short
pipe or pour himself out a glass of cognac; he practised remi-
niscence or introspection, or became absorbed in his little
museum of treasures, which he had gathered during many
years.

Shortly before his proposed meeting with Franz Lothar von
Westernach, he received an alarming letter from Christian's
mother.

Frau Wahnschaffe informed him that Christian had ordered
all his possessions to be sold—Christian's Rest, Waldleiningen,
the hunting lodge, the stables and kennels, the motor cars, the
collections, including the wonderful collection of rings. This
incomprehensible plan was actually being carried out, and no
one had an inkling of the motive. She herself was in the

utmost despair, and begged Crammon for some explanation and, if possible, to come to the castle. She besought him in God's name for some hint in regard to Christian's actions and state of mind. No news of her son had reached her for weeks; he seemed lost, and they were groping in the dark. The family did not, of course, desire his possessions to pass into the hands of strangers, and would bid in everything, although it was both difficult and hateful to oppose the impudent offers and the tricky manœuvres which the auction ordered by Christian would entail. 'Above all, however, there was her personal anxiety about Christian. She expected Crammon to stand by her in her hour of need, and justify the high opinion she had formed both of his friendship for her son and of his attachment to her family.

Crammon re-read the lines that mentioned the sale of Christian's Rest and of the collections. He shook his head long and sadly, pressed his chin into his hands, and two large tears rolled down his cheeks.

END OF VOL. I

CPSIA information can be obtained
at www.ICGtesting.com
Printed in the USA
LVHW081222031020
667846LV00008B/224